eBay the Smart Way

Third Edition

eBay the Smart Way

Selling, Buying, and Profiting on the Web's #1 Auction Site
Third Edition

Joseph T. Sinclair

⫶AMACOM

American Management Association
New York • Atlanta • Brussels • Chicago • Mexico City • San Francisco
Shanghai • Tokyo • Toronto • Washington, D.C.

Special discounts on bulk quantities of AMACOM books are available to corporations, professional associations, and other organizations. For details, contact Special Sales Department, AMACOM, an imprint of AMA Publications, a division of American Management Association, 1601 Broadway, New York, NY 10019.
Tel.: 212-903-8316. Fax: 212-903-8083.

Library of Congress Cataloging-in-Publication Data

Sinclair, Joseph T.
    eBay the smart way : selling, buying, and profiting on the Web's #1 auction site / Joseph T. Sinclair—3rd ed.
        p. cm.
    Includes index.
    ISBN 0-8144-7204-4
    1. Internet auctions. 2. Auctions—Computer network resources. I. Title
HF5478.S482003
381'.177—dc22   2003016751
                                                            CIP

Printing number
10   9   8   7   6   5   4   3   2   1

To my grandfather, Joseph Treble Sinclair, who was a master of commerce in Detroit in the first half of the twentieth century. And to my father-in-law, Ollie Jack Wallin, who was a master of retail in Oklahoma City during the second half of the twentieth century.

Contents

Acknowledgments

Many thanks to Don Spillane, who introduced me to eBay in 1998 and who is the quintessential retailer on eBay, first selling collectibles and now selling cars. Thanks to my agent, Carole McClendon at Waterside Productions, who always does a fine job, and to Jacqueline Flynn and the folks at AMACOM, including Mike Sivilli and Kama Timbrell, who contributed to the book. I certainly can't overlook the clever people at eBay, who have done a great job of creating a new marketplace—a huge and dynamic new marketplace now expanding rapidly internationally. And they continue to improve it. Good work! And finally thanks to my wife Lani, daughter Brook, and son Tommy, who endured the intense and lengthy effort it takes to write a book. Thanks.

I

Introducing eBay

1

Introduction to eBay

It's true that eBay holds auctions. It's also true that eBay operates only online. But put the two together and you start to understand the dynamic new international marketplace eBay has created. It operates 24 hours a day, 7 days a week. It's not like anything that has existed before. It excites the participants, it excites the imagination, and it offers you significant opportunities whether you buy, sell, or sell at retail.

3

How exciting is it? Quite exciting! In June 2003, eBay had 69 million registered users. Some of the following statistics come from the second annual eBay Live! conference, June 2003, in Orlando, Florida.

eBay's number of registered users, last quarter of each year:

1996	41,000
1997	341,000
1998	2 million
1999	10 million
2000	22 million
2001	42 million
2002	62 million

eBay members' sales for each year:

1998	745 million
1999	2.8 billion
2000	5.4 billion
2001	9.3 billion
2002	14.8 billion

Additional statistics derived from my own eBay books show the number of items for sale on a day for various months:

Jul 1999	2,400,000 items for sale in 1,600 categories
Jan 2001	5,000,000 items for sale in 4,000 categories
Jul 2003	16,000,000 items for sale in 27,000 categories

Not bad considering that the longest auction lasts only ten days, with many auctions lasting only three, five, or seven days.

If you check prices on eBay, you will find that prices are often a bargain for buyers. Yet, sellers can get more money for their used products and closeout products on eBay than perhaps anywhere else. How can this be?

Figure 1.1   The eBay home page.

Markets

It's actually easy to explain. Local markets do not operate very efficiently; they're not large enough. Typically a seller takes a used product to a local dealer to sell. For instance, a seller might take a used Nikon camera to a camera dealer. Because the local market is not huge, it will not include many buyers for the camera. The dealer takes a substantial risk that the camera will not sell in a timely manner. Consequently, the dealer will not pay much for the camera. The seller sells to the dealer at a low price.

On the other hand, the dealer has to charge a lot for the camera. He or she must seek a profit that covers the risk of the camera's staying on the shelf a long time. The profit must also cover the cost of doing business, which includes paying rent and employing sales clerks (overhead). The buyer buys from the dealer at a high price.

Thus, a low sales price (for seller) along with a high purchase price (for buyer) is the rule in a local market, particularly when most of the transactions take place through a local dealer.

Sometimes a periodic local show (or flea market) offers an exchange (or swap) that brings together buyers and sellers more efficiently, and prices grow a little higher for sellers and a little lower for buyers, particularly for transactions that don't involve a dealer. For instance, at a camera show with a camera exchange, a seller can get a higher price for the Nikon camera, and a buyer can buy at a lower price than in a transaction through a dealer. Nonetheless, even in a large city, for most products except the most popular, an exchange does not create the ultimate market. It simply never has a large enough population of buyers and sellers.

eBay has established an international marketplace with no peers except a few of the stock and commodity exchanges. The eBay marketplace rationalizes the sale and purchase of used goods—provides the best deal for both buyers and sellers. This is as much as such transactions will ever be rationalized (until more people join eBay). That is, eBay always has the maximum numbers of buyers and sellers compared to other smaller markets. The auction feature of the eBay marketplace provides a mechanism that dynamically establishes market values quickly and efficiently. The transactions do not necessarily take place through a dealer. Consequently, a seller can usually sell for a higher price than in a local market, and a buyer can usually buy for a lower price than in a local market.

You can say that the eBay marketplace promotes *disintermediation*. This fancy word means that the dealer (the intermediary) has been eliminated. Again, referring to the camera example, the seller should be able to sell the Nikon camera for more on the eBay market than to a local dealer, and the buyer should be able to buy the Nikon camera for less on the eBay market than from a local dealer.

The Dealer

A dealer can still fit into the eBay environment. If a dealer can count on turning over used goods quickly, the economics of his or her business practices change. Consequently, a dealer who sells on eBay can afford to pay more for used goods and sell such goods for less than in a physical location where overhead is higher and the market smaller.

Nonetheless, realize that every market is different. Dealers have been forced out of some markets on eBay and have thrived in other markets on eBay. What it comes down to each time a dealer looks at an eBay market is whether he or she can make money in that particular market. Sometimes the answer is yes, and sometimes it's no.

Keep in mind, too, that many dealers use eBay to sell new goods exclusively or in addition to used goods. Many dealers who sell new goods thrive. And many eBay members selling routinely have evolved into full-fledged dealers (retailers) themselves.

The more buyers and sellers for any particular product, the more the marketplace will rationalize the price. Thus, popular used items, such as popular brands, will exchange hands at a price closer to the price the items sell at retail (i.e., at discount stores). Less popular used items, such as less popular brands, will sell at a price well below their retail price at discount stores.

Law of Supply and Demand

Does the law of supply and demand work on eBay? Sure. When many sellers of a particular product want to sell to a few buyers on eBay, the price will go down. When many buyers want to buy a particular product from a few sellers on eBay, the price will go up. A huge market like eBay, however, has a maximum number of buyers and sellers compared to other markets. Due to the large number of buyers and sellers, the market will tend to be more balanced (more rational and stable) than a smaller market.

New Goods

Sellers sell new goods on eBay. In fact, new goods comprise a substantial percentage of the goods sold today. However, sellers usually do not sell new goods at full price or even at a discount price. More often eBay is a place to sell new goods at a deep discount. Consequently, buyers can expect to get a pretty good deal. But what about sellers? Can they get a good deal too?

Yes, a seller can sell a product new that he or she has not used or has decided not to use. These mistaken purchases happen to all of us sooner or later. What about that fishing reel you unwrapped at Christmas but never took out of the box? What about that food dehydrator you bought for making beef jerky but never got around to using? It's often difficult to return such merchandise for a refund, particularly after it sits in the garage for six months (or six years). But it's new, and if you sell it, you undoubtedly will sell it at a deep discount from the full retail price. eBay provides you the opportunity to sell it at the highest price you can expect to get.

Many sellers sell retail on eBay. This means they sell new goods as a business just like an offline retailer, albeit usually at lower prices. When eBay started its fixed price program, *Buy It Now*, the fixed prices gave eBay retailers a substantial boost. The fixed prices enable buyers to buy immediately just as they do in a retail store.

New goods also come from sources other than wholesale, such as distress sales and closeout sales by manufacturers and retailers. These are usually bulk sales. For instance, if you can buy 1,000 high-quality baseball caps for $500 at a closeout sale and sell them on eBay for $4 each, that price is substantially below the normal $8–$16 price in the retail stores. Both you and the buyer can consummate a satisfying transaction. The buyer buys cheap, and you make a reasonable profit.

Moreover, if as a dealer you do not have a retail store and an expensive website operation, you can afford to sell new goods on the eBay market in the regular course of business at even lower prices than a discount store (assuming you buy in large quantities). This provides a good deal for buyers and a profitable business for you.

Now, if you take a look at what's happening on eBay—if you haven't already—you will see the transactions described above happening every minute of every day. eBay has built a huge marketplace. At any moment in time, millions of items wait for bids, and millions of potential buyers look over the merchandise. If you were to put all of this in a physical setting, no building ever built could house all of this commercial activity. It would take about one hundred football fields to accommodate a marketplace of only one million people. Indeed, eBay has created a huge and rational marketplace.

An Important Insight

The interesting thing about goods is that each product has its own market. It may have a much different market than something closely related. For instance, insulated winter boots with rubber bottoms and leather tops enjoy a thriving market in the outdoor labor force. They keep feet warm and dry in winter—just what the working man or woman needs. You can buy them in stores that cater to outdoor workers. Insulated boots made entirely of leather enjoy a thriving market among skiers. They keep feet warm and dry in snowy weather—perfect for use after a day of skiing. Known as apres ski boots, you can buy them in ski shops. Although similar, these two products have much different markets.

This phenomenon holds true on eBay too. Every type of item has its own market and means of being advertised and sold. That makes it misleading to generalize about eBay. What you might say about one product may not hold true for a similar product. Some product sales thrive on eBay. Some don't. This phenomenon misleads and baffles people. But don't let it baffle you.

If you are thinking of doing a significant amount of selling on eBay, evaluate your potential market using the one sure method. Experiment, and experiment again. Don't attempt to apply logic. Don't make inferences. Just do it. You will find out soon enough whether your selling plan holds water.

Yet people want certainty. They want to know how to do it. They feel uncomfortable with the facts: 16 million items on eBay and thousands of different standard ways to sell each of those items. But the facts are the facts. You need to become knowledgeable about the products you buy or sell and you need to become knowledgeable about how they are bought and sold on eBay. Such knowledge leads to success. Generalizations do not necessarily lead to success on eBay.

Naturally, this book cannot cover thousands of different ways of doing things on eBay. It has to make generalizations. Just be advised that the most this book can do is lead you in the right direction. Only your experimentation will give you the insight you need for success with your particular products.

For instance, $300 digital cameras sell well on eBay, yet $300 couches don't. Digital cameras tend to be commodities. The one you buy on eBay exactly matches the one you might buy in a store. Couches tend to have much more variety, and you want to see them, feel them, and sit on them before you make a purchase. The $300 digital camera costs $8 to ship. The $300 couch costs $270 to ship. Yes, people have gone broke attempting to sell furniture online because they didn't know that UPS (inexpensive shipping) has size limitations, and you must ship furniture by truck (expensive). These differences seem obvious, but many other differences are more subtle, and only experimentation will expose them.

The way a particular market relates to the whole market also varies. For instance, many previously successful dealers were driven out of the collectibles market by losing customers to eBay. Yet antique dealers have thrived using eBay to both buy and sell antiques. Again, experimentation leads to discovering the anomalies of eBay markets.

Fitting In

Where do you fit in? eBay is simple. You sign up for membership, fill in an online form with some information on an item, and suddenly you're a seller. To be a buyer, you don't even have to fill in the information for an item. Just bid on something.

Thus, the question comes up, Why a book? The answer is straightforward. The more you buy and sell on eBay, the more committed you become to making eBay commerce a part of your life. Then things become more complex. Your activities start to look like significant dollars are at stake. Indeed, eBay commerce can add up to more than you expect whether you intend it to or not.

Many readers will buy and sell in volume for one or some of the following reasons:

1. They buy and sell as part of their hobby (e.g., coin collecting).

2. They run a side business on eBay one day a week.

3. They buy supplies and equipment for their business because they save money buying on eBay.

4. They use eBay as a convenient substitute for going to the local mall.

5. They wheel and deal in eBay items because it's fun, and there's lots of stuff.

6. They're eccentric and use eBay to buy lots of offbeat stuff they can't find easily elsewhere.

7. They sell on eBay to supplement their offline retail sales business in a physical location.

8. Or, they operate a full-time retail business selling exclusively on eBay.

This book is for people who buy or sell routinely, not occasionally. It's for people who want to make the most of their eBay activities. Consequently, it's for people who want to know about eBay as commerce more than eBay as a game or social activity. As you might expect then, this book has a quasi-business flavor to it.

Specifically, one purpose of this book is to be a primer for those who are serious about carrying on a substantial part-time or even a full-time business on eBay. My book *eBay Business the Smart Way* (AMACOM, 2003) takes up where this book leaves off and expands on the business of operating as an eBay retailer.

But this book is more than just a primer for eBay members who sell as a business. It also helps regular users. If you use eBay regularly, you will come to realize soon, if you haven't already, that eBay is a way of participating in commerce that requires skills and background knowledge to achieve your personal goals (e.g., saving money or making money). Thus, the business slant of this book will give you the edge to be successful and will thereby serve you well.

Other Online Auctions

What about other online auctions? eBay has had the lion's share of the online auction business. Most press accounts allege eBay's market share of the online auction market to be well over 90 percent. For any market to be highly rationalized, it must have a huge number of participants. Thus, so long as eBay has a major portion of the market, competitors (other online auctions) will have trouble competing effectively. The competitors will simply find it difficult to grow to a size where both buyers and sellers get the best deal. Size is perhaps the single most important characteristic of a successful online auction marketplace, and eBay got there first.

How did eBay get there first? That makes a fascinating story, but one which is beyond the scope of this book. Like other Web business success stories, eBay made customer convenience the primary goal for improving the eBay infrastructure. The result is a finely tuned system that works well and is reliable. But transactions require trust as well as procedural mechanisms. eBay outdistanced its competitors by using innovation to make auctions simple and effective and by creating a system that supports trust. Easy to use and trustworthy. What else do you need for a marketplace?

I encourage you to try other online auctions from time to time. Anyone can challenge eBay. Some specialty auctions will do well in spite of eBay. If someone can make a good market outside of eBay, it might be a benefit to you. But for the vast majority of consumer and small business goods, that seems unlikely.

Specialty Auctions

Because eBay has no effective competition, this book doesn't waste space covering other online auctions alleged to compete with eBay, even for comparative purposes. You can make the argument that some specialty online auctions will compete with eBay in their specific specialties. However, because market size is so important and because eBay caters to specialty markets, you can expect eBay to dominate even individual submarkets.

Specialized Auctions

Some specialized auctions are different from the general auction market because of artificial restraints. For example, to hold a legally binding real estate auction, you have to have a real estate license and satisfy real estate regulations. Consequently, eBay can't take over that particular auction market easily. Nonetheless, eBay has held *nonbinding* real estate auctions online for several years.

After becoming licensed in real estate in all the states, eBay has experimented with *binding* online real estate auctions in some states. If these binding real estate auctions work well, presumably eBay will expand its binding real estate auctions. Perhaps someday all eBay real estate auctions will be binding.

Will eBay continue to dominate? The eBay people are bright and innovative. They have well-financed potential competitors such as Yahoo! and Amazon.com breathing down their neck, which will keep them running at full speed. eBay has the momentum and the market. eBay made a successful public stock offering in September 1998. (Its stock went up 3,900 percent in value by the end of June 1999. It went down after the dot com crash but went back up to its high in the summer of 2003 and split.) This has provided the capital to remain successful, and eBay has been profitable. All signs indicate that eBay will continue to dominate the Web auction scene for the foreseeable future.

A Terrific Place to Shop

eBay is a terrific place to shop. Every time I forget this and go to the mall or somewhere else to shop, I am often disappointed. Customer service is too often terrible. Many minimum-wage store clerks seem to have no motivation to learn their retail merchandise, and they are all you have to rely on besides yourself. Stores are understaffed. Inventory is incomplete. Prices are sometimes unreasonably high. And you have to drive a ways to get such a buying experience.

It takes a long time to break old habits. I have been buying on eBay since 1998, and every year I buy more on eBay and other online stores and less locally. Now, I think of eBay first 75 percent of the time, and the other 25 percent I usually wish I had. And whatever you buy is delivered right to your door! If you're new to eBay, start training yourself to think of eBay first when you want or need something. You won't regret it.

And what a terrific opportunity for sellers! The millions of people training themselves to think of eBay first constitute a huge market— all the potential customers you could ever hope for. It doesn't get any better than this.

What's Up?

What do you make of all this? eBay is a new marketplace like none ever known before. It currently operates without a strong competitor. It features an efficient market for the exchange of used goods, good news for both buyers and sellers. It also brings with it new opportunities for those who want to wheel and deal in goods on a broader scale, especially new goods. In the true capitalistic spirit, it brings with it new opportunities to make money, lots of money.

Indeed, things happen today on eBay faster than they ever have. The rate of change is accelerating. eBay is not stabilizing, so to speak, but rather reinvents itself more often and continues to add features. A published book in print cannot keep up with the changes. Therefore, I try to paint a general overview and point you in the right direction to find the current information you need to be successful. That's all a book can do today.

Let Me Know

This book is not the final word on eBay. Not even close. Buyers and sellers and the ingenious people at eBay headquarters in San Jose, California, continue reinventing eBay daily. Those who create new businesses on eBay add to it. Join me in keeping up to date on this new marketplace. If you have a new idea about eBay or a new slant on eBay from personal observation—or an idea you dream up—and you want to share it, email me at *jt@sinclair.com*. If you mention it first and I use it in another edition of this book, I'll give you the credit. Thanks.

Check the BookCenter website (*http://www.bookcenter.com*) for additional information about using eBay and for information about my other book, *eBay Business the Smart Way*, which specializes in operating a business on eBay.

As in every marketplace, the knowledgeable reap the profits. Although eBay is simple and straightforward, it provides the infrastructure for complex business strategies and activities. And although eBay is simple to use, you need to know a lot to put it to profitable use. Whether you buy or sell one item, buy or sell in bulk, or buy or sell new or used goods, this book provides the information you need to operate intelligently on eBay. Even though easy to read, this book wasn't written for dummies. Indeed, it's for those who want to learn how to operate on eBay the smart way.

2

Opportunities for Buyers

The primary opportunity for buyers is to buy at the lowest possible price. That raises questions: Which buyers? What products? Tough questions to answer, because eBay evolves every day. Can an individual buy goods on eBay? Certainly. eBay got its start providing such a marketplace. Can a business buy goods on eBay? Today the potential for business purchases is greater than ever but still limited. Tomorrow, perhaps unlimited. See Chapter 26 for more information on business purchases; this chapter covers individual buyers.

Individuals

eBay attracts individual buyers (bidders) because such buyers can buy merchandise at a good price, sometimes at spectacular savings. A deal that's hard to beat! After all, this is the age of high-quality mass-produced consumer products. A Hoover vacuum cleaner works the same whether you buy it at full price from a retailer, at a discount price from a discount store, or at a deep discount price on eBay. Fortunately for buyers, there are plenty of sellers. eBay has grown into a huge market consisting of millions of people. Among those millions are many sellers. With a good balance between buyers and sellers, the market works well for buyers.

The bottom line is you can often buy things less expensively on eBay than you can elsewhere. This is a general statement that may not prove true in some cases. For instance, I usually price computer equipment on eBay and also at my local monthly computer show (*http://www.marketpro.com*). Sometimes eBay offers lower prices. Sometimes the show offers lower prices. They both offer prices significantly lower than elsewhere. At the least, eBay provides a good reference for price comparisons, and if I couldn't make it to the computer show, I would have no reservations about buying computer equipment exclusively on eBay.

eBay offers a wide variety of merchandise. Although eBay commerce seems to be top-heavy in things like collectibles, computers, and consumer electronics, this hides the fact that there are millions of products for sale on eBay that have nothing to do with such categories. Likewise, if you don't like used (pre-owned) merchandise, a substantial and growing portion of the merchandise auctioned is new.

eBay's Role

eBay is just a marketplace to buy and sell, nothing more. eBay does not get involved in the transaction. The seller pays a small fee to eBay—analogous to renting a booth at a flea market. As a buyer, you make your own arrangement with the seller for payment and shipping. The eBay auction process sets the price.

The Time Factor

The transaction time doesn't necessarily favor buyers. If you want something right now, you can't buy on impulse, except for *Buy It Now* items (growing to be a substantial part of the eBay marketplace). You have to wait until the auction is over, and you have to be high bidder too. In addition, you have to tend your auction; that is, you have to have a bidding strategy and follow it through. Once you win the bidding, you must arrange payment and shipping with the seller. Often the seller will wait until your check clears before making the shipment (unless you pay by credit card or PayPal). Thus, the total time of a transaction tends to be measured in days or even weeks.

All of the above assumes that a seller puts up for auction the item you seek. The item may not be available on eBay. When looking to buy microphones over a two-month period in 1999, I found that the number of microphones auctioned at any particular time varied between 110 and 215. When I looked for a copy of FrameMaker (specialized, expensive software) over the same two-month period, sometimes eBay had six copies up for auction and sometimes none. Consequently, you may have to wait to buy what you want to buy. It may not be continuously available on eBay, but due to eBay's huge size, sooner or later it will show up.

eBay Stores

Interestingly, you do not have to wait for some products. Some retailers running auctions have a URL (a link) in their eBay *About Me* webpages to their websites where you can order the merchandise immediately at a price comparable to the auction price. Don't overlook this opportunity when in a hurry. Many eBay sellers also have an eBay store where they sell items at fixed prices. Look for the eBay Store icon (red tag) by the seller's name.

Buy It Now

If you see the *Buy It Now* (fixed price) label on an auction listing, you can buy the item immediately for the price indicated. Your purchase terminates the auction. However, the *Buy It Now* price remains available only until the reserve is met.

The Market

The market for buyers is a smorgasbord. You can find almost everything you want. The enormous scope of the eBay market sets it apart from its would-be competitors. In a real sense, you should think of eBay as your personal asset. You can always turn to it to buy merchandise at good prices, merchandise that you otherwise might not be able to afford. And think of it as a long-term asset. No reason it won't work just as well for you five years from now as it does today. Probably better.

Risk

What risk do you take to buy merchandise on eBay? If it was risky, eBay wouldn't be so successful. Nonetheless, you need to keep your eyes open and always stay cautious. Never pay more for something than you can afford to lose, because you take a risk that you will lose your money to a commerce criminal (i.e., someone who doesn't deliver the goods or otherwise defrauds you).

If you can't afford to lose more than $500, you should take proper precautions for all transactions over $500. Fortunately, online escrow companies will protect you (for a fee) by handling the transaction. The escrow company doesn't pay your money to the seller until the shipper delivers the specified goods in reasonable condition. See Escrow Services in Chapter 4 for more on this.

eBay offers its own free insurance program that covers goods up to $200. It covers fraud but not shipping damage or loss. Some sellers (PowerSellers) now offer fraud insurance up to $500.

Con artists will always work eBay seeking to con you with means other than non-delivery of goods. But con artists work your local community too. You take a risk just by opening your front door. eBay may have even less fraud because eBay fraud is usually easy to trace online to the criminals responsible.

The good news is that eBay has a superb system for establishing reputations. In many cases, you will have full confidence that the seller will deliver the goods. The reputation (feedback) system comprises the heart and soul of the eBay system—truly a work of genius. You need to learn how to use it when evaluating sellers. See Chapter 7 for details. The eBay feedback system makes eBay a great opportunity for buyers because it decreases the risk of fraud significantly.

Transaction Overhead

Buying things on eBay entails some routine expenses. Although most of the items are nominal, they add up. What you thought you bought on eBay so inexpensively might start looking like a purchase from a store in your neighborhood by the time you take delivery.

Shipping and Handling

The shipping and handling charges are a fact of life on eBay just as they are for mail-order purchases. Don't forget to include them in your price calculations. Often a seller will charge a flat fee, so you don't have to estimate.

Insurance

What happens if an item you paid for is not delivered? At best it causes a mess. Insurance provides the best defense against this awkward situation. Unfortunately, insurance probably isn't cost-effective for cheap items. For costly items, request insurance. Or, if the seller offers insurance, take it (even though you may have to pay for it). Note that some shippers (e.g., UPS) include a minimal amount of insurance at no additional cost.

Sales Tax

As with mail-order purchases, one of the attractions of buying on eBay is that the seller is likely to be out of state, and you don't have to pay sales tax. Nonetheless, the shipping and handling costs often negate this savings; taken together, the shipping (cost) and sales tax (savings) often result in a wash, particularly for items between $30 and $100.

Don't forget, however, that when you make a purchase in your state (i.e., buyer and seller live in the same state), you have to pay sales tax (assuming your state collects a sales tax).

Escrow Fees

If you make a high-price purchase, make the effort to put the transaction in escrow. The fees seem expensive, but the process protects you from nondelivery of the merchandise. The escrow agent doesn't send payment to the seller until the buyer says that he or she received what was represented by the seller.

Payment by credit card may relieve you of the need for escrow because you can charge back (get your money back) the purchase within a certain number of days (e.g., 30 days) if you have good cause to be dissatisfied.

Payment

If you need to send a money order or cashier's check, you will have to pay at least a nominal fee for it (perhaps a relatively high fee). You will do better to use a credit card or PayPal (covered in Chapter 16). You can always ask for a charge-back to recoup your money if the seller doesn't deliver the merchandise as represented.

Rent or Buy at Auction?

Need expensive equipment for a project? Buy it used (in excellent condition) on eBay. Use it. Keep it in excellent condition. When you finish the project, sell the equipment on eBay (in excellent condition). You can probably sell it for about what you bought it for if you keep it in excellent condition. Looks like an inexpensive rental to me.

Summary

eBay provides solid opportunities for buyers to buy new and used goods, and even services, at low prices. eBay's system for establishing reputation takes much of the risk out of the auction transactions. In some cases buying, using, and reselling an item even simulates renting such an item at a low cost for a special project. eBay provides you with a new low-cost alternative for acquiring the goods and services that you need.

What About Businesses?

This chapter discusses individuals. To get some ideas about how businesses can buy on eBay, read Chapter 26 about eBay's business-to-business website.

3

Opportunities for Sellers

The primary opportunity for sellers is to sell at the highest price. After all, isn't that what auctions are for? eBay provides an excellent means of potentially getting the highest price because so many potential buyers look for merchandise in the eBay marketplace. On eBay, individuals can successfully sell to individuals, and retailers can successfully sell to individuals. This chapter covers such auction opportunities. For more information on business-to-business sales, read Chapter 26 about the eBay business website.

Individuals

Suppose you have a seven-year-old Sony TCM5000EV portable professional audio cassette recorder in excellent condition you want to sell. A radio news reporter uses this type of recorder to do interviews in the field. Sony has made the same model for many years. This fine piece of electronic equipment has a very limited local market. If you sell this to a dealer, chances are you will not get a good price. If you sell it through classified ads, you may not get many calls for it. But if you auction it on eBay, a few who appreciate the quality of the equipment and need it will step up from among the millions of eBay buyers to bid on it. Because of the immense size of the eBay market, you can find numerous people interested in what you have to offer. The more people interested, the more likely you can sell it for a higher price than elsewhere.

It doesn't have to be a specialized piece of equipment like the Sony TCM5000EV to get bids. Even more buyers will bid for a popular Sony consumer audio cassette tape recorder like the Walkman WM-GX552, and with the maximum number of buyers, you are more likely to get a maximum price.

With a quick trip to your garage, you can probably make $1,000 in the next week ridding yourself of things you haven't used in years by selling them on eBay. Maybe $5,000.

Advertising

How do you promote your auction on eBay? You advertise it. eBay provides you with an advertising section in your auction listing (a portion of the auction listing webpage). You use this section to present whatever information you want. You can even use Hypertext Markup Language (HTML), the simple markup language of the Web. Although this might sound like a chore if you don't know HTML, it's just the opposite. It's a substantial opportunity.

You can put anything you want to in your auction ad. There's no limitation. Naturally, you will want to describe the item you offer for auction. But you can also advertise your business (in effect), include a picture of the item for sale, and even include a link to your *About Me* webpage on eBay, which can include a link to your ecommerce website. Chapter 12 will show you how to use HTML templates for attractive ads without having to learn HTML.

The Time Factor

Don't look at eBay as a quick fix. You can take your Sony TCM5000EV, put it in the car, drive to a dealer, and perhaps get a check today, albeit a small check. eBay provides a longer process. The shortest auction lasts three days, and you might want to use a longer auction just to make sure you get the maximum number of bidders.

Nonetheless, creating an auction on eBay does not take long, and you do nothing during the auction period except perhaps answer a few questions via email from prospective bidders. Once the auction closes, you simply arrange with the winning bidder for payment and shipment, and the deal is done. The auction takes the negotiation out of the deal, and you will not have to waste time with offers and counteroffers.

Although not immediate, eBay does provide for a reasonably short sales period without a great deal of effort on your part.

The Market

Consider the market at least a national one and at best an international one. This means that you send the item being auctioned via normal shipping channels, or in the case of a foreign sale, you ship the item overseas. In other words, the buyer won't appear at your front door to hand you a check and pick up the item. Thus, to sell this way requires an additional time commitment on your part. You have to pack the item in a box and go to the post office or elsewhere to ship the item. But strangers won't knock on your door either (as they might with classified ads), perhaps a greater benefit.

You can assume that the market is full of serious buyers. Occasionally buyers will not complete the transactions for which they were the high bidders. Fortunately, eBay provides a system that discourages such behavior, and you shouldn't have to repeat an auction often.

The best news is that eBay has a vast market. Millions of buyers bid, and eBay keeps growing. You will always find a significant number of potential buyers for common goods in this market, and you will likely find buyers even for uncommon goods. This huge eBay market, always waiting for you, provides a convenient way to sell merchandise no longer useful to you.

Retailers

Retailers are businesses that have new merchandise to sell to consumers. Most retailers sell inventory in their stores at full price or run sales to sell at a discounted price. But retailers often have excess or outdated inventory that will not bring full retail price. For such inventory, eBay provides a potentially profitable new outlet. Indeed, many retailers do quite well auctioning on eBay, which provides a golden opportunity for excess-inventory sales and closeout sales. In addition, it provides a golden opportunity for retailers to buy at distress sales or closeout sales offline and turn around and profitably sell the inventory at retail for discount prices on eBay.

For retailers accustomed to fulfilling mail orders, selling on eBay is a natural fit. Retailers who have not sold via mail will need to get organized to conduct multiple auctions and fulfill eBay sales, not a overwhelming task, but nonetheless one that needs to be taken seriously.

Online Retailers

Retailers that exist only online will find eBay to be a natural extension of their online sales. Retailers that handle online commerce well will welcome eBay as an additional outlet. They can use their existing infrastructure to handle and fulfill orders easily and quickly.

eBay Retailers

A new breed of retailers has appeared that sells only on eBay. These retailers don't necessarily even have the expense of an ecommerce website and certainly not the expense of a store or warehouse. These people seek inventory at wholesale, distress, closeout, or otherwise low prices and then sell it on eBay at discount prices. In some cases, their overhead is so low that they can afford to sell at deep discounts even while purchasing their inventory through normal wholesale channels. Don't look at these sales efforts as fly-by-night retail operations. Many are serious businesses making big profits in this new marketplace.

Off Welfare

In the spring of 2000, President Clinton at a televised press conference claimed that by becoming eBay retailers, 20,000 people got off the welfare rolls. I wouldn't have believed it if I hadn't watched it myself. Where the president got his figures or whether they're accurate, I don't know. But there are definitely tens of thousands of people retailing on eBay, that is, auctioning merchandise routinely on eBay, whether part-time or full-time, as a source of steady income.

See my book *eBay Business the Smart Way* to get complementary information to this book on how to sell at retail on eBay.

Special Retail Sales Projects

What is a fly-by-night retail operation? Is it one where a one-person retailer purchases a huge inventory of a closeout item for a low price, spends two months selling it on eBay, goes on vacation for a month in Bermuda, and then returns to start the cycle over again? If so, I want to be a fly-by-night retailer. Indeed, eBay makes such special retail sales projects possible. Nothing requires that you have to have a store, warehouse, ecommerce website, or permanent address to be a reputable and honest retailer on eBay. You need to diligently find the inventory, run the eBay auctions, fulfill the orders, and keep after your travel agent to make the appropriate hotel reservations in Bermuda.

Offline Auctioneers

Some auctioneers, such as estate sale auctioneers, look to eBay to extend their auction activities. Why not? For certain types of merchandise, they may get more on eBay than they can in a normal auction offline. They make more money for their clients and more money for themselves in higher auctioneering fees. With a larger pool of buyers, they can sell for higher prices with potentially lower overhead costs.

Buyers Become Sellers

Many people routinely buy things for very deep discounts at local estate sales and garage sales and turn around and sell the merchandise on eBay for a profit. There are many other local sources where someone with an entrepreneurial inclination can buy at low prices and sell on eBay for a profit. For more inventory acquisition ideas, read Chapter 22.

Offline auctioneers who cannot take advantage of eBay tend to be ones who handle real estate or goods that require a lot of paperwork. For instance, state laws may prevent real estate from being auctioned effectively on eBay. In addition, real estate requires a lot of paperwork just to get ready for auction.

Another example is the Sotheby's type of auction. Sotheby's is an old line auction firm with offices in London and New York. The items (works of art and the like) to be auctioned by Sotheby's are so valuable that they require that written bills of sale, receipts, certificates of authentication, and other documents be provided for review by prospective bidders before the auctions take place. These kinds of auctioneers can extend their operations to the Web but perhaps do best via their traditional offline auctions, not via eBay. However, eBay provides a separate auction just for these types of auctioneers. See Chapter 27, which covers Live auctions.

Service Providers

No rule says you can't sell your services on eBay. However, this is a tough sell. Suppose you're an accountant seeking to pick up new tax clients. What do you sell? If you sell your services at a 30 percent savings from your usual fee of $120 per hour, you might find that you won't get much interest. Try a workable strategy. Offer a package of services at a reasonable price. For instance, you might offer to do a complete tax return for a $550 fee. For someone with a complex tax situation, that might look like a bargain (i.e., the kind of client you want to have for the long term). You might work inexpensively this year, but next year you can charge your regular fee. However, if that fee looks too expensive to someone, they probably don't need your services and will always be happy having their tax return prepared by H&R Block at a lower cost.

Marketing your services requires imagination and experimentation to find a magic formula that works on eBay. In the meantime, if you don't achieve success in selling your specific packages of services, you may find success in picking up clients just by the act of auctioning your packages (i.e., advertising—see Chapter 20).

Risk

As a seller, risk does not have to be a compelling concern. So long as you collect payment before you ship, you will protect yourself as well as you can in most circumstances. If you choose to ship before collecting payment, you will incur much more risk.

Keep in mind, however, that in purchasing via credit card a buyer can always ask the credit card company for a charge-back on an item with which he or she is dissatisfied. That creates the risk that you'll end up refunding the purchase price. I know of one retailer who not only lost in a charge-back contest (monitored by the bank), but the buyer didn't even return the merchandise. And the seller had a 99.8 percent positive feedback rating after thousands of eBay transactions. But for sellers like him, charge-backs are rare. They're simply a cost of doing business. After all, offline retailers get charge-backs too.

Perhaps the biggest risk you run is a dissatisfied customer. An unhappy customer can make considerably more trouble than he or she is worth. You will do well to make a refund or do whatever it takes to keep a customer from fuming. You risk your eBay reputation. With this consideration in mind, the threat of a credit card charge-back becomes almost meaningless.

Transaction Overhead

eBay auctions have their overhead costs. Some you can pass on to the buyer, and some you can't.

eBay Fees

Although modest, eBay auction fees paid by the seller still constitute a significant expense, particularly for items of low value (see fee schedules, Tables 6.1 and 6.2, Chapter 6).

Merchant Credit Card Charges

Like at most retail outlets, eBay buyers like to pay by credit card, and credit cards cost sellers money. Although you can get away without taking credit cards on eBay, serious sellers will want to offer credit card buying. Retailers need credit card merchant accounts to receive credit card payments. You may be able to get away with using special online payment services such as PayPal (explained in Chapter 16), which enables you to accept credit cards, in effect, without a merchant account. However, you must still pay PayPal a fee for credit card transactions completed through PayPal.

Shipping and Handling

Normally shipping and handling charges are a wash. The buyer pays them, and it costs that much to package and ship the item. Sometimes, however, sellers take a loss on shipping and handling.

The shipping cost is easy to determine. Look at the shipping rates. You will have a tougher time with the handling. That includes packaging materials and labor. It won't be accurate to the dime, but you have to calculate it anyway to avoid losing money on shipping and handling.

Profit?

Rather than a business chore, some sellers use shipping and handling as a business opportunity. You will see a lot of items selling for $8 on eBay with shipping and handling charged at another $6. Depending on the merchandise, a seller can make profit on the shipping and handling.

If you make an obvious profit on shipping and handling, though, you will irritate potential buyers and reduce sales. But you don't want to lose money on shipping and handling either, unless you plan to do so as part of your sales strategy.

Sales Tax

Don't neglect to charge sales tax to customers in your state. You will need a sales tax license too. If you make only an occasional sale, your state sales tax laws may exempt you from collecting sales tax on incidental items but probably not on expensive items. The buyer pays the sales tax, and the seller collects it and pays it to the state sales tax agency.

Customer Service

As a retailer, selling via eBay is no different than selling offline. The same laws apply. The same ethical guidelines apply. You need to be ready to take care of your eBay customers just as you would have to take care of your customers offline. Failure to do so may adversely affect your reputation on eBay (covered in Chapter 7). It doesn't matter whether you sell one item or dozens of items. Customer service is the name of the game. Read Chapter 10 carefully.

Responsibility

An auction where the buyer buys something used or something new at a low price has an aura of finality. If a buyer responds with a complaint immediately after receiving the merchandise, a seller needs to respond diligently. If a buyer complains two months later, however, unlike Target or other national retailers, few would expect a seller to take care of the problem, unless the seller had provided a guarantee. Thus, few buyers expect sellers to provide as much long term customer service on eBay as in a physical retail store.

An Individual

If you sell only occasionally, a buyer will not expect much in the way of customer support. A buyer will expect the item to be as the seller represented and to be usable (unless represented otherwise). But if a buyer receives something that won't work after you represented that it was in working order, regardless of the lack of guarantee you need to make it right. Otherwise your reputation on eBay may suffer. People have high customer service expectations when purchasing on the Web, even though such expectations may not extend long term.

The point here is that along with the opportunities on eBay come responsibilities. Buyers expect reasonable customer service from all retailers, even occasional sellers. Although overall customer service responsibilities may be less over the long term on eBay than in other markets, this does not mean customers don't have expectations. Failure to meet expectations can affect your reputation.

Opportunity

Look upon customer service as an opportunity rather than a responsibility. As in any other market, if you offer great customer service on eBay, you will get repeat business. Never make the mistake of thinking of eBay as a one-shot deal or as a temporary retail selling effort. You may sell on eBay for years to come. Perhaps decades.

Cost

If you're a retailer, customer service is part of your overhead. You have to expend the time, energy, and money to provide it, or your employees do. It's not free.

Summary

eBay provides solid opportunities for sellers, whether individuals or businesses, to sell used goods for higher prices than the same goods might bring elsewhere. In the case of services, auctioning can even mean inexpensive advertising. Another aspect of eBay is *retailing*. Retail selling on eBay provides huge opportunities to anyone who wants to provide good customer service and experiment with online auctions as a new type of retail outlet. Capital requirements and overhead remain low. The results can be spectacular. This is truly a prime opportunity for many people, and this book devotes much discussion directly applicable to eBay retail sales.

What About Non-Retail Businesses?

Can non-retail businesses sell on eBay? Sure. Non-retail businesses such as corporations, service providers, and the like certainly have the need to sell used equipment, overstocked supplies, and other items from time to time.

II

Learning to Use eBay

4

How eBay Works

You can operate an online auction hundreds of different ways. eBay was not the first auction online. Perhaps not even in the first hundred. But eBay has constructed a digital mechanism that accommodates both the potential of the new Web medium and the psychology of human commerce. It is this subtle mechanism—the heart and soul of eBay—which makes eBay successful. eBay does not merely translate a traditional auction into an online format. To understand eBay, you have to start with eBay values.

Community Values

eBay wisely sets what it calls *community values* that it expects to guide the behavior of everyone participating in eBay:

> We believe people are basically good.

> We believe everyone has something to contribute.

> We believe that an honest, open environment can bring out the best in people.

> We recognize and respect everyone as a unique individual.

> We encourage you to treat others the way you want to be treated.

These statements of values set the tone for the conduct of auctions and the transactions that follow. Should you have trouble dealing with other people on eBay, it might be wise for you to review these guideline values. You might find in them some ideas on how to resolve your conflicts.

Values alone are not enough, however, and eBay requires you to sign its User Agreement, which sets forth the rules of the road for eBay members.

User Agreement

The following is not a reprint of the eBay User Agreement (*http://pages.ebay.com/help/policies/user-agreement. html*), which does change occasionally. Rather it's my impression of the high points. Your impression of the high points might be different than mine, and I urge you to take the time to read the Agreement in its entirety.

1. The information you provide for registration, bidding, or listing must be accurate and must not infringe on another's copyright or trademark.

2. eBay is only a venue. This means that eBay is only a place for

people to conduct their transactions. It does not take part in the transactions.

3. You release eBay from liability for any claims arising out of the transactions in which you take part on eBay. You indemnify eBay from any claims by third parties arising out of your breach of the Agreement.

4. High bidders have an obligation to buy.

5. Sellers have an obligation to sell once a bid above the minimum (or the reserve) has been made.

6. Bid manipulation or interference is prohibited for both buyers and sellers.

7. You may not use any software that will adversely affect eBay's website.

Additionally, the User Agreement incorporates the following documents by reference:

Privacy Policy

Outage Policy

Board Usage Policy

Nonbinding Bid Policy

Listing Policy

Half.com Policy

Investigations Policy

Prohibited, Questionable, and Infringing Item Policy

Real Estate Policy

Nonpaying Bidder Policy

Read the entire User Agreement and its incorporated documents yourself to get a full and complete understanding of what is expected of you and of the people with whom you will deal.

Trust

If you're new to eBay, you should now understand after reading the preceding two sections that trust lies at the heart of the eBay system. When you deal with someone a couple of thousand miles away, you have to trust them. Without trust, eBay would cease to function. Chapter 7 covers the feedback system, which builds the foundation for trust on eBay. Chapter 8 covers recourse against those who don't deserve your trust.

In 2003, eBay claimed that only one transaction in 10,000 was fraudulent. This indicates that fradulent transactions are hardly a commerce-threatening number. According to eBay, about 800 employees at eBay worked on security and enforcement in 2003, showing eBay's commitment to making eBay safe. Thus, one must conclude that trust does work when reinforced with the proper rules, regulations, and enforcement. The remainder of this chapter covers the general website mechanism that makes eBay bidding work. But don't lose sight of the fact that the most important ingredient of the eBay magic digital formula for success in buying, selling, and Web commerce is trust.

Navigation

The words at the top of the eBay home page are links that take you to various parts of the eBay website (see Figure 4.1).

home	sign out	services	site map	help ⑦

Browse	Search	Sell	My eBay	Community	Powered By IBM

Figure 4.1   Page-top links.

Site Map

Above the navigation bar perhaps the most important link is *site map*, which takes you to the eBay Site Map, a longer list of links. This map shows you everywhere you want to go on eBay, and you will find it quite handy (see Figure 4.2).

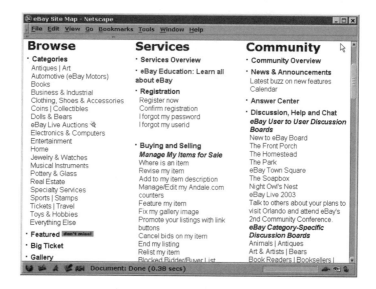

Figure 4.2   Site Map's list of links.

I often use the Site Map rather than the other links on the top of the page to find where I want to go on eBay.

Browse

The Browse link takes you to a short list of featured auctions. These are auctions for which someone has paid extra money in order to get extra attention. (In most cases, they're not very interesting primarily because they are featured by sellers, not elected by buyers.) A better way to get to the auctions you seek is to go below the featured auctions to see a more detailed list of categories than is displayed on the home page—a list that's quite useful. In addition, the sublinks under Browse take you to some specific sets of auctions (see Figure 4.3).

Figure 4.3   The Browse link and sublinks.

The sublinks enable you to browse auctions via local selection (*regions*) or even by *themes* (e.g., cooking). And there is a sublink to eBay Stores.

Search

The Search link is handy because it provides you with a comprehensive searching mechanism. You can search by item number, words, price range, categories, location of seller, seller, bidder, and eBay Stores. In addition, you can do an "advanced" search with even more comprehensive criteria including "completed items." This will help you do sophisticated searches without using the Boolean operators covered later in the Search Aids subsection.

Any Page

You can search from almost any eBay page, but that search input is limited. The Search link on the navigation bar takes you to the Search webpage that is much more complete (see Figure 4.4). You will find it useful from time to time.

Words

Searching on "words" is undoubtedly the most popular type of search. The eBay search engine searches through the item titles (see Chapter 12). You can elect, however, to include the item descriptions in the search too. Consequently, if a seller had a "5 megapixel Sony digital camera" in the title and you searched for a Sony DSC-V1, you might miss the auction. If the seller included the model number in the auction ad and you elected to include the item description in your search, you would find the auction.

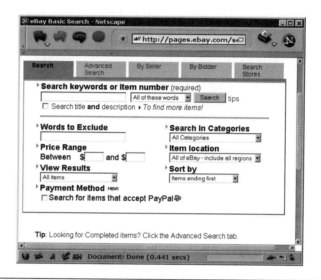

Figure 4.4   eBay Search page.

Search Aids

You can use certain symbols to help your search. Don't worry about memorizing them, because you can search well without them. When you get frustrated and can't find what you're looking for, however, you might want to try them.

No symbol Lists all auctions with all the included words in the auction title in any order. Thus, *Shure microphone* will list all auctions with both *Shure* and *microphone* in the auction title.

Asterisk (*) Use as a wild card. For instance, a search on *mic** will list all auctions that include *mic*, *microphone*, or *microphones* in the title. It will undoubtedly list some other unexpected auctions too (e.g., Mickey as in Mickey Mouse).

Quotations (" ") Restricts the search to the words in the exact order quoted. For instance, a search on *"Shure microphone"* will list only the auctions where *Shure* and *microphone* are contiguous and in the same order. Thus, such a search would miss *Shure dynamic microphone* or *microphone Shure*.

Minus Sign (–) Does not include titles with the word after the

minus. For example, *microphone –Shure* would include all auctions with *microphone* in the title except the ones that also had *Shure* in the title.

Parentheses ( ) Searches for both words in the parentheses. Hence, *(microphone,mic)* lists all auction titles with either *microphone* or *mic* in the title. You can use with a word outside the parentheses. For example, *microphone (Shure,Sony)* will list all auctions with *microphone* and *Shure* or *Sony* in the title.

Comma (,) Searches for either of the items separated by the comma (uses no spaces between words, only commas). You need this to use parentheses.

Keep in mind that the searches are not case-sensitive; that is, it doesn't matter whether you use upper- or lower-case letters in your words. Don't use the words *the, and, an, or,* and the like. The search engine ignores these words unless inside quotations. To keep your searches narrow and fast, search inside eBay categories, not in all of eBay.

Find Members

Another election is the Find Members search. It simplifies your search to find another eBay member whose eBay ID you know.

Favorite Searches

This election keeps a list of your searches that you want to use again and again. One click, and you can add a search. It even uses some artificial intelligence to automatically list your favorite categories. I discovered this feature while writing this book and have found it very handy for searching for rare items over long periods (e.g., a certain brand or model of electronic equipment).

Don't Give Up

Having trouble finding something you need or want? Don't give up until you've tried searching several different ways. The eBay search engine is quite powerful and makes it as easy as possible to find items. Taking a little time to learn to use the eBay *Search* will save you a lot of time in the future.

Sell

The Sell link takes you directly to the input form where you enter an auction. See Chapter 6 for information on entering auctions. The sublinks under Sell take you to useful information (seller guide), auction accounting (seller account), and eBay software services for sellers (seller tools).

My eBay

This link takes you directly to an accounting of everything you do on eBay. It's very handy, particularly when you lose track of what you've done or what you're doing. If you sell regularly, you will find this invaluable, at least until you choose to use a third-party auction management service. See more on *My eBay* later in this chapter.

Community

The Community section provides access to news sources, Discussion Boards, Chat, and even an Answer Center. You can read about the newest devices and procedures on eBay. You can get support, even live support. You can read stories about other eBay members. The eBay community is alive and dynamic.

Figure 4.5   The Community link and sublinks.

Services

In the Services section (link over the navigation bar) you can register to be an eBay member, find buying and selling aids, check feedback, or enter your About Me information (see Figure 4.6). From Services you can also access the eBay security sections.

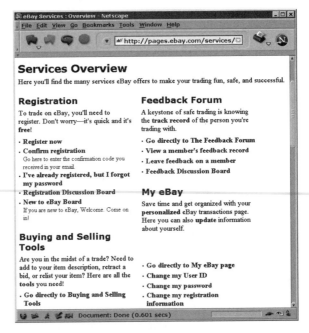

Figure 4.6   The top of the Service webpage.

Help

The Help section, or Help Center (link over the navigation bar), has information for rookies and old hands alike (see Figure 4.7).

Figure 4.7   The Help window.

Although when evaluated in isolation the Help Center appears to be a clever and helpful system, it has its drawbacks. On my browsers, the Help Center comes up in a small screen that I must manually expand to read easily. It has its own navigation system different from the eBay website. It always seems a little irratating to use. Nonetheless, it's a useful resource.

The Help Center has a lot of useful information. Time spent learning how to use it will save you lots of time in the future. Especially take a look at the A-Z Index. Perhaps most helpful is the quick access to information for buyers and sellers and to eBay rules and policies.

The Buying section takes you to a substantial amount of information about bidding auctions on eBay. If you are primarily interested in being an eBay buyer, this is an excellent place to start learning about eBay. It's also a reference that you can use anytime you have any questions. Go *Help, Buying* for buyer's information.

The Selling section link takes you to plenty of information on auctioning items on eBay. Use it to get started, and then use it as a reference. Go *Help, Selling* for seller's information.

Preparation

Starting with registration (discussed in the next section), you will be required to fill in forms on the eBay website for one thing or another. This section is a short tutorial to assist you.

If you have a broadband Internet connection, you simply fill out the form at your own pace while online. With broadband, you're always online until you turn off your computer. If you have a dial-up connection, however, you may feel uncomfortable spending a lot of time online. Perhaps your daughter wants to use the phone. Before filling out any eBay form, you can visit the form and save it. You can read it and even fill it in casually offline. In addition, with a few techniques, you can more effectively fill it in online.

Save As

Go *File, Save As* to save any webpage. This comes in handy for reading eBay information casually offline. After you save a webpage, remember where you saved it and what the file name is. Then access the webpage on your hard disk with your browser. With this technique, however, you can't fill in the forms and submit them.

Frozen Browser

After accessing an eBay form with your browser, simply go offline without closing the browser. The webpage will remain in the browser.

You can fill in the forms at your leisure. Then get back online and submit the form. This usually works, but not always.

Paste In

You can write text almost anywhere (e.g., in a word processor), highlight it, copy it to the clipboard, and paste it into a form in a webpage. This technique enables you to read, offline, an eBay webpage you have saved that includes forms. You can draft the input for the forms in a word processor offline. You can then get online, go to the forms, and copy and paste the text from the word processor into the eBay forms.

Registration

Registering to be a member of eBay is easy, fast, and free. Just fill in the registration form. You will choose an ID (your eBay name, which is a log-in name) and a password.

Welcome New Users

On the eBay home page you will notice a blue bar (see Figure 4.8). It's for new users and includes the following buttons: buying tips, selling tips, and register now. If you're new to eBay, this gives you quick access to appropriate information that will get you started.

Figure 4.8   The blue welcome banner.

The *Register Now* button will take you directly to the registration form where you can register immediately.

Before You Register

eBay is a lifelong asset. Before you register, take the time to understand how it works. More importantly, take the time to understand what it means. If you register immediately, thinking that eBay is some sort of a game, that attitude may lead you to activities that are unacceptable to eBay and the eBay community. As a result, you may have your eBay rights terminated indefinitely. The loss of rights for perhaps the most dynamic and powerful commerce marketplace of the new century will undoubtedly be a loss that you will regret sooner or later. Read Chapters 7 and 8 to be sure that you know what you're getting into and what the consequences will be if you abuse the system.

Registering

To register, you simply fill out the eBay online registration form. You'll know all the information requested except for your ID and password. You will have to dream those up.

Although you can navigate around the eBay website and even visit all the auctions, you cannot buy (bid) or sell anything unless you are a registered member. At least 69 million members have registered ahead of you. How difficult can it be?

ID (Log-In Name)

Pick an ID. Some people pick "cool" names such as *soaringeagle*. Others pick straightforward names like mine: *sinc* for Sinclair. Some use their email address so that people can always contact them. That, however, is no longer allowed.

Password

Don't take your passwords lightly anywhere, especially on eBay. If someone can find out your password, they can cause you much damage on eBay, financial and otherwise. Never use the same password for more than one website or service, and don't use short passwords (eight characters minimum). Mix lower case and numbers in your password but don't use words. If you follow these suggestions, it will be practically impossible for anyone else to use your account at eBay.

But it's a large burden to remember a lot of passwords, particularly for websites and services that you don't use often. I use Password Keeper (*http://www.gregorybraun.com*), a shareware program, to keep all my passwords. When I forget a password, I can always look it up in Password Keeper. If you protect yourself well by choosing long passwords, you'll need to look them up often.

Registration Form

The registration at *Services, Register now* is straightforward (see Figure 4.9). Choose your ID and password before you register so that you don't have to make a hurried decision. The registration will ask you for the usual name, address, and phone number as well as some personal questions (optional).

Figure 4.9   Top half of the registration form.

Confirmation

Click at the bottom of the form to submit your registration. Next you will have to wait. eBay will send you a confirmation number at your email address. You then take the confirmation number and follow the instructions (e.g., enter the confirmation number at the eBay website). The instructions will explain the remaining steps to complete your registration (e.g., enter ID and password). After you finish the registration process, you're legit. You can now buy and sell.

Auctions

You can use four types of auctions for over 27,000 categories of goods and services.

Categories

The general categories are on the home page. By clicking on a category, you get to lower-level categories as you go deeper and deeper into the category directory. The number of items currently up for auction are in parentheses after each category (see Figure 4.10). Chances are you will find a low-level category that will fit well what you want to buy or sell.

For instance, a click on *Music* (under *Entertainment*) takes you to a level of subcategories in which a click on *CDs, Blues* takes you to auctions featuring blues music on CDs.

When you finally get to a category you can use, you will see a list of auctions (see Figure 4.11). The listings you see are one-line each (eBay calls them titles) from eBay auctions (a limit of 45 characters). This one line, created by the seller who entered the auction, should indicate exactly what is being auctioned.

Figure 4.10   Categories on the eBay home page.

The One-Line Title

As you read the list of titles looking for what you want, you'll find it helps quite a bit if the list is easily readable (see Figure 4.11). It helps you to skim through the listings quickly. Titles that have poor-quality typesetting (e.g., all caps) create an impediment to reading.

People use poor-quality typesetting out of ignorance. They think that a technique like all caps will draw attention to their listing. Instead, it makes their listing less readable and creates a barrier to easily skimming the list. They think that if they are selling a Ford pickup truck that all caps will, by some magical attraction, draw in buyers who are looking for a Dodge van. Unfortunately, it doesn't work that way. Someone looking for a Dodge van will not buy a Ford pickup truck no matter what the title says and no matter how it is typeset. Instead, the person looking for the Ford pickup truck will have a more difficult time spotting the title because the title is all caps and more difficult to read.

The eye and brain together can easily pick out of a readable list whatever they look for. The more readable the list, the easier it is for you to find what you are looking for. The less readable the list, the more difficult it is to find what you are looking for. The one-line titles enable you to spot the auction of an item you are looking for. Then the specific auction page is just a click away. Remember this when, as a seller, you enter your auction ad.

Figure 4.11   eBay auction listing webpage.

Search

Once you have reached the lowest subcategory you can find, you can further refine your quest by using the search input near the top of the page on the left. For instance, suppose you have reached Blues and you see a long, multiple-page list of blues titles. But you're interested only in John Lee Hooker's music. Just type John Lee Hooker in the search input, and it will quickly and effectively search the Blues subcategory for John Lee Hooker's music.

Individual Auctions

Click on a title, and you will go to that auction. The auction is one webpage featuring one auction item. It has:

1. Standard information at the top

2. An auction ad (*Description*) created by the seller in the middle of the page

3. A place to bid at the bottom

For bidders, Chapter 5 covers the standard information and the bidding section. For sellers, Chapter 12 covers creating eBay auction ads.

Types

The four types of eBay auctions provide you some flexibility for your auctioning activities.

Normal

The normal auction is similar to a silent auction. The seller sets a minimum bid to start things off. Some sellers set the minimum bid low, some set it high. If it's low, it will probably be bid up to market value. If it's high, it will probably be bid up to market value, too. If the minimum is over market value, it's unlikely to get any bids at all. The normal auction is for one item (or package) only.

Reserve

A reserve is like a secret minimum. You can still use a minimum bid just as in a normal auction, but the reserve is the secret minimum. As soon as the reserve has been exceeded by the current high bidder (assuming it is exceeded), eBay publishes the fact that the reserve has been met. It doesn't make sense to use a reserve unless the reserve amount is higher than the minimum bid. The reserve auction is for one item (or package) only. If no bidders bid the reserve amount or higher, the seller does not have to sell the item.

Dutch

The Dutch auction is for multiple identical items. Bidders bid in the normal way, specifying how many of the identical items they are bidding on. The top bidders win the auction but pay only the bid of the lowest successful bidder. For instance, suppose you auction five identical new toasters. The bids follow in Table 4.1.

Table 4.1 Bids on Five New Toasters at a Dutch Auction

Alias	Number of Toasters	Bid ($)
sinklily	1	34
punkypete	1	33
livefive	2	32
laxtrainer	1	31
bynite	2	29
stonerich	1	27
rainmore	4	26

The bids of sinklily, punkypete, livefive, and laxtrainer take all five toasters. All the winning bidders pay only $31 each for the toasters, the lowest bid of a successful bidder (i.e., laxtrainer's bid). The seller sets the minimum bid, but no reserve is allowed in a Dutch auction.

Private

Anyone can bid at a private auction. What makes it private? The auction display keeps the bidders' identities secret. Of course, eBay notifies the seller of the winning bidder's identity, but that's the only bidder that even the seller will know.

Comparison

The four types of auctions are briefly compared in Table 4.2, showing the advantages and disadvantages of each.

Table 4.2 Four Auction Types

Type	Advantages	Disadvantages
Normal	Lets market set price	No minimum guaranteed price (except minimum bid)
Reserve	Minimum guaranteed price (unpublished)	Item may not sell
Dutch	Can sell numerous identical items at once	If minimum price too high, no bids is a possibility
Private	For bidders who want anonymity	Fewer potential bidders

Restricted Access

This is not a separate type of auction. It's a restricted category. The only restricted auction currently is adult erotica. eBay attempts to ensure that anyone accessing this category is 18 or older by requiring a credit card number prior to access.

Duration

Auctions run for three, five, seven, or ten days. They end exactly at the same time of day as they started. For example, a three-day auction that starts at 7:47 PM on Monday night ends at 7:47 PM on Thursday night. A seven-day auction starts and ends on the same day, same time. Consequently, you choose when you want your auction to end by entering it at the requisite time three, five, seven, or ten days earlier.

Prohibited Auctions

eBay has rules prohibiting certain things from being sold on eBay. The rules make sense, and eBay adds to the forbidden items as experience dictates. The list below includes some, but not all, of the items prohibited:

- Alcohol
- Child pornography
- Current catalogs
- Counterfeit items
- Securities (e.g., stocks and bonds)
- Human body parts
- Credit cards
- Controlled substances (i.e., illicit drugs)
- Prescription drugs
- Tobacco
- Forged autographs
- Autographed items
- Embargoed goods
- Military weapons
- Bootleg recordings
- Firearms and fireworks
- Locksmith paraphernalia

- Animals and wildlife products

- TV descramblers

- Surveillance equipment

- Replicas of government IDs or licenses

- Law-enforcement IDs and badges

- Current license plates

- Stolen things

- Lottery tickets

- Academic software

- Spam lists or software

- Beta software

- Postage meters

- Things that infringe on a copyright or trademark

For an updated list, go to the Help Center and start with eBay Policies.

In addition, eBay treats some items as questionable. They are not prohibited absolutely, but you will have to be careful that you don't break any rules by selling them. A partial list of items includes:

- Used medical equipment

- Contracts

- Tickets

- Weapons and knives

- Autographed things

- Food

- Batteries

- Used clothing

- Offensive and adult items

- Artifacts

- Freon

- Pre-sale listings

- Police-related items

- Hazardous materials

- Non-FCC-compliant electronic equipment

- International transactions

If something on these lists catches your attention, you need to investigate the details. Incidentally, eBay no longer keeps these prohibited items listed separately. It intermingles both the absolutely prohibited and the questionable items. You need to seek out the reasons for and the degree of prohibition of each item on the lists that may affect your selling efforts.

The prohibition against infringing materials bears some additional comment. They include copyrighted items such as copies of music, movies, television shows, software, written works, games, photographs, artwork, images, and promotional items. But infringement is more complex than just stating a simple list of banned copies, and you will do well to read what eBay has to say about infringement, or potential infringement, if there is any possibility at all that you might be auctioning items for which this might be an issue.

VeRO

If you are an owner of copyrights—manifested in copyrighted materials—and sellers are auctioning infringing copies of your works on eBay, you can join the Verified Rights Owner (VeRO) program. This enables you to work together with eBay to curtail the infringing sales. Software developers and recorded music companies are active VeRO program members.

Finally, eBay treats real estate in a special way. Real estate auctions are allowed but not binding on either party. eBay also has a special fee for real estate auctions.

Gallery

eBay also presents auctions in a way different from just a list of one-line titles. It presents auctions in a photo gallery. Go *site map*, *Browse*, *Gallery*. This applies, of course, only to auctions that include a photograph and have been placed in the Gallery. If anything, the Gallery points out how important text (which it does not have) is in identifying items that people seek to purchase. Nonetheless, the Gallery is another place for your item to be displayed. But you can't get there without a photograph in your auction ad.

Keep in mind that, for certain items, looking at photographs is the best way to find what you're looking for. For instance, you might find it more convenient to look at Japanese prints in the Gallery than to hunt them down in individual auctions.

To have your auction listing (together with a photograph) included in the Gallery costs a little extra, but if your item justifies such a display, the Gallery may help you sell it.

After the Auction

eBay is not a party to the auctions. It is up to you as either the buyer or seller to contact the other party to consummate the transaction. As a buyer (high bidder), I sometimes have an urgent need for the merchandise. Therefore, I contact the seller by email immediately to ask about exact payment, mailing address, etc.

However, contacting an eBay retailer can affect their follow-up system. Some sellers look upon unsolicited communications from buyers as an unnecessary interference with their auction management systems. Regardless, I still contact a seller when I need an item urgently. Otherwise I wait for the seller's email.

As a seller, you want to send a communication as soon as possible to the high bidder after an auction. This is especially important if you run many auctions. You need an email follow-up system that works so well that you discourage unsolicited email messages from buyers. Individual email from customers is time-consuming to handle, inefficient, and unprofitable, particularly for transactions involving inexpensive items. Naturally, when a problem arises, you are happy to get it sorted out by communicating with your customers. But, otherwise, you don't have the time and energy to exchange email with them any more than is necessary.

Communication Management

Note that both eBay and most auction management services send email to the buyer immediately after the auction concludes. The official eBay notice is just background noise and will not keep a buyer from contacting the seller. However, the seller can elect to send the buyer an additional invoice via eBay. If the seller does so immediately after the auction, the invoice will keep the buyer from making an unnecessary communication. Best of all is an auction management service which will automatically and immediately send the buyer an invoice. Thus, the buyer will not make any unnecessary communication to seller.

Escrow Services

eBay no longer provides escrow services. It recommends Escrow.com (*http://www.escrow.com*). However, you can go *Services, SafeHarbor, Escrow services* to find additional recommendations for other countries. (A company that provides buyer-seller protection and intends to provide escrow services in the future is eDeposit, *http://www.edeposit.com*).

You must go through a series of steps, which Escrow.com spells out, to complete your escrow. Escrow.com will charge you 3 percent on the first $5,000 of value, 2 percent on the next $10,000 up to $15,000, 1 percent on the next $10,000 up to $25,000, and 0.85 percent on the value above that. If the buyer uses a credit card for payment, the fees go up substantially. This is not inexpensive, but it's worth it to a buyer who writes a big check.

What about sellers? Is it worth it? My position has always been that it is, indeed, worth it to sellers. If a buyer accepts an item in escrow, it's difficult for that buyer to come back later and claim that the merchandise is unacceptable. He or she has already accepted it. That's a decided benefit to sellers. Therefore, I believe that buyers and sellers should split the escrow fees. Nonetheless, many sellers disagree with me, as you might guess.

eBay recommends an escrow closing for transactions over $500. Everyone has their own opinion about this threshold amount, and the opinions of the buyer and seller will dictate the amount. Quite frankly, escrow closings are more trouble for sellers, and most sellers would like to see a higher threshold than $500. As a seller, one way to make yourself look good but raise the threshold is to put your escrow policy in your auction ad boilerplate. For example:

> No escrow closings acceptable for items with a sales price under $2,000.

A buyer of a $1,300 item might be disappointed, but he or she will still get a comfortable feeling that you don't make a blanket prohibition of escrow closings. A seller who does make a blanket prohibition of escrow closings is suspect and will lose some potential bidders.

Wanted Page

Where do buyers without an auction to bid go? If you can't find something you want up for auction, go to an appropriate Discussion Board and ask the Board participants. eBay used to have a Wanted bulletin board, but apparently it wasn't very popular. I can't find it any longer. Go *Community, Talk, Discussion Boards* for a list of forums you can join to ask about an item you want.

Researching an eBay User

You can research another user's feedback (see Chapter 7 regarding analyzing a user's feedback). Go *Services, Feedback Forum*. You will need the user's ID.

You can also research another user's history of aliases and email addresses or full contact information (including address and phone). Go *Search, Find Members*. Again, you will need the user's ID. In this case, eBay notifies the user. This can provide you with a wealth of information on another eBay user for evaluating a seller or buyer or for making a transaction work.

Researching Market Values

Because market value is so important to success on eBay and because research is so important to determining market value, use the following list of sources to find the market value of items. Keep in mind that obtaining list prices is a good place to start in determining the used value of manufactured items.

Catalogs Look through printed catalogs and catalogs online of offline retailers and manufacturers.

eCommerce Look through the online catalogs of retail businesses that exist only online.

Completed Auctions You can access completed auctions on eBay where they are archived for a few weeks. You will find the winning bid amounts.

Shop Get in your car and go shopping.

Magazines Read specialty magazines. Many collectibles magazines feature compilations of values, and all specialty magazines have retail ads, many of which feature prices.

Manufacturers Go to manufacturers' websites. Often suggested retail prices are posted.

Books The library has reference books that are price guides. They are usually old news but still may be useful.

Appraisers Chat with an appraiser who knows market values.

Dealers Chat with a dealer who knows the market well.

eBay Resources Go *Community* on the navigation bar and try the following: (1) specialty Chat sessions where you can get advice from eBay retail experts; (2) Discussion Boards where you can also get advice.

Web Search Engines Use Google to look up items, and you will get to some of the sources mentioned earlier. It's a quick and efficient way to research.

Research—meaning the determination of market value—is the one most effective technique for success on eBay for both buyers and sellers. How do you know what to do unless you know the market value?

Completed Items

If you go through the categories and subcategories until you narrow down your quest for an item to a list of auctions, you can reach the eBay archives by doing a search.

For instance, suppose you go Jewelry Boxes, Vintage and find 800 items. You're looking for Lady Buxton jewelry boxes. In the search entry, type "buxton" and check the *in titles and descriptions* check box. You will get a more narrow selection of auction listings as a result. In addition, a link *Completed items* will magically appear on the left near the top.

Click on that link, and you will get several weeks of completed auctions with winning bid amounts displayed. These are "comparables" for appraisal purposes.

Representing Yourself

As you will read in Chapter 7, your reputation on eBay generates the trust you need to make successful transactions. If your reputation fails—due to your bad behavior—you will have a difficult time getting anyone to do business with you. You always want to be conscious of how you treat other people and be careful that you don't violate any eBay rules.

Feedback System

You can rate other eBay members with positive, neutral, or negative feedback and also make comments. Such ratings, however, are limited to transactions; that is, buyers and sellers rate each other.

There is no requirement that buyers and sellers rate each other for each transaction, but many do. So, there are plenty of ratings on each active member (except rookies) to establish a reputation. The feedback system works well. A person can't treat other people unfairly or with abuse without incurring negative feedback.

If One Doesn't Behave

The positive feedback ratings (for each positive rating you get a +1) and negative ratings (for each negative rating you get a –1) are added. If a person gets to a rating of –4, eBay automatically suspends his or her membership.

About Me

The feedback *comments* tend to be valuable when they are negative (assuming they provide the facts) and useless when they are positive (mostly ridiculous praise), although the *ratings* are always valuable. However, eBay gives you a chance to tell people something about yourself. You can make an entry in About Me, and everyone can read it. If you do make an About Me entry, an About Me icon goes next to your name so that people will know that your information exists to be read. This eBay device gives you a chance to tell your story and increase your credibility.

If you sell regularly on eBay, your *About Me* webpage provides you with an opportunity to advertise. You can even include a link to your ecommerce website if you have one.

You can't be sure about trusting someone based on his or her About Me profile, but it's significant information that together with other information (e.g., feedback) you can use to make an informed judgment.

Be Prepared

Before you start your About Me entry, prepare your information ahead of time offline. Look at a dozen or more of other people's About Me presentations and decide how you want yours to read. Write the information. Find a graphic you want to include (e.g., a digital photograph of yourself). Then log onto eBay to make the entry in the form at *Services*, *About Me*. You will find a handy form to fill in. Copy and paste the information you have prepared into the inputs in the form. Your photograph, if you use one, will have to be available on the Web somewhere (see Chapter 11), and you put the URL of your photograph in the appropriate input in the About Me form.

A webpage

If you are not satisfied with what you can enter into the form casually, create a webpage about yourself instead. Submit the webpage into the input in the form. Remember to copy only the *<body>* portion of the webpage when you copy and paste. Do this the same way as when you submit the template for advertising as outlined in Chapter 12 or as covered in Chapter 18 in regard to using a Web authoring program. In other words, cut off the top and bottom of the webpage.

Submitting a webpage

Because Chapters 12 and 18 show you the general means of submitting a webpage for an input in a Web form, this chapter does not duplicate such information. You can also use the HTML tutorial in Appendix IV.

Edit

Don't worry about making your About Me perfect the first time. You can always go back and edit it or completely revise it.

Security

eBay has started a security program—ID Verify—wherein they check a member's application against the facts in an Equifax Secure, Inc., database to ascertain that a person is really who he says he is. It requires that a person submit via secured transmission (Secure Sockets Layer or SSL—built into Web browsers) certain personal information and a $5 fee. *This program is optional*. It is an excellent program that all honest and forthright eBay citizens should embrace. It provides an extra measure of protection against fraud and other criminal behavior. Although it's a voluntary program, eBay members can make it a compulsory program, in effect, by refusing to deal with anyone who isn't verified. That, of course, will not happen. Nonetheless, you can refuse to deal with anyone for large transactions whose ID is not verified. This is part of eBay's SafeHarbor program to ensure that eBay is a safe place to do business.

Not a Credit Check

The eBay Equifax check is not a credit check. It's just a check to verify name, address, and other basic data.

The additional security fostered by the ID Verify program should encourage the growth of the membership and the additional participation of the members in eBay auctions, particularly auctions for more expensive items.

Naturally, people who are properly identified are more likely to behave well (i.e., be trustworthy). You would like to deal with people whose identities have been verified, and that works both ways. Buyers would like to know that sellers are who they say they are. After all, buyers are making payment and trusting that sellers will send the merchandise. Sellers would like to know that buyers are who they say they are. Invariably, sellers have problems with bogus bidding by people who hide behind their unverified eBay IDs. Accommodate both buyers and sellers. Have your ID verified.

ID Verify

To have your ID verified, go *Services*, *Buying & Selling Tools*, *Trade with Confidence*, *ID Verify*. The process takes you through a questionnaire that includes questions about your affairs that only you and Equifax would know. You are later notified as to whether you have been approved (verified).

This provides more assurance to other parties that you are unlikely to be a con artist. Most criminals do not want their true identities known. Unfortunately, for some reason this verification has not caught on. You can make it more popular—and perhaps eventually compulsory—by having your ID verified.

eBay does require ID Verify for buyers for transactions over $15,000. I believe this threshold should be lowered considerably ($500?) and applied to sellers as well. eBay has matured into an important national marketplace. eBay is no longer a place for con artists or miscreants who want to play games. ID Verify will go a long way toward reducing the number of both.

eBay requires a credit card or bank account from sellers. This is a sort of verification process, even though its purpose ostensibly is to ensure payment to eBay for seller's fees. If eBay cannot verify your credit card or bank account for some reason, you will have to use the ID Verify process instead in order to be permitted to sell on eBay.

Should you be afraid of the ID Verify process? My experience was that I didn't have to give any information that Equifax didn't already know. Giving your Social Security number is optional (and I didn't give mine), but, in any event, Equifax probably already knows it.

If you are a regular eBay user, either buyer or seller, I strongly recommend that you get ID Verify and require it of the other eBay users with whom you deal, particularly on high-dollar auctions. Widespread use of ID Verify will reduce the risk in the eBay marketplace for both buyers and sellers.

PayPal Verification

PayPal requires verification for you to become a PayPal member. This is a feature of membership that makes PayPal a safe payment system. There are various levels of verification, and you should opt for at least one level above the normal in order to increase your credibility.

Privacy

An objection can be raised that ID Verify is an invasion of privacy—your privacy—by eBay. Indeed, you do have to trust eBay when you give bits of personal information. In my opinion, eBay has earned your trust, although everyone must remain alert to be sure it doesn't abuse your trust in any way. The risk of abuse compared to the advantage of greater security seems to be a risk worth taking.

Quality of Protection

A verification merely helps ascertain that a person is who he says he is. But John Larkspur (a name I made up) can be who he says he is and still be a Web ecommerce criminal. Therefore, all a verification does is identify a person.

I suppose if you start chasing a Web ecommerce criminal for recovery of stolen funds, it's best to know who he is. Presumably without the verification it might be difficult to know the true identity of the person you want to chase. But knowing the true identity of someone is no guarantee that you will catch him or recover stolen funds. In the final analysis, you have to rely on other indices of trust to do business with a person on the Web.

That's why the eBay feedback system is so valuable. It provides you with an eBay member's reputation. That, together with a verification, is perhaps better protection than you get offline for dealing with someone you don't know.

By-Product

A by-product of the eBay verification and feedback system may be the use of eBay as a general commerce reference. In other words, suppose you want to do some business with an appliance dealer (either on or off the Web) that involves a certain degree of trust (e.g., installment sale). The dealer can run a credit check on you. But perhaps that's not enough. The dealer can also look up your feedback on eBay. If you're verified, perhaps the dealer will have even more confidence that you are who you say you are without checking your driver's license. Will your ID on eBay be requested on credit applications in the future? That's something to think about.

Community

eBay is a community of people who are drawn together to take part in ecommerce. Many are just occasional community members, but others pursue selling activities that make it profitable to take part in eBay often. If you are one of those who uses eBay often, you may be interested in one of the communities supported by eBay.

Chat

To visit Chat on the eBay website, go *Community, Talk, Chat*. You will find a variety of chat rooms where people talk in real time with others currently signed into the chat room. The "talk" is in writing and appears on the chat board.

You can also use Discussion Boards (aka forum, mailing list, discussion group) to communicate with other eBay members. Go *Community, Talk, Discussion Boards* to find a variety of online Boards. The Boards discuss various aspects of eBay and other topics. If you want more specific information regarding buying and selling, eBay also features Boards on specific ecommerce topics. If you deal in certain types of goods, eBay may sponsor a Discussion Board that has created a community in regard to such goods. For instance, there are Boards on jewelry, toys, and photography, among many others.

And don't overlook the International Boards. That's your ticket to expanding your sales to other countries.

If you need help, need to understand a certain process, or want to help others, you can participate in the Answer Center, which covers a variety of topics regarding eBay operations. Go *Community, Talk, Answer Center*.

When you're having trouble contacting another eBay member, you can go to the Emergency Contact chat room and get some assistance. This is handy after the seller gets your check for $125 and is suddenly out of touch.

Finally, you can participate in a Workshop Board, a temporary Board on a very specific topic. You can even read past Workshop Boards. This a type of Web-based training.

And that's not all. There's news and event schedules and stories about eBay members all under *Community* on the navigation bar.

Help

It cannot be over emphasized that participating in an eBay online community when you need help can be very productive. You can return again and again as you run across new problems. Of course, don't forget that someday it will be your turn to give help instead of get it.

Is a Community for You?

Many of us do not have enough interest in the goods we use to join a community (unless we are professionals or collectors). Nonetheless, communities can be meaningful. As a buyer, you can join a community, albeit temporarily, to seek advice for making a purchase. Have your eye on a 30-year-old Nikon 300mm telephoto lens on auction and want to find out if you can use it on your 15-year-old Nikon camera body? Join the Photography Board and ask the experts. While you're there, have some good conversations, make some new friends, and enjoy the community in addition to getting the information you need.

As a seller, your participation in specialty Boards will put you in touch with prospective customers and increase your credibility. It's a natural for promoting your business so long as you don't practice blatant com-

mercialism. Promote yourself and your business very subtly. Be helpful, be friendly, and give advice (based on your expertise as a retailer or
user). People will recognize your contribution and remember you
favorably.

Not Free

Being a member of an eBay community does not come free. If you
participate regularly, it will take a lot of your time.

Education

There are user tutorials. Look for them via *Site Map*, *Services*, *eBay
Education*. That will take you to the eBay Learning Center where tons
of fun and education await you. If you haven't used eBay before, it will
help you get going. In addition, you can attend eBay University in a
city near you as eBay goes on the road.

Visits to the Auctionbytes (*http://auctionbytes.com*) website will keep
you up to date on a host of eBay-related topics. Sign up for the two free
email newsletters about online auctions. Ira Steiner, the editor and
publisher, does a nice job of producing high-quality information.

Attend eBay Live!, the annual eBay conference, which features three
days of enlightening seminars and a great opportunity to meet other
eBay members. In June 2004 it will be in New Orleans. Check the
eBay website for information on the conference for subsequent years.

eBay Customer Service

eBay seems a little weak in customer service for eBay users. True, it
has a wide range of assistance features well presented. If, however, you
have a special problem to solve, it's tough to find a place to get assistance. For instance, I signed up for ID Verify, went through the procedure, and was approved. Nonetheless, nowhere was it indicated that I

had ID Verify. It's supposed to be noted with a special icon in your feedback section. (Eventually it appeared.)

When I checked my feedback, not only was the ID Verify icon missing but I had at least four positive feedbacks that were not mine. (They could have been negative feedback!) When I tried to get the mess straightened out, I spent a considerable amount of time trying to find where to contact eBay about these problems. Finally, I found a place to email eBay buried in a suggestion box somewhere on the site map. In other words, eBay doesn't encourage custom handling of user problems. Unfortunately, sometimes custom handling is the only way to solve problems.

In answer to my email, eBay told me that the ID Verify icon would be added to my eBay persona immediately but that it was my problem to get the erroneously filed feedback straightened out. Since the erroneous feedback is positive, I have no incentive to correct it. Were it negative, I would be incensed over eBay's unwillingness to take any responsibility.

One strategy for finding the proper place to go for getting help when you need it is to consult the Answer Center. Go *Help*, *Ask eBay Members*, *Answer Center*. Ask a question and get an answer from a fellow eBay member.

My eBay

eBay is a great mechanism for buying and selling, and it does provide a variety of online customer service devices mentioned throughout this book. A very useful one is *My eBay*. Note that the link *My eBay* is found on the navigation bar on every eBay page.

My eBay is a customer service device that features the following:

- Bidding record
- Watch list

- Selling record

- Recent feedback

- Account status

- Favorite categories and searches list

- Feedback status

- Sign-in preferences

The records of your bidding and selling show what you've done on eBay. The watch list shows the auctions you've marked to watch.

Watching

In the basic information on each auction page, you will find a link labeled *watch this item*. You can put any auction on your "watch" list. You can see your watch list in *My eBay*. The list helps you keep track of items in which you're interested but have not yet bid. When an auction starts to look interesting, you can join the bidding.

The recent feedback shows a partial record of your feedback. The account status shows how much, if anything, you have on deposit with eBay to pay your auction fees. It also can show a record of all your fees paid (going back to your first day, if you're willing to wait for the eBay database to crank out archived data). The favorites list gives you quick access to your favorite categories and saves you some navigation time. Try it. If you're a heavy eBay user, it can save a lot of time.

The sign-in preferences enable you to pick eBay functions for which you will not have to input your ID and password after you sign in. *This is especially valuable for automatically entering your ID and password for bidding; it saves time in bidding contests during the final minutes of an auction.*

Thus, *My eBay* provides you with convenient one-stop service to review your activities on eBay and even set up navigation and bidding shortcuts. Try the *My eBay* link over the navigation bar. You may find it's just what you've been looking for.

Anywhere

If your question is, Where can I access eBay? the answer is, Anywhere! Indeed, eBay even supports portable wireless devices including:

- WAP (wireless application protocol) cell phones
- Pagers
- PDAs (personal digital assistants)

Go *Site Map, Services, Buyer Tools, eBay Anywhere - Wireless*. See Figure 4.12. This gives you the opportunity to keep up with your eBay commerce even when you're away from your home or your job. eBay's support for these technologies is through the normal vendors such as AT&T and Sprint.

Support for these devices means, of course, that as a buyer you never have to miss a final-hour bidding competition, nor as a seller will you miss answering questions by potential bidders in a timely manner.

Charity

Yes, eBay even provides you with opportunities for charity. Go *Community, Overview, Charity*. You will find fund-raising auctions sometimes affiliated with celebrities such as Rosie O'Donnell.

Summary

eBay works well and is easy to use as this chapter demonsttrates. If you have difficulty getting started, you can get plenty of help. Once you get rolling, you can get even more help. Amazingly, almost everything discussed in this chapter is free. What a deal!

Trust is the foundation of the eBay system. Once you understand that and come to have confidence in eBay, you will feel free to sell or bid and then complete eBay transactions. But you must still be wary to protect yourself, and eBay provides some devices that you can use to do so.

Yes, the system does have some complexity. Much of the complexity, however, addresses problems you may never have. So, learn the basics, but at least skim over some of the exotic features; you'll know they're there when you need them.

Figure 4.12   eBay Anywhere.

5

Bidding

Bidding is where the fun is. It's a kick to bid and win, particularly when you have some competition. But the fun is the frosting on the cake for most people. Most people seek to purchase an item because it's at a good price or because they can't find it elsewhere. And no matter how much fun it is, it's also serious business just as any commercial transaction is serious business. Hence, enjoy your bidding, but don't lose sight of the fact that the winning bidder is obligated to buy the item auctioned.

Bidding

There is a string of steps to go through to bid on an auction. The first step is finding something to bid on.

Finding What You're Looking For

You can use the eBay auction categories, which are organized into a tree, starting on the home page. This is perhaps the easiest way to find what you are looking for. The eBay search mechanism can be useful too.

Categories

Follow the categories from the most general on the eBay home page (or Browse page) to the more specific (see Figure 5.1). When you get as far as you can go, look at the listings. You will find some items that you are looking for.

For instance, to get to microphones, start with *Musical Instruments* on the eBay home page. Then select *Pro Audio, Wired Microphones*. That will provide you with a listing of microphones. In many cases, you may find more items than you want to look through. You can narrow the search even further.

Searches

Once you get to a listing that contains the item you are looking for (e.g., wired microphones), you can plug a keyword into the search input and narrow the listings even more. For instance, while at the *Wired Microphones* auction listing page, input *Shure*. Check Search only in Wired Microphones (see Figure 5.2).

You will get a new listing of auctions that will be all Shure microphones, or, to be more accurate, all the auctions in the listing will have *Shure* in the title (401 auctions the day I tried this search in August 2003—see Figure 5.3).

Figure 5.1 The eBay auction category *Pottery, Glass and Porcelain*.

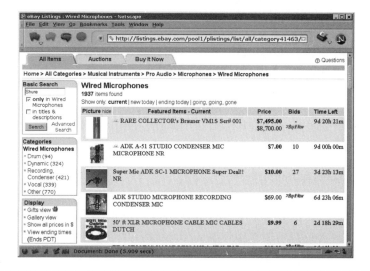

Figure 5.2 Using the search input to narrow the listings for a microphone.

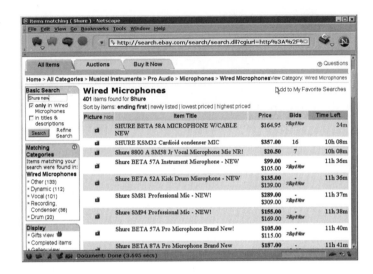

Figure 5.3   Using the search input for further search refinement.

You can refine your list with the search function as much as you want to. You don't necessarily have to do it in steps. Try *Shure new* to view only auctions that offer new Shure microphones.

eBay Search Tips

Sometimes the keywords for searches are obvious. Sometimes you have to figure out the not so obvious. And sometimes more than one keyword works. For instance, a microphone is also a *mic*. If you used mic as the keyword in the preceding search, you got 610 *mic* auctions out of a total of 1937 *microphone* auctions.

Misspellings

Sellers misspell words. Sometimes if you try some misspellings, you can find items that don't get much traffic specifically due to the misspelling. For instance, if someone misspelled *mic* as *mike*, they would have gotten only 12 microphones listed out of a total of 1937. If you can find items that are misspelled, you may find an auction with very little bidding competition.

Plurals

Oddly enough, there's a difference between singular and plural in the eBay search. Plural words can leave items out in the cold. For instance, if someone uses *microphones* instead of *microphone*, the items will not get as much traffic (only 83 auctions out of 1937 *microphone* auctions).

Pure Searches

You don't have to begin with categories. You can use the eBay search engine right from the start. Go *Search* and pick the type of search you want to do. The various search menus are self-directing.

International

Select the *Advanced Search*. You can search in more than one country. In fact, you can search all the eBay auctions in 27 countries. Of course, because of the words you use, you're likely to find listings only in English-speaking countries.

Reminder

There's a more detailed explanation of pure searching in Chapter 4, which covers advanced searching techniques.

eBay Stores

Don't forget eBay Stores. You can search eBay Stores as well as eBay auctions. Go *Browse*, *Stores* and look for the *Search Stores* entry in the upper left of the webpage. Stores offer you fixed-price items for which you don't bid. You just pay your money to buy instantly.

Reading the Listing

Many sellers, surprisingly, can adequately specify what an item is in 45 words. Consequently, when you skim the list of auctions, you will be able to easily spot what you are looking for. Only the poor typesetting and bizarre titles will impede you. Auctions with photographs will have a picture icon beside the title.

New

You can have the listing arranged a variety of ways (e.g., ascending or descending based on closing date). New auctions have a new icon beside them. If you see the new icon at the top of the listing, you will know that the auction listing is arranged in descending order. However, the default is ascending order (oldest auctions first).

Reading the Auction

When you click on an auction title, the first thing you see is the basic information on the auction (see Figure 5.4). The basic information includes many links, which lead to more information.

The words *Current bid* show the current bid. This is accurate. (The bid amount in the listing for a particular auction title is often inaccurate—a delayed posting.) If you want to know the latest bid, refresh the auction webpage (use the refresh button in browser) and look at *Current bid*.

Reserve

If the auction is a reserve auction, once the reserve has been met or surpassed, the term (reserve met) will appear beside the bid amount. Until that happens, the reserve has not been met and the caption will read (reserve not yet met). If you don't see either of these, it's not a reserve auction.

The term *History* shows the number of bids and links to a list of bidders. There will be no bid amounts shown by the bidders, however, until after the auction is over.

Figure 5.4   The basic information is at the top of the auction webpage.

The word *Location* indicates where the seller lives or does business. That will determine whether you will have to pay sales tax if you win the auction. It also places the auction in a regional auction.

The word *Seller information* shows the seller. Click on the seller's ID and you will get a screen that provides the seller's email address, after you log in. Sometimes a seller's name is an email address in which case a click on the name will bring up your email client. After the seller's name is a link, in parentheses, to the seller's feedback rating. A summary of the seller's feedback appears just below.

The term *(View seller's other items)* links to a webpage that shows all the current auctions that the seller operates.

Notice that the auction title and the auction number are at the top of the page.

Those are the highlights, but there is other information there too. Look around and check things out. But that's not all. Scroll down the page, and you will get to the auction ad. eBay provides space for an auction ad—a long one if desired by seller.

Auction Ad

The auction ad is whatever the seller wants it to be. See Chapter 12 for details. This is a seller's chance to provide all the information necessary to help the buyer make a decision to bid. As a bidder, this is your chance to get all the information you need to make a decision to bid. If you don't get the information you need, you have three choices. First, you can pass, as will many other potential bidders. Second, you can bid without proper information, a choice you may regret. Third, you can contact the seller to get more information. If you have considerable interest in an item, contacting the seller is sometimes the only way you can get adequate information.

Making a Bid

At the bottom of the auction webpage, you can place a bid. Above the input is the current minimum bid. Your bid must equal such an amount plus one increment higher. Click on the *Place Bid* button when you are ready to submit your bid (see Figure 5.5).

Then you get a webpage that requires your login and password. You need to input your ID and password before you finally enter your bid by clicking the *Submit* button (see Figure 5.6).

Sign In Prior to Bidding

You can avoid this step by signing in when you first visit the eBay website. Above the navigation bar is a sign-in link.

Figure 5.5   Bidding on the auction webpage.

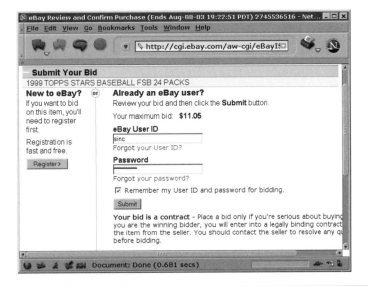

Figure 5.6   The password page.

Set Preference for Quick Bidding

Once you have signed in, you do not have to enter your ID again for the duration of your eBay session. But you will still have to enter your password wherever it's required on eBay unless you take the further step of setting your sign-in preferences. For whichever preferences you check under *My eBay Preferences*, you will not have to provide your password for that procedure during the current session. One preference is bidding, and not having to enter your ID and password for each bid can give you an advantage in the final minutes of a contested auction.

See Chapter 9 for the Double Window technique that saves additional time submitting bids.

Bidding Increments

The bidding increments are automatically enforced by the eBay system. See Table 5.1.

Table 5.1 Bidding Increments

Bid ($)	Increment ($)
to 0.99	0.05
1.00 to 4.99	0.25
5.00 to 24.99	0.50
25.00 to 99.99	1.00
100.00 to 249.99	2.00
250.00 to 499.99	5.00
500.00 to 999.99	10.00
1,000.00 to 2,499.99	25.00
2,500.00 to 4,999.99	50.00
5,000.00 and over	100.00

After All

After all this talk about bidding, sellers can now give you a fixed price too. Look for the *Buy It Now* icon (see Chapter 6).

After Your Bid

Chapter 9 provides much information on bidding, including strategies and tactics. After you bid, you will probably want to keep track of the auction in order to bid again or perhaps just to see the final outcome of the bidding.

Checking Your Email

When you bid, eBay sends you an email acknowledging your bid. This makes a good record. Don't discard it. You can find much information in this email message that you may need later.

Reviewing Your Activity

You get the best information—and the latest high bid—by refreshing the auction webpage. In fact, this is essential to do in the last minutes of competitive bidding for an item in order to keep up with the bidding. This is the only up-to-date source of the latest high bid.

Current Auctions

You can always check the record of the auctions you have bid on (that are still open) should you lose track because you are bidding on several items. Go to the *Search* page and search *By Bidder* using your ID.

My eBay

Another place you can check is the more comprehensive record called *My eBay*.

Bidding

Go *My eBay* on the navigation bar. It features a record of your bidding. This is a good place to keep track of your bidding since other eBay convenient services are readily available.

Watching

eBay provides a way to make a list of auctions you want to keep track of but have not yet bid on. You put them on the watch list at *My eBay*. Thus, you can keep track of your bids and auctions you watch in one convenient place.

Being Outbid

As soon as you are outbid, eBay sends you an email message acknowledging you have been outbid. However, this is not a very good way to keep up with the bidding, particularly in the last hour of the bidding.

Winning the Auction

If you win the auction, eBay will send you a message informing you. Thereafter, it's up to you and the seller to get together to consummate the transaction.

Following Up

Traditionally, it's the seller who emails the high bidder to inform him or her of the details regarding payment and shipping. Nonetheless, if you don't hear from the seller in a timely manner, take the initiative to contact the seller. Keep following up until the transaction is completed.

For most transactions, the eBay checkout scheme works well. It's for your convenience. Use it unless the seller directs you to do otherwise. The checkout will lead you through the payment procedure.

Retracting a Bid

You can retract a bid if you desire, but you open yourself to negative feedback. You better have a pretty good excuse. Don't retract a bid. A little forethought will prevent unnecessary retractions. Go *Services, Buying and Selling Tools, Buyer Tools, Retract My Bid* for instructions on retracting your bid.

Optional eBay Bidding Features

This section mentions some of the eBay devices that are available to help you reduce your risk as a bidder.

What For?

This section is for collectibles, antiques, jewelry, and the like. It isn't for recently manufactured mass-produced consumer items. You don't have to have a Minolta digital camera authenticated. No one is likely to counterfeit one.

Grading and Authentication

Although grading and authentication are not eBay services, they are services you can get from third parties and are well advised to do so in many cases. These processes require third-party experts and usually cost money. They are your best protection against receiving phony merchandise. If a collectible is worth more than you can afford to lose, have it authenticated before you pay for it.

A seller will usually take the position that he or she knows the item is authentic; thus, the buyer must pay for the authentication. Sometimes the seller will offer an authentication that's already been done. This may be acceptable, but be cautious.

Grading

Grading is simply the evaluation of the physical condition of a manu-factured item. Unfortunately, grading is different for different items. You have to know the market for a particular item to understand the grading. Grading is subjective (in the eyes of the beholder). And grad-ing is subject to honest mistakes and, yes, even to dishonesty. This all adds up to a situation where a buyer has to be very careful. Investigate carefully the condition of any item being auctioned.

Quality

For some items, grading is a determination of quality, not necessar-ily physical condition, and should by done by an expert.

Some other books about eBay assume that there's an agreed grading scale on eBay. Don't believe it. Even if there was, most eBay users would not know exactly how to use it, and it would be unreliable. Always play the detective when it comes to ascertaining the condition of an auction item.

Authentication

Authentication is a process whereby an item is verified to be genuine (and in the condition represented). Is a Beanie Baby really a Ty Beanie Baby? Or, is it a forgery? A third-party expert verifies an item. A verifi-cation is an opinion by an expert and subject to being incorrect. Even experts make mistakes. If you are a collector or are buying jewels, for instance, authentication is your best protection against forged or phony items. Go *Help, Safe Trading, Chose Items Confidently, Authenti-cation Services* for a list of experts who provide authentications. Go to Make Sure It's Real (*http://makesureitsreal.com*) for authentication of watches, diamonds, and jewelry and to review the website's authenti-cation procedures.

Verification

Verification is a means of establishing that an item is authentic in a way that "travels" with the item. For instance, suppose you have a Ty Beanie Baby authenticated by an expert. How can you make that authentication stick with the Beanie Baby itself? One way is to put the Beanie Baby inside a plastic display case. The third-party authenticator seals the case with his or her unremovable seal attesting to the authenticity of the Beanie Baby.

The Switch?

Unfortunately, the following is a common scenario based on an actual case (in the late 1990s). A person buys a rare Beanie Baby via eBay for $1,800. She receives it, and it turns out to be a forgery (worth $3). She informs the seller. The seller says it was authentic when he sent it and will not refund the money.

This is a sad case. The seller may not have known that the Beanie Baby was a forgery. Now he has the buyer telling him that it is. How does he know that she didn't switch it with a forgery and is pulling an $1,800 scam? The buyer is stuck for $1,800. She doesn't know whether it was an honest mistake on the part of the seller or a scam. But it doesn't matter. She's the one who is stuck.

Is a prosecutor going to pursue this case? (See Chapter 8 for more discussion on remedies for fraud.) Probably not. The case may be impossible to prove, and the prosecutor will not waste taxpayer resources on such a weak case.

Authentication would have protected the buyer in this case. Authentication is best set up as part of an escrow arrangement. Yet, the buyer could have protected herself in another way. Suppose, instead of opening the package received from the seller, she took the package directly to her local Beanie Baby dealer (expert). There the package was opened by both of them together. The expert examined the Beanie Baby and found it to be a forgery. Now the buyer has a witness.

Assuming the dealer has a good reputation, he or she will be a credible witness. The witness makes a much stronger case, and the seller may find it prudent to take back the phony Beanie Baby and refund the $1,800.

Appraisal

It's tough to decide whether to put a discussion of appraisal into the buyer's or seller's chapter because it can serve both. An appraisal is an estimation of value that usually includes an authentication. Naturally, the estimate of value has a date. Market prices go up and down. Thus, an appraisal is good for only a limited period of time. Certainly an appraisal can be valuable to a buyer who may need to rely on a third-party expert opinion of value and who needs authentication as well. Then too, a seller can use an appraisal as a selling tool to verify market value for prospective bidders and to provide authentication.

With over 27,000 categories of items, a short list of appraisers in this book wouldn't make much of a splash. However, the following resource may be helpful: International Society of Appraisers (*http://www.isa-appraisers.org*). What's It Worth to You (*http://www.whatsit-worthtoyou.com*) provides inexpensive appraisals on a wide range of items. It essentially acts as a clearing house for hundreds of experts who do appraisals.

Unfortunately, it's sometimes difficult to determine whether an appraiser is qualified. Certainly, membership in specialty professional organizations that certify appraisers provides some credibility, but for many categories of items, there are no professional organizations. Always look into an appraiser's credentials.

Physical?

Generally, if there is no physical inspection of an item, an appraisal is merely an estimate of value, based on information the owner has submitted to the appraiser, and does not include authentication.

For authentication, usually the appraiser must physically inspect the item. Keep in mind, in the absence of an inspection, the appraiser relies on the information the owner provides. As a buyer, you will want to know what that information was.

eBay Insurance

Currently eBay does furnish fraud insurance free. The insurance covers up to a $200 loss ($25 deductible). PowerSellers offer $500 of eBay fraud insurance (free). This insurance doesn't cover shipping damages or losses, only the nonperformance of seller after payment has been made (e.g., seller fraud). This is a good program because it covers the inexpensive items where escrow would be relatively inconvenient. For the expensive items, eBay leaves the parties to make their own arrangements (e.g., escrow), which makes more sense for higher-priced items.

Escrow

eBay recommends the Escrow.com escrow services. This is your best bet to protect yourself against fraudulent sellers. Don't send a check for an auction item that's more than you can afford to lose. Put the transaction in escrow instead. You then send the check to the escrow agent. The funds are held by the escrow agent until you have received and examined the auction item. If everything is satisfactory (as represented by the seller), you inform the escrow agent, and the funds are released to the seller. If not, then you can return the item to the seller and get your money back.

Is Escrow Enough?

If you review the scenario under the preceding The Switch? subsection, you will find that an escrow by itself could not prevent that situation. However, an escrow together with an authentication is the ultimate assurance that you will enjoy a successful transaction in which you are well protected. In such a case, you make arrangements acceptable to the seller to have an expert authenticate the item before it is released from escrow.

Also take a look at eDeposit (*http://www.edeposit.com*). It provides services that make transactions safer for buyers and sellers and plans to offer an escrow service in the future.

eBay Tool Bar

Try the eBay Toolbar; go *Services, Buying & Selling Tools, Buyer Tools, eBay Toolbar*. It locates right in your browser, tracks your bidding, gives you desktop alerts, and provides a search engine without being at the eBay website. This is a great tool for keeping an eye out for items that you want to buy. And it's free!

Illicit Merchandise

Sooner or later you will be presented with the opportunity to buy illicit merchandise. This is an opportunity you don't want to take. If you knowingly buy what you know to be stolen or pirated goods, you may be guilty of a crime in either your own state or the state in which the goods are offered.

In addition, such participation undermines the integrity of eBay. It's to your advantage to keep eBay a marketplace free of criminal activity. After all, as a buyer, you can get great bargains today and for many years in the future. Why would you contribute to activities that undermine the marketplace that provides you such an advantage? Avoid illicit merchandise, and preserve eBay as a corruption-free, long-term personal asset.

The tougher test comes, however, when you have illicit merchandise sent to you unknowingly. For instance, there are a lot of inexpensive CDs containing expensive software for sale on eBay. Many are legitimate, not pirated. Yet in one transaction, I bought a book via eBay (in a Dutch auction), and in the process of communicating with the seller,

I was offered a copy of Adobe PhotoShop, a $700 program, an unspecified version on a CD, for just an additional $15. I had in the past bought legitimate expensive software (old versions) for very deep discounts on eBay (on CDs) just as I am able to do at local computer shows, so I accepted the offer without thinking much about it. When I received the book, the additional software (an up-to-date version of the PhotoShop) was on a recordable CD, not on a manufacturer's CD (i.e., the additional software was pirated). The seller maintains low visibility by not offering the pirated software on eBay. Rather she offers it via email in the course of arranging the payment and the shipping of the book for a winning bidder.

The hard question is, What do you do? This kind of practice is very troubling and is not healthy for eBay and its legitimate users. In this case eBay accepts reports. So, you can file a report directly with eBay. Look in the SafeHarbor area of the eBay website for information on filing reports. By the time I got around to researching how to report this illicit offer, however, the incident was a few months stale.

Then about a year later I bid on a version of Adobe PhotoShop in a current auction. Afterward I received a deluge of email from people offering to sell me current copies of the program for $15–$50 (undoubtedly pirated). This is called *bid skimming*. I went to eBay SafeHarbor, which provides current guidelines on reporting violations. As per instructions, I forwarded copies of the email solicitations to SafeHarbor. Once you learn what to do, it's easy to do it.

Procedures

eBay checks the skimming email to see if the perpetrators are registered with eBay. I was notified in every case except one (sender warned but not kicked off eBay) that they were not registered.

eBay suggested that I forward copies of the emails addressed to *postmaster* at the ISPs from which the emails were sent. I didn't think that would generate any result. But I did it anyway (easy and quick to do). It did produce results. I received an email from Yahoo! indicating that it had kicked a sender off the Yahoo! email service. Ironic that Yahoo! kicked off the offender but eBay gave only a warning to another offender.

I also forwarded the illicit email to support at Adobe and received an automated reply, which meant that such was a wasted effort. Then I tried to find an email address at the Adobe website where I might forward the illicit email. That was also a waste of time. Adobe provided only a long form for reporting piracy. It would have taken me an hour to fill out the form for all the incidents of the illicit email. So I declined. Thus, I ended up not getting through to the one organization that might have done something about it. Adobe ought to wake up.

Summary

Find what you're looking for. There are plenty of goods on eBay. Make your bids. The eBay system is easy to use. When you win an auction, follow up, and make your payment promptly. You'll find eBay to be a reliable source of things you need at reasonable prices, often at deep discounts.

6

Selling

The life of a seller is easier and more passive than that of a bidder, that is, until the follow-up. The follow-up is where the work is for sellers. This chapter covers the basics up to the follow-up. Chapter 10 provides considerable additional information on follow-up and fulfillment (customer service).

The selling opportunities on eBay are unlimited because the buyers are so numerous and have such varied interests, and the market is continuous 24 hours a day, 7 days a week. But many sellers run auctions, and you will not find a lack of competition.

Prior Chapters

Chapters 4 and 5 include many basics about auctions at eBay. Such basics are not necessarily repeated in this chapter. Consequently, you need to read Chapters 4 and 5, too, to develop a firm understanding of eBay auctions.

Sellers (Auctioneers)

The first step toward becoming a seller is registering to be an eBay member. Only members can auction (sell) or bid (buy). Chapter 4 covers registration, which is the same whether you are a buyer or seller. The next step for sellers is arranging payment to eBay.

Payment Arrangements

eBay makes its revenue by charging sellers at least two fees. The first is the Initial Listing fee. The second is the Final Value fee based on the winning bid.

You arrange to pay eBay by giving your credit card or bank account number to eBay. Then eBay immediately attempts to authorize your card or verify your bank account. Assuming you're approved, eBay will bill you via credit card or debit your bank account each month for the previous month's fees.

eBay requires a credit card (or other verification) to sell in order to:

- Ensure sellers are a legal age
- Ensure sellers are who they say they are
- Protect others from fraudulent or irresponsible sellers

If you do not have a credit card or bank account, you can alternatively use ID Verify to establish your identity. See Chapter 4. (eBay users registered prior to October 22, 1999, do not have to meet this requirement.)

You calculate the Insertion fee based on the minimum bid or reserve amount according to Table 6.1.

Table 6.1 Insertion Fee

Minimum Bid or Reserve ($)	Listing Fee ($)
to 9.99	0.30
10.00 to 24.99	0.55
25.00 to 49.99	1.10
50.00 to 199.99	2.20
200.00 and up	3.30

The spreadsheet formula for calculating the Initial Listing fee amount is:

```
=IF(E5<10,0.3,IF(E5<25,0.55,IF(E5<50,1.1,I
F(E5<200,2.2,3.3))))
```

In the spreadsheet, E5 is the cell where you enter the minimum bid or reserve amount.

You calculate the Final Value fee (cumulative) based on the high bid according to Table 6.2.

Table 6.2 Final Value Fee (Cumulative)

High Bid ($)	Fee
to 25.00	5.25%
25.01 to 1,000.00	2.75%
1,000.01 and over	1.5%

The spreadsheet formula for calculating the Final Value fee amount is:

```
=IF(E8<=25,E8*0.05,IF(E8<=1000,((E8-
25)*0.025)+1.25,((E8-
1000)*0.0125)+25.625))

[Attributed to Eric Slone by author Neil J.
Salkind in eBay Online Auctions.]
```

In the spreadsheet, E8 is the cell where you enter the high bid. Note that the fee calculation is cumulative; that is, it's 5 percent on the first $25, 2.5 percent on the next $975, and 1.25 percent on the excess. For the total auction fees, add the Initial Listing fee and the Final Value fee (see Figure 6.1).

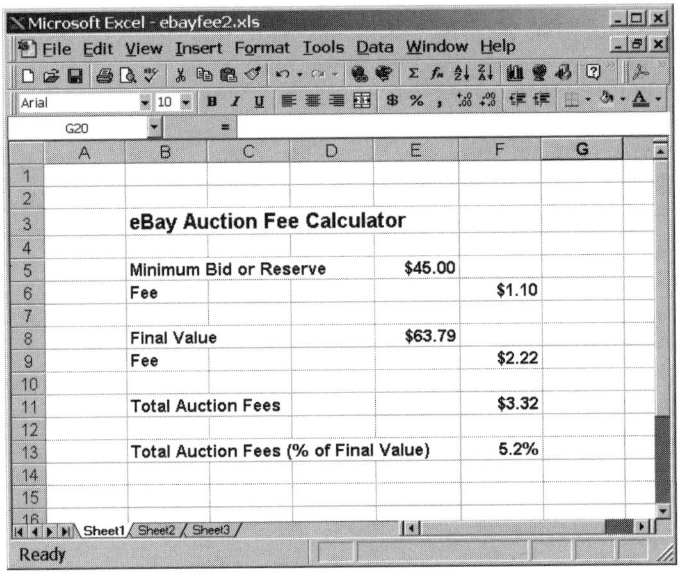

Figure 6.1   Spreadsheet calculates total eBay fees for running an auction.

Of course, you don't have to calculate these fees. eBay does it for you automatically and charges your account. The calculation formulas provided in the preceding paragraphs serve to educate you and provide you with a planning tool should you care to use it.

This is a general view of the eBay auctioning fees. There are additional special fees for special features.

Bold Title in bold. $1.00

Home Page Featured Auction placed in Featured section reached via the Browse button on the navigation bar. $99.95

Featured Plus Auction placed in Featured list at the top of the page in its category. $19.95

Highlight Auction title highlighted with yellow. $5.00

Gallery Auction goes into eBay photo gallery (must have photograph). $0.25

10-Day Auction Longest auction gets a surcharge. $0.10

Reserve Price For reserve price, there's a surcharge; refunded if item sells. $0.50 (under $25) and $1.00 ($25 and up)

Fixed-price For *Buy It Now*, add $0.05.

For a more complete review, go *Help, Selling, Listing Your Item, Fees.*

Setting the Minimum

Before you submit your auction, you must determine a minimum bid. If you run a reserve auction, you must determine the reserve. These decisions require general knowledge of the market for the item and, in particular, specific knowledge of the eBay market for the item.

One way to get this information is to research eBay auctions and past auctions. A survey of similar current auctions will tell you a lot. Use the archive of past auctions *Completed Items* to get a selection of completed auctions from which to derive market prices for items identical or similar to the one you will auction.

Research is a powerful means to get the appropriate information to set the stage for success. A minimum or reserve price too high or too low will probably not achieve the purpose of auctioning your item for the highest bid possible. Research can help you set the price at an intelligent value. See Chapter 5 for more details.

Rating the Condition of the Item

It's your job as the seller to accurately evaluate the physical condition of the item being auctioned. Misrepresentation could lead to disputes.

As Is

There are legal ways in many states to sell merchandise as a seller and have no further obligation to the buyer (e.g., the "as is" sale). Those ways may work legally, but they may not work on eBay as a practical matter. (See a detailed explanation of "as is" in Chapter 10.)

You get the impression from the verbiage in the auction ads on eBay that many sellers are selling merchandise "as is." So long as the merchandise works, there is no problem. But if something doesn't work and there's a resulting dispute, the dispute will be harmful to the seller regardless of the legalities.

The best advice is that if something doesn't work, don't sell it. If you choose to ignore this advice, at least indicate very clearly that the item doesn't work. Statements such as, "I don't know whether it works or not, sold as is," are an invitation to disaster. Statements such as, "Item doesn't work, being sold for parts," may be OK so long as they are prominently displayed.

Know the Market

Each item has a different market. Items within a certain market are often evaluated a certain way using certain terminology. Before you evaluate something, know the terminology. In many cases, you will have to know proper evaluation procedures too.

What's the penalty for ignoring proper evaluation? It might be a misrepresentation that carries liability. If you sell items outside your area of expertise, take a look at some of the auctions for identical or similar items on eBay to determine if there is special terminology or evaluation procedures you need to use.

Common Sense

Absent other terminology, use commonsense terms. Don't stretch the truth.

New This means *unused*, not *used only a little bit*.

Like new or **mint condition** This means *in perfect condition* and *used only a little bit*. If an item has been used more than *only a little bit*, it's not in mint condition unless it's a heavy-duty machine (e.g., auto).

Excellent condition This means *no blemishes and works perfectly*. The assumption is that this item has been used considerably.

Factory refurbished or factory rebuilt This means that the item has been unused since being overhauled at the factory into *like new* condition. These items are usually in a factory-sealed box. If the item has been used since coming from the factory, that fact should be disclosed.

OEM This means original equipment manufacturer. OEM can be either the manufacturer or a reseller. Doesn't shed much light does it? Well, what the reseller does is add value to a piece of equipment it buys from the manufacturer by putting a private label on it, bundling it with other equipment or intellectual property (e.g., software), or providing it bundled with set-up, service, or training. Such equipment is usually supplied in bulk to the reseller, not in consumer boxes with accompanying manuals, etc. Or, it might be a component inside another piece of equipment. Thus, when someone on eBay offers a piece of OEM equipment, it usually means that it does not come in a consumer box with all the marketing trimmings. That doesn't mean it's not new; it usually is, or it should be described as used.

These are my definitions. Others may have other definitions. Therein lies a significant problem.

Grading

By using commonsense words to describe the condition of an item, you may be inadvertently grading it. See the Grading section later in this chapter. Always provide further detailed explanation for the condition of an item that you auction on eBay, not just common-sense words, grading words, or grading abbreviations. Grading is best left to experts.

Misunderstanding

Some will tell you that there are standard words or abbreviations to use on eBay in describing items. Those are usually the eBay "in" people who comprise a small percentage of eBay members. Such standard words will be understood only by a certain percentage of all potential bidders, usually under 50 percent if they are common sense words. If they're not common sense words, they will be understood by far less than 50 percent. You don't have to use such words at all, and you are ill advised to use them without additional explaination. In fact, a detailed explaination of the condition of an item avoids problems with both grading and misunderstanding.

Don't use abbreviations for anything. You will lose a significant per-centage of your market, OHPG.

Blemishes or malfunctions should be disclosed. A photograph is a good means of disclosing blemishes. If you disclose something, it's unfair for a buyer to complain about the very defect that you disclosed. If you don't disclose blemishes, defects, and malfunctions, you are begging for a disputed sale and negative feedback.

Keep in mind that there are buyers for all items in whatever condition. The potential bidders looking for new goods probably will not buy used goods. The buyers looking for used goods are bargain hunting and probably will not spend extra money for new goods.

OEM Example

A reseller builds computers from components she buys from manufacturers. She buys DVD drives in bulk without consumer packaging to install in some of the computers she builds. She sells all the computers but has four DVD drives left over. She sells the DVD drives to consumers without consumer packaging. She advertises them as OEM DVD drives. They aren't in a pretty package. They may not even include an owner's manual or cables.

Entering an Auction

How do you start an auction? It's simple. You just input the information in the Seller's section on the eBay website. Go *Sell* in the navigation bar. Follow the instructions you find there (see Figure 6.2 for entry of auction information).

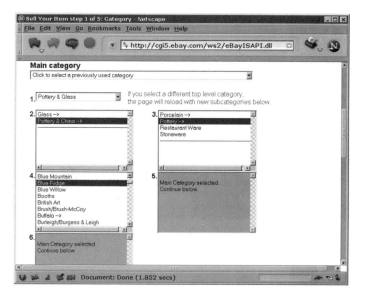

Figure 6.2   Enter an auction and begin by specifying the category.

Types of Auctions

Chapter 4 covers the types of auctions (normal, reserve, Dutch, and private) you can run on eBay. You will have to pick one.

Input

You input all the basic information for your auction directly into the *Sell Item* form (see Figure 6.3).

Although the input is not burdensome, it takes time. If you run numerous auctions, the input requirements add up. You will start looking for a more efficient way of entering the auctions. Chapter 14 covers eBay bulk uploads.

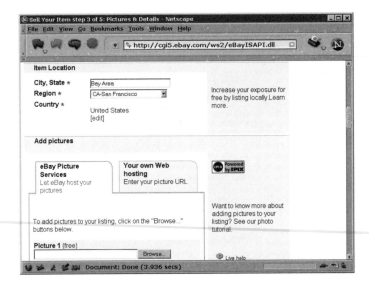

Figure 6.3   Entering auction information.

Length

You control when your auction ends by entering it exactly three, five, seven, or ten days earlier at the same time of day. Those are your choices. It seems to make sense to have your auction end at a busy time on eBay. Perhaps that will get a last-minute bidding frenzy going.

Auction Ad

One of the inputs is for the middle section of the auction webpage. This is the auction ad (*Description*—see Figure 6.4). This is your opportunity to sell your item. You should be well prepared ahead of time to enter the appropriate information here. Chapter 12 shows you how to make an HTML template (webpage template) to make your auction ads look professional. You can enter such a filled-in (completed) template in the Description input window in the form via copy and paste. (You can get free templates at *http://www.bookcenter.com*).

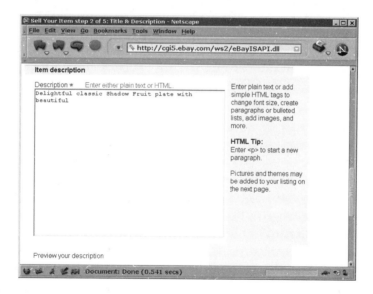

Figure 6.4   Auction ad (Description) input.

Photograph

Photographs sell goods. Chapters 11, 12, and 19 provide you with the skills and knowledge you need to successfully handle digital photographs for your eBay ads.

Bulk Upload

The ultimate time-saver for numerous auction ads is a bulk upload. eBay provides the Turbo Lister (bulk uploading procedure), and Chapter 14 provides you with background on the bulk uploading process, which enables you to run many auctions with a minimum of effort.

Buy It Now

eBay gives sellers the option to charge a fixed price for their auction items as an additional feature to an auction, not in place of an auction. An icon indicating it's a *Buy It Now* item appears with the auction title, and the fixed price goes to the top of the auction webpage.

Sellers usually set the *Buy It Now* selling price higher than the initial bid. So long as no bids have been made, a bidder can elect to take the fixed price.

If the buyer has a credit card on file or has an ID Verify, the auction automatically terminates; the parties proceed to complete the purchase transaction at the fixed price. If not, the buyer is prompted to register a credit card or obtain the ID Verify. Once the buyer completes this procedure successfully, the auction automatically terminates. If a buyer does not or cannot qualify by registering a credit card or obtaining an ID Verify, the buyer cannot buy the item via the fixed-price procedure and will, instead, have to bid on the item.

Once the minimum bid or reserve price has been met, the fixed-price alternative is no longer available.

Don't underestimate using a fixed price. Less than 250 years ago, a negotiated price was the common practice. The fixed price came along and started a retail revolution. Today both auction prices and fixed prices have their place in the eBay marketplace. Many buyers prefer fixed prices. Buyers especially like fixed prices when they're in a hurry and don't want to wait to make a purchase until the auction ends.

Me, I'll wait until the auction ends to see if I can buy the item for less money. But like everyone else, sometimes I'm in a hurry. Then fixed prices look good, assuming they're reasonable.

Counter

Many sellers have used counters on their auctions ads (auction webpages) to determine how much traffic they get. That usually entails going to a counter website and following the procedures for installing a counter (try Andale at *http://andale.com*). eBay now offers a convenience. You can elect to have an Andale counter installed when you enter your auction information for your auction ad. There is no charge for this device.

Authentication and Other Protections

Chapter 5 covers authentication and verification. Review that chapter before reading this section. Pay particular attention to the subsection The Switch? which outlines a situation as potentially devastating to the seller as it is to the buyer.

Authentication

Authentication protects sellers as well as buyers. If you have your item properly authenticated as part of an escrow arrangement, the buyer will have a difficult time claiming that you sold counterfeit goods. You can avoid the situation outlined in The Switch? (Chapter 5) by endorsing authentication for expensive items.

Verification

Use verification wherever possible. Make sure that the verification is accepted within the particular market for the item. For instance, for the Beanie Baby example in Chapter 5, there were a number of verification services on the Web. If someone wants to know about the particular verification that travels with the Beanie Baby, you can point to a verification website.

Grading

It is a mistake to think that there is some agreed grading scale on eBay. Different types of items have traditionally used different words and different grading scales. Never use abbreviations for grading. Many eBay users won't know what you are trying to communicate. Abbreviations are a convenience for you but are terrible customer service. Even words like "mint" and "excellent" do little to communicate properly except in the context of a particular commerce (e.g., antiques, stereo equipment, farm implements). The trouble is that different categories of items use different words or assign special meanings to commonsense grading words.

The better practice is to explain the condition of an item you auction. The explanation is more useful to potential bidders and won't eliminate those who do not understand the jargon or abbreviations for a particular type of item.

If you are determined to use grading, make sure the grader is an expert in regard to the item graded. That might be you or an appraiser you've hired to authenticate the item. Explain that the item is being graded according to traditional custom for such items. *And then also provide an explanation of the grading as well as the grading words or abbreviations.* Thus, every potential bidder is informed.

Appraisal

An appraisal can be a useful selling tool. It indicates market value for potential bidders and lends the authority of a third-party expert. Many appraisals also include authentication. See Chapter 5 for more information.

Shipping Insurance

Insurance that insures shipments against loss or damage is essential for both buyer and seller. If a package disappears or is damaged, who sustains the loss, buyer or seller? Who knows what the answer is to that legal question? It will depend on state law and the circumstances of the particular case. As a practical matter, however, the seller will probably sustain the loss. If not, the seller will surely get negative feedback. Don't try to split hairs here. Get insurance, or be prepared to be self-insured. Don't think the buyer (consumer) will sustain this loss.

On inexpensive items, self-insurance makes sense. That means you replace anything lost or damaged in shipment. For expensive items, buy the insurance. UPS and FedEx Ground automatically provide $100 insurance, and additional insurance is relatively inexpensive. US Postal Service insurance is relatively expensive. If you state your shipping policy as part of your auction ad, you can charge the entire cost of insurance (or half) to the buyer, although putting the responsibility for insurance on the buyer is probably not wise.

Receipt

Provide a receipt. Make sure it contains all the details of the sale, such as date, price, description of item, buyer's name, and shipping address. The receipt is a summary of the transaction. As such, it protects you as well as the buyer.

eBay Insurance

The insurance offered by eBay is insurance for fraud. Although free, the insurance does not necessarily benefit you. You know you're not fraudulent, and you don't need the insurance. But you have to keep in mind that such insurance is a customer service.

The insurance pays $200 with a $25 deductible. For PowerSellers only there is new eBay insurance coverage up to $500. This can be a convenient selling point.

Escrow

An escrow transaction protects the seller as well as the buyer, as the example in The Switch? subsection (Chapter 5) demonstrates. You are asking for trouble if you don't use escrow transactions for expensive items. In contrast to the buyer, however, you have a different interest in the escrow arrangement.

Authentication and Escrow

Escrow without authentication is not important to sellers. It's like fraud insurance, and the seller does not need it. However, an escrow arrangement can provide sellers with protection against credit card charge-backs and fraud. Go *Help, Buying, Trusting the Seller, Escrow.*

Consequently, you have to ask yourself: Does this item require authentication? If the answer is no, then the escrow arrangement is not a priority for you as a seller.

As illustrated by The Switch? example, a Beanie Baby needs authentication. There are certainly plenty of counterfeit collectibles around. To do a transaction for an expensive collectible without escrow and authentication is asking for trouble.

Nonetheless, there are plenty of items that don't really require authentication. For instance, does a factory-refurbished brand-name camcorder need authentication? Probably not. It will come in a factory-sealed box and is unlikely to be a counterfeit. For the buyer to claim it had been used or was a counterfeit would take a blatant act of fraud, which seems unlikely.

What about a used camcorder in excellent condition? Does that require authentication? Suppose the buyer claims it is in average condition and worth less? This is not a disaster as long as you have the serial number on record. Ask the buyer to return the item, and refund the purchase price. It's not like the Beanie Baby where the value goes from $1,800 to $3. Therefore, an escrow and authentication (that the camcorder is in excellent condition) may not be necessary from your point of view as the seller.

However, suppose the buyer runs out and misuses the camcorder (out of ignorance) the first day he or she receives it. Now the camcorder is not in excellent condition any longer, and the buyer blames you. In this case, it is possible that the camcorder is permanently inoperable and worth little. To escrow and authenticate, or not? In this case, there's no easy answer, but raising the question at least makes you aware of the risk.

For expensive collectibles or even for expensive used appliances (are they in the condition specified?), an escrow together with an authentication will protect you as the seller as well as protect the buyer. For new or factory-refurbished items in sealed boxes, escrow and authentication may be unnecessary.

After You List the Auction

Once you have entered the input for your auction, you have nothing further to do. The bidding action is up to the bidders. You don't even have to watch. The auction will end three, five, seven, or ten days after you have entered it and at the same time. Only then do you have to follow up. In the meanwhile, you may get email from prospective bidders asking questions. If so, answer them promptly.

Changing an Auction

You can change anything you want to before the first bid. After the first bid, you can only add information to your auction listing. It will appear at the bottom of your auction ad, dated. You can change your item's category too. If you do something outrageous or unfair, expect to hear bad things from fellow eBay members.

Retracting an Auction

You can retract an auction for which there are no bids at any time. Who are you going to irritate? Probably no one. If there are bids, however, you face a different procedure. You must cancel the bids. There is a specific procedure for canceling bids. The cancellation goes on your record. Therefore, be very cautious about retracting auctions. It's probably not worth risking your reputation in most cases.

Auto Auctions

eBay Motors, in my opinion, should be an exception to the rule. A seller should not be allowed to retract an auction. Many potential bidders cannot make serious bids on autos without taking the time to prearrange financing and to develop strategies for making intelligent purchases in faraway cities. After making such preparations, to find an auction retracted is not fair. It wouldn't be so bad if this happened occasionally, but it seems to be the common practice of many used car dealers.

No Bids

When your auction runs its course and receives no bids, you lose the listing fee but do not have to pay the Final Value fee. If you want to run the auction again, you can take advantage of eBay's relisting policy for no additional fee. This policy, in effect, guarantees your first try. However, you need to be reasonable in your offering as there is no further fee-free relisting after the second auction fails.

When you relist an auction that received no bids, you can get back the listing fee if the auction is completed on the second try. When you're about to relist an auction for which there were no bids the first time, it's a good time to rethink the minimum bid or reserve. You may want to lower it.

Relisting

You can relist any auction automatically without going through the process of entering it again. This is a convenient service when you auction the same items on an ongoing basis.

Follow-Up

Follow-up is the most important role of the seller. After all, you must contact the buyer and arrange payment. Then you must ship the item.

Accounting

Losing track of your auctions? You'd better get things under control, or your eBay operation will start to self-destruct. That will invariably result in negative feedback. See Chapter 17 for auction managemenet services that will keep you efficiently organized.

Seller Search

Input your own ID and password in a *By Seller* search (via the *Search* link), and you will get a list of all your current auctions. This can be quite handy.

My eBay

Access *My eBay*, at *My eBay* over the navigation bar, and you will get a record of all your selling and bidding activities on eBay. This is an even more complete record than the Seller search. *My eBay* also includes recent feedback, your eBay account records, a list of favorite categories, your sign-in preferences, and other information. Thus, it makes a great place to hang out on eBay, a place where you have a lot of convenient information at your fingertips.

Customer Service

Chapter 10 covers customer service thoroughly. The fact that customer service occupies its own chapter instead of a section in this chapter indicates its importance. Your success as a retailer on eBay will ride on the quality of your customer service. Even for casual sellers, the quality of your customer service will directly affect your eBay reputation. Customer service is not an activity to take lightly.

When an Auction Is Not a Sale

Why would someone want to hold auctions on eBay yet not necessarily want to make a sale? Advertising! eBay makes a viable advertising medium. Indeed, what many retailers do is to use a hybrid strategy. They offer one product a week at a serious discount as a draw to their auction ad. They sell the product at a profit (or perhaps at a loss), but the effort is not really a selling effort. It's essentially advertising. As mentioned earlier, a similar strategy can even be effective for advertising services that are difficult to sell via an eBay auction. Read Chapter 20 for more information on this special use of eBay.

Then there are those who want to find out what the market is for a particular class of merchandise. What better way than to sell one item on eBay. In this case, the item is sold, but the act of auctioning is essentially for the purpose of appraisal, not necessarily to make a profit. This is an especially useful technique to use for test marketing where the item has never been sold before, and an appraisal is needed to set the price.

Summary

Auctioning merchandise is as simple as inputting information into a form at the eBay website and including an auction ad (*Description*).

Read Chapter 13 for more details on conducting eBay auctions. The more laborious task is the follow-up: corresponding with the buyer and shipping the goods.

7

Reputation

Reputation is often a subtle thing. A bad reputation doesn't keep you from doing business. Many business transactions are straightforward and essentially risk-free for each party. For instance, in an office supply store, you hand your $155 to the person at the counter, and you get a fax machine. The transaction takes place directly without much risk on either side.

However, if a transaction requires trust, a bad reputation creates an obstacle. For instance, suppose you take delivery of the fax machine but pay the $155 for it in installments over a six-month period. The seller has to trust you to make the payments. If you have a bad reputation (a bad credit rating), the seller will not make this arrangement with you.

Or, suppose you pay the $155 to the seller, who promises to order the fax machine and deliver it to you as soon as it comes from the manufacturer next week. You have to trust the seller. If the seller has a bad reputation, you will probably not agree to pay for the fax machine until delivery.

eBay transactions require trust. eBay sellers and buyers need good reputations. The idea of an international marketplace with a transaction mechanism that works well is great, but it won't work unless the buyer feels confident that he's going to get the Sony camcorder, for which he won the bidding, when he sends his $425 check to the seller. Why would anyone send a check to another person he or she doesn't know hundreds (or thousands) of miles away? For eBay, the answer is the eBay reputation system, the Feedback Forum. This is the heart and soul of the eBay system. This is the firm foundation on which the whole eBay transaction process rests.

eBay Feedback System

How does eBay establish reputations for its sellers and buyers? Simply, it enables sellers and buyers to rate each other. The ratings are simple: positive, neutral, or negative.

In addition, sellers and buyers can make comments. These comments often include fluffy praise resulting from successful transactions. When not fluffy, however, they can provide useful information of interest to the eBay community.

Positive, Neutral, Negative

Some scenarios follow that illustrate how you might enter feedback based on your eBay transaction experiences. These are solely my opinion. Everyone will have their own notions about the feedback that the other party deserves. I think, however, that you have to be reasonable.

For instance, suppose you visit eBay almost every day to pursue your hobby of collecting antique mirrors. You buy a mirror, send a check to the seller, but don't receive the mirror immediately. Understandably, you get frustrated. The seller, however, happens to be a person who works long hours every day at a demanding job and only frequents eBay on the weekend as an occasional buyer or seller. She tends to think of eBay as a weekend activity. She gets your check and subsequently finds out on a Monday that the check has cleared. In all likelihood she is not going to get around to shipping the package until Saturday. Is this unreasonable? Not for her. But if she were a person operating a retail business on eBay instead, it would be an unreasonable delay. Thus, one must determine reasonableness in an overall context.

Positive

Transactions often run into problems and are not always on time. *A positive performance by the other party is one that completes the transaction within a reasonable time (not necessarily on time) and according to the terms of the agreement (as defined by the auction offering).* Sometimes additional negotiation based on some reasonable circumstances may alter the agreement.

Case #1 Seller Enters a Positive

A buyer says he sent a check the day after the auction, but when the check gets to the seller, the envelope shows a postmark a week after the auction. Give the buyer a neutral or negative rating? No. Whenever a transaction consummates, rate the other party positive unless there is a compelling reason not to do so. A check sent a week late is not a compelling reason.

Case #2 Buyer Enters a Positive

The seller represents that he will charge the winning bidder $20 for shipping and handling. The buyer pays the bid plus $20. When she gets the product, she notices that the package has a UPS charge of $5 on it, not $20. She complains to the seller, but the seller won't budge. Give the seller a negative rating? No. Whenever a transaction consummates, rate the other party positive unless there is a compelling reason not to. The buyer has a right to complain perhaps, but it doesn't make sense to quibble with a charge that was stated before the auction closed.

Note also that shipping and handling are different from just shipping. Handling does cost money; it's not free. If a seller states in advance a charge for shipping and handling, it doesn't provide the basis for neutral or negative feedback that the buyer thinks the seller set the shipping and handling charge too high. The shipping charge is just a portion of the total shipping and handling.

Neutral

Even when the transaction closes, a party may have caused so much distress that he or she does not deserve a positive rating. *A neutral performance by the other party is one that completes the transaction but not without a good deal of seemingly unnecessary frustration-causing or unpleasant behavior.*

Case #3 Seller Enters a Neutral

Here the story is the same as earlier (see Case #1 Seller Enters a Positive subsection) except that the buyer takes three weeks (instead of one week) before sending the check. The transaction closes, but the seller doesn't receive the check until almost a month after the auction ends. Give the buyer a neutral rating? It depends. If the buyer had some problems with making the payment but kept the seller informed, a neutral rating is probably not appropriate. If the buyer kept putting off the seller with misrepresentations or no responses, a neutral rating may be justified.

Case #4 Buyer Enters a Neutral

The seller represents that he will charge the winning bidder a reasonable shipping fee ("handling" is not mentioned). The transaction closes. The seller charges $20 and ships the product in an old cardboard box stuffed with newspaper. The buyer (high bidder at $45) sees the UPS charge of $5.75 on the box and complains about the $20 shipping charge. The seller won't budge. Give the seller a neutral rating? Perhaps not. After all, the buyer could have tried to pin down the shipping fee via email before the auction was over, but she did not do so. Then too, the seller might mistakenly think that "shipping" really means "shipping and handling."

On the other hand, it looks as if the seller has attempted to augment his profit by unexpected gouging on the shipping charge. That deserves a neutral rating.

Negative

Negative ratings should be reserved for situations where the transaction does not consummate or grievous problems remain unresolved indefinitely or for a long period of time. *A negative performance by the other party is one that does not complete the transaction, completes it only after a very long delay, completes it only after causing a great deal of aggravation, or completes it according to different terms than defined by the auction offering.*

Case #5 Seller Enters a Negative

Here the story is the same as earlier (see Case #1 Seller Enters a Positive) except that after several promises to pay, which extend the transaction for three weeks, the buyer finally admits that he cannot scrape together the money to pay for the product. Give the buyer a negative rating? Whenever a transaction does not close based on the irresponsible behavior of one of the parties, a negative rating is appropriate. The buyer should not have bid without the capacity and willingness to pay the winning bid, and now he deserves a negative rating.

Case #6 Buyer Enters a Negative

The seller represents that he will charge the winning bidder a reasonable shipping fee but nothing is said about handling. The seller asks the buyer (high bidder at $45) to pay $20 to ship the product (lightweight and not fragile) via UPS ground (about $6). The buyer contacts the seller to complain about the high cost of shipping but never refuses to complete the transaction. The seller immediately reenters the item into eBay for another auction. Give the seller a negative rating?

The seller is not only gouging on the shipping but is apparently unwilling to be responsive to or to negotiate the buyer's legitimate complaint. The transaction does not consummate due to the seller's unreasonable behavior; he deserves a negative rating.

No Rating

No rule requires that a seller or buyer must give the other party feedback. Unfortunately, failure to do so sometimes undermines the system. If a transaction does not reflect adversely on either party and neither party enters feedback, I suppose the system can survive without the information about that transaction. Indeed, such cases are the norm not the exception, as many parties are too lazy or distracted to enter feedback. (I'm guilty of that myself, I'm sorry to report.) When a feedback rating would be adverse to a party, however, and the other party (the offended party) does not enter it, that constitutes an irresponsible act.

For instance, suppose a seller operates a bait-and-switch scam. He offers one item of merchandise but substitutes another of inferior quality. A failure on the buyer's part to report such an offense via feedback undermines the system, particularly when it turns out that the seller routinely acts unfairly to other eBay members.

Special Cases

Special cases will always come along where the transaction did not close because the seller and buyer agreed that it should not close.

Case #7 No Closing

Suppose the seller auctions a model MX54-A chain saw. After the auction the seller informs the buyer that he has made a mistake. He has only the model MX54-C, which looks the same but is generally worth 35 percent less. He offers the different model to the buyer for the bid price less 40 percent and offers to ship it for free. The buyer decides not to close the transaction (not to buy the substituted item). Should the buyer provide negative feedback on the seller?

If the seller makes an honest mistake, don't rate him or her negatively. After all, in the above case the seller seems to have offered the buyer a favorable deal to atone for his "mistake." In such a case, assuming she believes the seller, the buyer will probably not enter feedback. Probably in most cases where the seller and buyer agree not to complete the transaction, no feedback is reported.

Unfortunately, feedback should be reported in such a case. It can be valuable to fellow eBay members, not for its rating value (e.g., neutral) but for its commentary. For instance, in this case, the buyer can rate the seller neutral but also include the following facts:

> Proper comment: He mistakenly did not have the item but made a reasonable offer to substitute.

If the mistake was sincere, this rating will not hurt the seller. If the mistake is routine, ratings like this will eventually expose the seller as a careless or shady operator.

Comments

Using positive, neutral, or negative feedback provides little information. Only a straightforward comment makes any sense out of a rating. Just stating the facts gives your comment the maximum impact it deserves.

Negative or Neutral Feedback

Always just state the pertinent facts. Don't make any judgmental, accusatory, or speculative comments. If you do, you may be wrong, and you may lose credibility with other eBay members, presumably just the opposite of what you want to do.

If you make a judgmental, accusatory, or speculative statement, you may defame the other party, thus incurring legal liability. Seldom do you have all the facts you need to establish legally sound grounds to make such a statement. But you can state the facts as you know them. The truth is always a defense to defamation. If you stick to the facts that you know, you will make it impractical for someone to challenge you legally thereby making a lawsuit unlikely. Fairness also dictates that you cool down and determine what the facts really are before you make comments about someone.

The facts will damn the other person more in any event. Anytime you make an opinionated negative statement about someone else, people take it with a grain of salt. But facts are facts, and people pay attention to facts.

Improper comment (about seller): He intentionally aggravated me by taking far too much time to ship the vase.

Proper comment: He didn't ship the vase until 25 days after he received my money order.

Improper comment (about winning bidder): This gal's a deadbeat who needs a psychiatrist to get herself straightened out.

Proper comment: She promised to pay during three weeks after the auction but never did.

Improper comment (about seller): This lowlife tried to triple his profit by gouging me on the shipping.

Proper comment: He required a huge shipping fee, refused to discuss it, and then killed the sale.

eBay provides you with only 80 characters (about 15 words) to make your statement. So, make it concise and factual. Save the expletives for telling the story to your friends.

Positive Feedback

Most positive feedback doesn't mean much. Just to give someone a positive rating is enough if the transaction went well. You see a lot of fluffy praise among the comments for positive ratings. Here again facts speak the loudest. Just state the facts.

Improper comment (about winning bidder): Winning bidder is the greatest. Will do business again.

Proper comment: Winning bidder paid promptly and was pleasant to deal with.

The improper statement boosts the bidder's ego, which is fine. Nothing wrong with that. And it does convey the message that the bidder did something right. But it doesn't tell us much. The proper statement has more impact because it conveys facts. Incidentally, the improper statement sounds canned, which it probably is.

Informational Feedback

Occasionally, the use of a comment is primary, and the rating is much less important. In the earlier Case #7 No Closing subsection example, the seller made a mistake and didn't have the item auctioned. He made an offer to sell a similar item at a good price and pay the shipping. On one hand, if the seller seems sincere, you don't want to give him a negative rating. Even a positive rating might be justified. On the other hand, if he's a con artist pulling the old bait-and-switch trick, you would want to give him a negative rating. You don't know for sure which he is. So, give him a neutral rating. Here the comment you make is more important than the rating, and the comment must be factual to be of use to anyone.

> Proper comment: He mistakenly did not have the item but made a reasonable offer to substitute.

When people look at this comment together with all the other comments, they will get a more accurate picture of the seller. If this situation shows up as an anomaly, people will excuse it. If together with other comments it shows a pattern of undesirable behavior, people will catch on quickly.

Fairness

You can give a neutral or negative rating without making a comment, but fairness requires that you give a good reason to support neutral or adverse feedback. If you cannot give a good reason (state a fact or set of facts), then you should rethink why you are giving a neutral or negative rating.

Communication

Always attempt to work out any differences with the other party. Direct communication works well for resolving problems. Get the other party's phone number and address immediately after an auction finishes. Call, write, or email him or her. Get the problems resolved.

Probably most adverse ratings result from a lack of communication or from one party's total failure to communicate. Make sure that you communicate. When the other party attempts to contact you, respond in a timely manner. When a problem arises, initiate communication.

Making a neutral or negative rating does not motivate the other party to live up to his or her agreement. It warns eBay patrons that you couldn't work things out with the other party because he or she acted unfairly, unreasonably, or fraudulently. Never threaten the other party with an adverse rating as a negotiation ploy (blackmail?). Reasonable people do not threaten others, and if the other person reports your threat, it will make you look like the bad guy.

Reporting negative feedback is not the last resort. You report negative feedback after you've reached the last resort to get the transaction completed and the transaction continues to have problems.

People make mistakes. In a transaction, reasonable people work together to minimize the impact of a mistake on each party. If that can't be done and the transaction doesn't take place, reasonable people walk away and get on with their lives. Getting angry at the other party doesn't serve much purpose. (By definition a mistake is unintentional.)

If the mistake happens beyond the point where the buyer and seller can cancel the transaction, reasonable people understand that life is full of risks and try to work out the best solution to the problem. Assume the other party acts reasonably until specific facts indicate the contrary. If you do so, communication will serve you well when your transactions run into problems.

Few eBay transactions end up with the parties unreconcilable or involve fraud where one party disappears. Yet one must assume that many eBay transactions run into problems. When people communicate, the problems get solved.

Negotiation

Interestingly, the auction process takes all the negotiation out of making a deal. Otherwise, a third of this book would have to be devoted to negotiation. Nonetheless, problems sometimes arise. Buyers and sellers must negotiate. Good-faith communication gets the negotiation done. But you need to be careful in your communication when you negotiate. Always keep things open. Never close off communication with unproductive statements like "Take it or leave it." Never stop keeping an open mind; never stop looking for a solution.

Name-Calling

Some people deserve to be called names because they act so badly. Still, you can never let communication degenerate into a name-calling session. The only reason to communicate with someone you don't know who lives far away is to complete the auction transaction. Name-calling will bring an end to the communication and is self-defeating. Reasonable people don't resort to name-calling.

Anger

When a transaction becomes frustrating usually due to the other party's abject stupidity or felonious behavior, you can get pretty mad (I know I do). Never take any action against the other party in the heat of the moment. You will surely regret it. Cool off first. Then do something rational. If the other party deserves the "worst," you will be better able to administer the "worst" when you are rational. If it turns out that the other party really isn't that bad, you will save yourself some grief or guilt and will certainly save yourself from looking vengeful.

Public Record

The feedback ratings and comments constitute a public record. Anyone using eBay can see them anytime. The ratings are set in concrete. Once made, you cannot change them. You can add information to them later, but you cannot change them. They remain in the public record permanently for all to see. Consequently, a bad reputation on eBay will probably hurt you more in regard to eBay than a bad reputation where you live will hurt you in regard to your locale. Anyone who wants to know your reputation can find it in one click.

The great genius of this system is that eBay doesn't care about any-one's reputation. eBay just makes a permanent public record of it. If you're a big eBay customer, eBay doesn't care. If it's your first time on eBay, eBay doesn't care. eBay just publishes the reputations in a public record, and it enables the sellers and buyers to make or break each other's reputations.

eBay Action

If your feedback rating reaches a –4 (positives plus negatives), the eBay system will automatically shut you down as a member. You can have your case reviewed, but eBay can put you out of business (on eBay) permanently.

On the Positive Side

If you accumulate positive feedback, you earn stars, which go beside your name (see Figure 7.1).

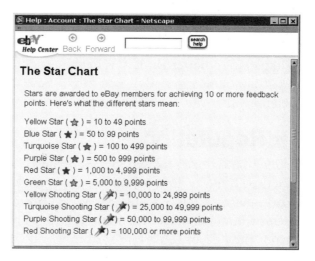

Figure 7.1   eBay Star Chart.

It's Your Reputation

Does your reputation on eBay seem artificial? Does it seem more like an attribute in a digital game than the real thing? Can you break your agreements with impunity and walk away without consequences? If you develop a bad reputation on eBay, can you just erase the entire experience? Can you be sure your eBay reputation won't spread beyond eBay?

The answer to these questions is no.

Your reputation on eBay is perhaps more real than your offline reputation. After all, more people can access it. It's the real thing. But how can a bad reputation on eBay hurt you in the world outside eBay? Easy to answer. What will prevent your banker from looking up your reputation on eBay before he or she loans you $23,000 for a new car? Nothing. In fact, a smart banker might do just that. (Will your alias on eBay be a question on future loan applications? Will the day come when you won't be able to get a loan unless you have a reputation on eBay?) Look at eBay as another credit bureau. Your reputation on eBay is not something to take lightly.

What about other creditors? What about potential employers? With 69 million people on eBay, you might have difficulty claiming with credibility that you don't have an eBay account.

It's Their Reputation

Reputation is not a problem for you because you're a good person who practices honesty, honors agreements, and treats others fairly. The good news: the eBay feedback system protects you against all the creeps who deserve bad reputations and get bad reputations on eBay just as they do offline. The system works for you, and you have a vested interest in maintaining the integrity of the system and making it work well.

The system relies on you to *tell it like it is*. This means that you must give people a negative or neutral rating when they deserve it just as you give people a positive rating when they perform as they are obligated to perform. By failing to give negative or neutral ratings when deserved, you undermine the system.

Retailers

The retailers on eBay who also sell at retail offline understand reputation. They know that reputation is everything when it comes to selling. They have built their businesses on their reputations. Ironically, many are reluctant to give adverse ratings to eBay buyers who abuse them. They reason that negative feedback given to a buyer who doesn't honor his or her agreement to purchase may result in retaliatory negative feedback. Thus, an aborted transaction can potentially hurt an innocent retailer perhaps more than a guilty buyer who doesn't care about reputation. This is an unfortunate weakness in the system, but the system has survived in spite of it.

Don't Hesitate

Give negative feedback in situations where the other party deserves it. The system depends on you to do so just like you depend on others doing so to support this wonderful ecommerce machine that eBay has turned out to be.

Non-Retailers

This situation is not limited to retailers. Almost anyone of goodwill who cares about his or her reputation might fail to post negative feedback on the other party. This natural propensity warps the entire feedback system.

Warp Effect

On one hand, if you see a retailer who has 79 positive ratings and 2 negative ratings, it most likely reflects a normal situation. You can't please everyone no matter how hard you try. Most likely those two negatives represent people who will never be happy.

On the other hand, if you see someone on eBay who has ten positives and four negatives, it seems probable that the warp (referred to above) has an influence. For each negative rating, there may have been one or more additional parties who should have given a negative rating but didn't. A person who has a substantial number of negative ratings is suspect, particularly when the ratio of negative to positive is high.

Indeed, when a person gets to a feedback rating of -4 (adding together both positive and negative feedback), eBay will terminate his or her membership.

How the System Works

The system invites you to enter ratings on the people with whom you've done business in regard to an eBay auction. To access the reporting section, go *Services, FeedbackForum, Leave feedback about an eBay user* (see Figure 7.2)

Check the appropriate radio button to choose a rating. Then enter a comment in the input below.

If giving negative feedback, write your comment on a piece of paper offline before entering it as part of the rating. That will allow you plenty of time to avoid making a blunder you might regret. Remember, the rating and comment remain posted forever, and you cannot change them.

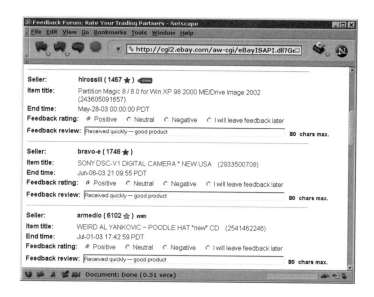

Figure 7.2   Leaving feedback.

Comment on a Rating

Occasionally, you will need to comment on a rating you've already posted. eBay permits this, but it shows as an addition to the posted rating and does not take the place of the posted rating. Such a comment also becomes part of the permanent public record.

Comment on the Other Party's Rating of You

If someone makes an adverse comment about you, you can answer it. Never answer when you're mad. Cool down and carefully draft an answer. Follow the advice in the next section; just state the facts.

If the adverse comment by the other party is justified, you may be better off not making any comment. If you're guilty as charged but have a reasonable excuse, admit the charge but state why you felt you were justified in doing what you did. This will at least show you to be a reasonable and honest person.

Comment on Your Rating of the Other Party

There will be times when you want to comment on the other party after you've already commented once. Suppose as the seller you accepted a credit card for payment of the item sold. You rated the buyer positive for paying promptly. Later the buyer asks his bank for a charge-back on the credit card based on a complaint about the item bought. The buyer never contacted you to discuss the problem, if there really was a problem.

The buyer may be attempting to beat you out of payment for the item. If you can't get the matter straightened out with the buyer, you may want to add a comment onto the original rating you made explaining what happened after you thought the transaction had been completed.

A follow-up comment need not always be negative. Suppose you are the buyer in Case #6 Buyer Enters a Negative subsection earlier. Your negative rating of the seller catches the seller's attention. The seller tells you that the shipping costs so much because the sale includes a set of heavy batteries which have to be shipped separately, a situation of which you were not aware. You complete the transaction and receive the batteries as well as the item. At this point, you can reasonably add a favorable comment to your original negative rating.

Bickering

When the parties bicker back and forth with add-on comments to the original ratings, it usually makes both parties look like a couple of loonies. Never attempt to answer the other person's add-on adverse comment. Just let it go if you have nothing new to add. It has to stop somewhere. Sometimes broken transactions get to the point where the best thing to do is just move on. People looking at the public record of your ratings and comments can read between the lines very skillfully.

If you have conducted yourself reasonably in a transaction, that fact will probably emerge from the comments, even if the other party has the last word. Don't risk your reputation (and your sanity) by getting into a bickering contest.

Public or Private

You can choose to make your feedback public or private. Why would you do business with a person who kept his or her feedback private? Why would anyone do business with you, if you keep your feedback private?

Recently I communicated with a seller for a few days about an item (several emails). Then I didn't bid on the item as I had indicated to him I would. He sent me an email to ask why. I told him that just before I would have placed the bid, I checked his feedback. It was private, so I didn't bid. He took the time to reply and berate me for acting crazy. What would you have done?

Liability for Defamation

eBay's permanent public record of feedback will generate lawsuits. If you make false or derogatory statements about someone, you may find yourself at the wrong end of a lawsuit. However, truth is always a defense. As long as you make factual statements in your feedback, you minimize your risk of being sued. So, if you find yourself heading for the feedback section on eBay very angry at someone, you'd better stop and cool off before you type in something you'll regret later.

Evaluating a Person's Reputation

You can easily and quickly evaluate a person's reputation. Just read his or her ratings. Start with the negative ratings. Then read some of the positive ratings. You will probably get a good idea of whether you want to do business with the individual.

Buyers Beware

When reading negative ratings, I am always struck by how many seem to be about winning bidders who just didn't understand their obligations and made unreasonable demands on the sellers, mostly out of ignorance. That leads me to advise that if you're a buyer, read the auction ad carefully, and don't complain if a careless reading gets you into a bind.

To fine-tune your analysis of a buyer or seller, pay attention to the percentage of transactions that are auctions and the percentage that are purchases. Then look specifically at the feedback for each. It's possible that a person can be a great seller but a lousy buyer, or vice versa.

If you buy, remember that you're going to send the seller payment. The risk of the transaction is yours. If the seller proves unreputable, you're the one who's out the money. However, you must decide before you bid. Reviewing the seller's reputation and refusing to pay after you win the bidding will expose you to a justifiable negative rating.

If you sell, remember that if the buyer doesn't pay, you will waste your time and energy and become frustrated. In the end, you will have to put the item up for auction again with the requisite delay in selling the item. Also, remember that you don't have to sell to anyone so long as you have an acceptable reason. If the winning bidder has a poor reputation, you can sell to the next-highest bidder. Should you decide to do so, however, you should advise the winning bidder of your reasons and remind him or her of your right to refuse a sale. Be tactful. Keep in mind also that the second-highest bidder has no obligation to buy.

Up Front

If you want to be particular about who you will sell to, state it up front in your auction ad. For instance, you might say, "Will not accept buyers with a feedback rating below 20."

SafeHarbor

eBay's SafeHarbor program exists to ensure that buyers and sellers can carry on commerce with the confidence that they will not experience an unreasonable level of the risk of fraud. The Feedback Forum, eBay's reputation program, is part of the SafeHarbor program. Take a look at the SafeHarbor program to see what else it offers. Go *Services*, *SafeHarbor*.

Conclusion

This chapter deals with a lot of negative situations. Does that mean they will all happen to you sooner or later? Not necessarily. Most transactions resulting from eBay auctions close sooner or later despite occasional neglect or slow performance by one or the other party. Most people act reasonably, communicate competently, and have the skills to conclude a long-distance transaction. Most deals close, and presumably the parties walk away happy. eBay provides you with a great way to sell stuff and buy stuff. But as for every public activity, the parties must follow rules of conduct. When a person flagrantly violates those rules, you should warn the eBay community about such an individual.

8

Reporting and Recourse

Report on the other party to eBay, and ask the other party to report on you via the eBay feedback system. Thereby, you build up your eBay reputation. Most transactions go smoothly, giving you your chance to pat the other party on the back and receive the same in return. Occasionally, however, transactions go bad. Chapter 7 covers eBay reputation and feedback. This chapter reports on what additional you can do to deal with the other party if the other party treats you unfairly or commits fraud.

145

Most People Are Honest, But …

Most people are honest, but occasionally a real loser comes along and grabs your money (or merchandise) and runs. eBay has seen scams in the past. eBay has scams today. And eBay will experience scams in the future. Kind of reminds you of real life, doesn't it? Well, cyber life ain't what it used to be.

If You Are a Bidder

How can you get zapped? Let me count the ways:

1. Merchandise damaged in shipment

2. Merchandise lost in shipment

3. Defective merchandise

4. Merchandise not in the condition represented

5. Merchandise substituted without your approval

6. No merchandise delivered

You should foresee a few of these and take the necessary precautions. For instance, merchandise lost or damaged in shipment can be covered by insurance.

If You Are a Seller

What can happen? After all, presumably, you control the transaction by withholding the merchandise until payment has been assured. But these four things constitute risk:

1. Insufficient funds for a check. You can get a report about a person's checking account (whether there has been prior trouble), but you will never know whether there are sufficient funds until the check clears.

2. Credit card charge-back. Any buyer can have his or her credit card bank nullify a purchase for good reason usually within a

90-day period. Some banks extend that period up to a year.

3. Forged or phony financial instrument (e.g., money order).

4. Shill bidding (see below).

Usually, prior trouble with a bank account warns you about a bad check; but when no prior trouble shows, you can still get stung when there are insufficient funds to cover your check. If a buyer does a charge-back on his or her credit card, you may have trouble getting your money or even getting the merchandise back. Then, of course, stolen credit cards cause ongoing problems. Counterfeit financial instruments cause problems offline. Online, where counterfeiters are easier to trace, counterfeit financial instruments do not cause so many problems; but beware.

Fraud Online

Interestingly enough, although fraud occurs at about the same rate online as offline according to some financial experts, more criminals get caught online than offine. Law enforcement can trace them easier online.

Shill Bidding

Shill bidding is collusion between two or more bidders working an auction. Online, it can be one bidder working with two ISPs and two eBay accounts. Unfortunately, this probably happens more than anyone will admit. If you suspect shill bidding, report it to eBay.

Adverse to Buyers

Shill bidding affects bidders when the seller (with two ISP accounts and eBay accounts) bids up the price on an item. This is illegal and also is not permitted by eBay. Nonetheless, many people have second or third ISP accounts and eBay accounts. A seller with more than one eBay account can bid up an item without being discovered. If you have good reason to suspect this, report it to eBay.

Adverse to Sellers

Shill bidding affects a seller when the first bidder bids up the item to a high price to smoke out the reserve amount (the lowest price you are willing to accept) and to preempt honest bidders. The first bidder then retracts his or her bid late in the auction. The second bidder (who can be the same person using a different account) then bids slightly over the reserve. You, the seller, are left with the second bidder's lower bid. Anytime a high bidder retracts a bid, make an analysis to detect shill bidding. If you think it is, report it to eBay.

Negotiate

Should you find yourself in a situation where you have a problem, negotiate. Don't get mad. Don't make unreasonable demands. Don't threaten. Just keep asking the other party to do what he said he would do. Be monotonous. Discuss whatever, but always return to asking the other party to do what he said he would do. That means do what he advertised or what he represented he would do. In the alternative, ask for a refund and offer to return the item auctioned (buyer); or offer a refund and ask that the item auctioned be returned (seller).

It doesn't pay to quibble. As you will see from the remainder of this chapter, your remedies may not work well nor be cost-effective. Consequently, if the other party unreasonably disagrees with you, you may have to make the best of a bad situation and cut your losses.

eBay is not a moral forum; it's a commercial milieu. If you want to fight, blame, or determine right and wrong, you can probably do so better someplace else on the Web. For buyers and sellers, the marketplace has always been fraught with risk. eBay is no different. You have to roll with the punches. I recommend that you stand firm and insist that the other party perform as agreed, but you have to take a practical approach, too, due to the difficulty of finding an adequate remedy. For instance, you can't march down to small claims court and expect to get the matter effectively resolved when the other party lives 2,000 miles away in another state.

Remember the Telephone?

You don't have to negotiate by email. Pick up the telphone and call the other party. Get the telephone number from eBay. Go *Search, Find Member, Contact Info*. eBay will email you the information. (Your request for the telephone number will be reported to the other party.)

Remedies

When negotiations fail to reach an acceptable solution to whatever problems arise, you must consider taking other action. This section covers some things you can do.

Receipt

A receipt can protect each party to a transaction. It should specify the seller, the buyer, the date, the price, and the merchandise. The receipt should specify the merchandise in detail, and the specification should match the merchandise described in the eBay auction ad.

Absent a receipt, what do you have? Well, you have eBay's email notification regarding the winning bid for the auction. And you have the eBay auction ad itself. These documents establish the terms of the transaction absent a receipt.

Buyer's View

From the buyer's point of view, the receipt is a legal document that summarizes the transaction. If you have to go to court, it's handy to have. Always check the receipt for accuracy, especially in regard to the

specification of the merchandise and the price. If the receipt is not correct—and the transaction is large enough—demand an accurate one.

Save all information in regard to the transaction, including the receipt.
That means the eBay auction ad, the eBay email notification, and
email correspondence. Alas, you may not remember to do so, but if
you find yourself in a jam, you'll wish that you had done it.

Seller's View

Always provide a receipt that accurately summarizes the transaction. If
a buyer does not dispute the accuracy of the receipt within a reasonable time, the receipt may come in handy later when a buyer starts
making unreasonable demands. It also makes you look like a prudent
and honest businessperson.

Just as for the buyer, save your eBay auction ad, the email notification,
and all other information in regard to the transaction, such as any
exchange of email.

Refund and Return

When there's dissatisfaction, a refund and a return of the merchandise
often become a good remedy for both buyers and sellers.

Buyer's View

If something unacceptable goes wrong with the transaction and the
seller doesn't cooperate, try to get back to the starting line. That means
request a refund and return the item. Don't quibble about who will
pay the shipping cost (but there's a difference between asking and
quibbling). Make sure you send the item back in the condition in
which you received it, if possible. This is often a disappointing remedy
but a far more practical one than some of the others available.

Seller's View

Sure there are unreasonable buyers. Nonetheless, offer a refund when problems arise as the best way to preserve your reputation and build a following of loyal customers. That is not to say that if problems arise you shouldn't try to get them resolved in other ways, if possible. But a dissatisfied and determined customer will waste your time and sap your energy.

Occasional Seller

Even if you sell only occasionally on eBay, you may have to act like a retailer to preserve your reputation. Your auctioning of 15 or 20 items over the next five years makes you look like a retailer once the time element is removed (e.g., the Feedback Forum).

Oddly enough, it is the seller who usually suggests a refund and return. It's a good way to resolve a problem, keep everyone happy, and reserve your energy for other business endeavors.

The tough case comes along when you've sold something in an "as is" condition with a stipulation that it has defects, and then the buyer wants to return it because it doesn't work due to the defects mentioned. In this circumstance, you have plenty of reason to hang tough with the buyer. But you may find it more trouble to hang tough than to just make a refund.

When you offer or agree to make a refund, always insist that the buyer return the item as a condition of making the refund, even in those occasional cases where you don't want to get the item back. Faced with having to ship the item, the buyer may decide the perceived problem isn't quite as bad as imagined. Just offering to make a refund often defuses the buyer's anger and sets the stage for resolving the situation in another way.

Mediation

When you can't resolve a dispute, sometimes mediation helps. Now we have e-mediation? Well, whatever. Actually, SquareTrade (*http://www.squaretrade.com*) provides dispute resolution. It uses some online techniques to resolve disputes through mediation, but if such techniques don't work, SquareTrade stands ready to use a hands-on effort to resolve arguments. This service is available to all at a low fee, but both parties have to agree to use it. The seller can pay a low monthly fee to SquareTrade for the use of their logo. The logo in the seller's auction ads signifies that the seller agrees to use SquareTrade should a dispute arise. This is an excellent service. Give serious consideration to using it, especially on large transactions.

Report to eBay

Negotiated remedies don't always work, and sometimes you have to take action. In addition, nonperformance by one party (i.e., a buyer doesn't pay or a seller doesn't ship the merchandise) requires action.

Unresolved Dispute

When you have a dispute that you cannot resolve, you have to decide what you will do about it. Making a negative feedback that affects the other party's reputation on eBay may be appropriate, but it is not a remedy. However, it may force the other party to resolve the dispute just to make a credible reply to your negative feedback.

Report the problem to eBay as another step in seeking a remedy. Go *Services, SafeHarbor, Fraud Protection*. However, eBay has no interest in resolving commercial disputes. That's up to the parties. Only when an act clearly amounts to criminal behavior, or at least to a shady business practice, will eBay have an interest in hearing from you. eBay's action against the other party, if any, will not provide a remedy for you unless it somehow forces the other party to resolve the dispute.

Nonperformance

If one party changes his mind about buying or selling in spite of the occurrence of a valid auction, you can usually convince the other party to perform just by standing firm and insisting. If nonperformance is due to fraud or a deliberate contracting with no intent to perform, you probably won't hear from the other party (i.e., they won't answer you).

Nonperformance is a deliberate act. In some cases, it may be a criminal act. In any case it's unacceptable behavior, and you should make a negative feedback comment. In addition, if criminal behavior, you should report it to eBay.

Not Optional

Don't think of reporting nonperformance as an option. It's your duty as a good eBay citizen, so to speak, to report such behavior. Most (99.99 percent) of the people who use eBay act honestly and reasonably. If eBay works for you, you have an obligation to make it work for other people. Your feedback on nonperformance warns other eBay members. Your report to eBay on nonperformance (in the case of suspected criminal behavior) may help eBay eliminate bad actors sooner rather than later.

Whether such a report to eBay will result in a remedy for you is not certain. In some cases, it may force the other party to perform. In other cases, it will simply result in the other party being barred from participation in eBay or in no action at all.

Insurance

eBay does provide insurance against fraud. The limit is $200 with $25 deductible. PowerSellers can offer $500 insurance. Although this insurance doesn't cover *very* inexpensive items, it does cover *moderately* inexpensive items on which you normally wouldn't willingly spend much money to get protection against a loss. For items over $200 (or $500), eBay probably figures that the parties can and will protect themselves adequately in regard to these more expensive items; that is, they will purchase fraud protection. This seems a reasonable assumption.

The insurance is automatic, and you collect on a loss by filing a claim. Although similar to filing a complaint, an insurance claim comes with a cash remedy. Too bad that the upper limit isn't $2,000 instead of $200 (or $500).

This insurance doesn't cover damage in shipment. You need to purchase shipping insurance to cover such a potential loss.

Better Business Bureau

Although not the appropriate place to register a complaint against an individual, the Better Business Bureau (*http://bbb.org*) provides a mechanism for filing a complaint against a business. First, the Bureau will refer you to a local Bureau organization if one exists in the locale where the company operates. Not being a governmental agency, the Bureau has limited power to pursue complaints, but for grievances against established businesses, this alternative might work.

Civil and Criminal Liability

Before the discussion of remedies goes further, you need to distinguish between civil and criminal liability.

Civil Claim

A civil claim is one between the parties to an eBay auction transaction. A court will resolve the dispute between the parties if one of the parties files a complaint. This provides the basis on which the court will resolve most transactional disputes. If the claiming party wins, the court usually grants an award of money to compensate for the damages incurred.

Criminal Complaint

Where one party commits fraud or theft, the act is an offense against the public (based on the victim's complaint). Once you file a criminal complaint, it's out of your hands. Only the prosecuting attorney (district attorney or DA) has the authority to prosecute or not to prosecute the complaint.

As a practical matter, the DA will probably not prosecute your complaint should you withdraw it. After all, you may be the only witness; if you don't cooperate, the DA may not find the complaint worth pursuing. If you do not withdraw your complaint, the DA might decide not to prosecute it for lack of adequate evidence or other reasons. Nonetheless, the DA can choose to prosecute based on your criminal complaint resulting in an arrest warrant being issued for the other party.

No Threats

Don't threaten the other party. Courts like reasonable people. Courts take a dim view of unreasonable people. You want to make sure a court always sees you as a reasonable person. This presents a dilemma: You always want to let the other party know that you intend to file suit; it may entice him or her to be more reasonable. But you don't want to threaten the other party because it will make you look unreasonable. Thus, you have to walk a fine line. In other words, tone down your threats so they seem like reasonable statements.

Improper: If you don't send my refund immediately, I'm going to sue you for everything you've got and report you to the Better Business Bureau.

Proper: Your refusal to be fair is forcing me to consider seeking remedies other than negotiation.

If you feel this low-key approach has had no effect, repeating it may make it more convincing to the other party.

In many states, the improper statement above is unethical for an attorney. An attorney could make the following statement without violating bar ethics:

> Proper (for an attorney): If you continue to refuse to be fair, you will leave me no choice but to recommend to my client that she file a lawsuit.

Remember, reasonable people file lawsuits only as a last resort.

Although not making threats is important in civil cases, it is particularly important in criminal cases. People who threaten to make criminal complaints if the other party doesn't do this or that do not favorably impress judges. Never overtly threaten to file a criminal complaint against someone if he or she doesn't agree to your terms. It will sound like you're abusing the criminal justice system for your own advantage. Be very subtle; the other party won't miss the point you make.

If you threaten, however subtly, to make a criminal complaint against the other party where such a complaint is not justified, it may have the opposite effect intended. The other party may become indignant and prove even more difficult to negotiate with. Moreover, as long as you can communicate with the other party routinely, chances are you cannot justify criminal action. Real criminals tend to disappear or become incommunicado.

Civil Suit

You can file a suit against the other party in your local small claims court without hiring an attorney. This makes a cost-efficient way of suing someone, if you have the time to handle the case yourself. You can use this kind of legal action particularly effectively against a resident of your state because when you get a judgment (award of money), you can collect it much more easily. As mentioned earlier in the chapter, however, you will have a difficult time using the small claims court against a party in another state.

To conduct your own case in small claims court, buy a book on doing so. Nolo Press (*http://www.nolo.com*) publishes a series of self-help legal books that can assist you.

Small claims courts have an upper limit on the jurisdictional amount. In other words, if the damages you seek are over a certain amount, you cannot get full satisfaction in small claims court. For instance, suppose you seek a refund of $4,000 and the small claims court has financial jurisdiction for $3,000. You can't collect more than $3,000 in the small claims court. To recover the entire $4,000, you will have to hire an attorney and file your case in the regular court (the court of general jurisdiction).

Attorneys can be expensive. You need to make a determination as to whether it's worth it to pursue a lawsuit requiring the services of an attorney. With enough at stake, it may make sense. Otherwise a legal remedy may not be a cost-effective option.

Criminal Prosecution

When the other party makes a blatant misrepresentation or does not perform at all, it might be a criminal act. But criminal acts require criminal intent.

Suppose the seller represents that a computer printer prints at 12 pages per minute. It turns out the printer prints at only 4 pages per minute. The seller got the information from the manufacturer and then passed it on to bidders and potential bidders. The seller may have misrepresented the facts but presumably without intent. And without intent, there's no crime. This points out that you have to be very careful before you accuse anyone of a criminal act.

Suppose you send a check for the computer printer after exchanging email messages with the seller. You don't receive the printer in two weeks and you try to get in touch with the seller to no avail. How long do you wait to take action? Suppose the seller happened to go on vacation for three weeks just after your check arrived and was deposited, and the printer was mistakenly not sent. It may not be a good business practice to close the doors, in effect, for three weeks, but it's not criminal.

You need to consider it very carefully before you file a criminal complaint against someone. Make sure he or she has committed a criminal act, not just done something with which you don't agree. Make sure he or she intended to commit the act. Don't take filing a criminal complaint lightly. Keep in mind, too, that unless you have convincing evidence that the other party has committed fraud, the police will not have much motivation to take action.

However, when you've been had by someone, sooner or later it becomes painfully obvious. Don't be reluctant to file a criminal complaint. In such a case, it's not only your duty as a good eBay citizen, it's your duty as a good citizen of society. Usually, you will find that you are not the first victim. If you are the first victim, though, perhaps your complaint will save others the pain of being defrauded.

Is a criminal case a remedy for you? Not in most cases. You can probably best use it as a threat, albeit a subtle threat as explained earlier in the No Threats subsection. In a criminal case, however, the judge imposes a jail sentence, and that will not necessarily benefit you.

Out of Touch

If someone defrauds you, he will almost certainly take the money (merchandise) and run. He will be out of touch, and your biggest clue that you've been bamboozled will be that you can't communicate with him. Can law enforcement eventually catch up with him? Apparently the police have an easier time finding criminals who have committed crimes online than offline, but it takes aggressive law enforcement to catch such criminals in any event. Whether you can enlist such aggressive law-enforcement investigators on your behalf is the question.

Across State Lines

Conducting a lawsuit or even filing a criminal complaint across state lines is likely to be more complicated than filing one at home. It's probably not worth your time unless it involves a large amount of money. Attorneys typically charge over $100 per hour.

State Court

For instance, suppose you are in Michigan and file a claim in small claims court against the other party who lives in New Mexico. You get a judgment in Michigan. What will you do next? You may have to file an action (which requires a hearing) in court in New Mexico in order to enforce the judgment in New Mexico. This will probably require an attorney. Then you have to collect the judgment, often the most difficult part of the process. And you have to do all this over a thousand miles from home. Note, too, that in some cases by law you may not be able to enforce a small claims court judgment in another state.

Suppose you want to file a criminal complaint against the other party in New Mexico. You will file the complaint from a long ways away. To get a conviction, the local DA will have to trust that you will travel to New Mexico to testify. The local DA may not show great enthusiasm about prosecuting such a case. Even if the DA prosecutes the person, a criminal conviction does not necessarily resolve the problems in the transaction (i.e., you don't get a remedy).

Attorney General

Some states handle fraud cases through the state Attorney General's office, not through the local DAs. The Attorney General may have a permanent fraud office or a fraud task force.

Federal Agencies

Under federal statutes you can file a complaint against the other party with the US Postal Inspection Service (*http://www.framed.usps.com/postalinspectors*) if US mail was used by the other party, the Federal Trade Commission (FTC — *http://www.ftc.gov*), or the federal Attorney General. Again, this might result in penalties to the other party but no benefit to you. The subtle threat of doing so, however, may have an effect on the other party, if such a complaint is justified.

You can also file a report with the National Fraud Information Center (*http://www.fraud.org*). The Center transmits this report to the National Fraud Database maintained by the FTC and also to the National Association of Attorneys General. Where this will lead is anyone's guess, but it beats doing nothing if criminal behavior seems apparent.

Federal Court

You can conduct a lawsuit between parties from different states in federal court. You will need an attorney, however, and conducting a lawsuit in the federal court tends to be more expensive than doing the same in a state court. To justify the expenses to conduct such a suit, the amount you seek to recover must be large.

You can also file a criminal complaint in the federal court via the FBI (*http://www.fbi.gov*) if you believe that federal criminal laws have been broken. Whether the federal DA will pursue the case is out of your hands, but often this is the most realistic way to prosecute criminals who operate across state lines.

eBay

Go to *Services*, *SafeHarbor* to report fraud to eBay. It's the best way to protect your fellow eBay members and maintain eBay as a viable and enduring marketplace.

Collecting a Judgment

Just because you get a judgment against someone doesn't mean that you realize a remedy. You still have to collect the judgment. Often that is impossible.

- The other party disappears.

- The other party's assets disappear.

- The other party has no assets.

- The other party is difficult, perhaps impossible, to locate.

You can go to all the expense of conducting a lawsuit (e.g., attorney fees), get a judgment, and then never collect a dime. This is a sobering thought when you consider initiating a lawsuit.

Prevention

This chapter will probably not help you much except to make you realize that prevention is your best defense against an unfair or fraudulent transaction. If you will recall, this book recommends that as a buyer you never bid more than you can afford to lose. If you bid more than that, make sure that you protect yourself with an escrow arrangement. If a seller, never deliver the merchandise until the buyer pays you.

Unfortunately, you cannot eliminate all risk. You can only take commonsense precautions. If you go overboard as a buyer, you may be asking for negative feedback. For instance, if you insist on paying by credit card when a seller has stated in his auction ad that the only acceptable payment method is by money order, you're asking for trouble. The seller may not even have a credit card merchant account.

If you go overboard as a seller, you will put a damper on your business. For instance, if you take only money orders, you don't run the risk of charge-backs on credit cards. But you eliminate a lot of honest potential bidders who want or need to pay by credit card. And money orders have their own risks anyway.

Although precautions do not provide an absolute guarantee, they will considerably reduce your chances of becoming a victim of an unfair or fraudulent transaction. So, practice prevention as your best remedy for the acts of those unsavory predators lurking on the auction grounds.

Forget It

There comes a time when you may just have to forget it and get on with your life, not a pleasant thought when someone has treated you unfairly or defrauded you. But as you have learned from reading this chapter, conducting a lawsuit is expensive and time-consuming with negligible chances of collecting in most cases.

If you do get taken by someone, report it to all the proper places, but prepare to absorb the loss.

eBay Offenses

eBay lists a number of prohibited offenses in its SafeHarbor section of the eBay website. See *Services, SafeHarbor* for more detailed information. Some of these actions may constitute criminal activities. Some do not. Regardless, eBay will take action (e.g., indefinite suspension of an offender) on any of these offenses reported. The following subsections list some of the eBay offenses.

Feedback Offenses

You cannot use second registrations or associates for the filing of positive feedback to boost your own feedback record (shill feedback).

You cannot use second registrations or associates for the filing of negative feedback to impact the feedback record of another person (shill feedback).

You cannot threaten negative feedback to demand from another person some undeserved action (feedback extortion).

You cannot offer to sell, trade, or buy feedback (feedback solicitation).

Bidding Offenses

You cannot use second registrations or associates to artificially raise the level of bidding to extremely high levels temporarily in order to protect the low bid of an associate (bid shielding).

You cannot email the bidders in a currently open auction to offer the same or similar item at a lower price (bid siphoning).

You cannot email bidders in a currently open auction to warn them away from a seller or item (auction interference).

You cannot retract a bid to manipulate the bidding.

You cannot use second registrations or associates to artificially raise the number of bids to the level required for a "HOT" designation.

You cannot chronically bid on items without completing the transactions for which you are the high bidder.

You cannot persist to bid on a seller's items after a warning from seller that your bids are not welcome (e.g., seller doesn't want to do business with you due to your negative feedback rating).

Selling Offenses

You cannot use second registrations or associates to artificially raise the bidding on your item up for auction (shill bidding).

You cannot represent yourself as an eBay seller (another person) and intercept the ended auctions of that seller for the purpose of accepting payment (auction interception).

You cannot manipulate the system to avoid paying fees.

You cannot sell items (accept payments) and not complete the transactions (not deliver the items).

Contact Information–Identity Offenses

You cannot represent yourself as an eBay employee.

You cannot represent yourself as another eBay user.

You cannot provide false information such as name, address, and telephone number to eBay.

You cannot use an invalid email address.

You cannot be an eBay user if you are under age 18.

Miscellaneous Offenses

You cannot use any device, software, or procedure to interfere with the proper operation of eBay.

You cannot send unsolicited email to past bidders or buyers.

You cannot threaten another eBay user with bodily harm via email.

You cannot publish the contact information of another eBay user on any online public area.

You cannot offer pirated intellectual property or illegal items for sale.

You cannot use profane, vulgar, racist, hateful, sexual, or obscene language on any online public area.

How Seriously?

Does eBay take fraud seriously, and if so, how seriously? eBay hired an ex-federal district attorney to oversee its security operations. One can assume from that act alone that eBay means business when it comes to dealing with fraud.

Verified Rights Owner Program

eBay operates a program with publishers (software publishers as well as publishers of books and other intellectual property) that helps keep counterfeit materials off eBay: Verified Rights Owner (VeRO) program. If you are a victim of a fraud involving a counterfeit product (e.g., pirated software), a complaint to eBay (or to the copyright holder that is a VeRO) should result in some action.

Summary

This chapter does not attempt to define every transaction on eBay that is unfair or fraudulent. Indeed, when it comes to fraud, some criminals are ingenious. Nor does it attempt to define everything you can do to prevent someone from defrauding you or otherwise dealing with you unfairly. The chapter simply explores the potential of resorting to eBay or the legal system for a remedy. Unless large amounts of money are at stake, however, the prospects do not look good for recovering a loss through the legal system. Therefore, you have to be conscious that prevention provides your best remedy for the losses you would likely suffer, sooner or later, by being careless. But don't act so overly careful that you increase your potential for offending potential bidders.

Millions of people use eBay each week. They include a few crooks who do their best to prey on others for their own personal gain. But overall, nice people like you and me who just want to make mutually beneficial transactions comprise all but a very small part of the huge eBay marketplace.

III

Bidding Strategies

9

Timely Bidding

There are no bidding guarantees, only strategies and tactics. This chapter will help you develop an eBay strategy and give you some tactics to improve your bidding success.

Realities

No bidding practices will guarantee that you will win an auction, except perhaps overbidding by a considerable margin. Another bidder can come in and outbid you at any time by offering a price that you do not wish to match.

At times eBay (or the Internet) slows down, making the precise timing of bids difficult in the final moments of the auction. When you get set up ahead of time to carry on a last-minute bidding frenzy, you may unexpectedly get called away to do something more important and thereby miss the final minutes of the auction. I've done this on numerous occasions.

The bidding process itself may yield information about the item being offered—information that provides a basis for changing your bid limit at the last minute—but you may be unavailable or unprepared to make the adjustment necessary to win the bidding. Or, the bidding process in the heat of the last moments may overwhelm you; it's sometimes difficult to make decisions when the window of opportunity is measured in seconds.

The underlying assumptions of the prior paragraphs are:

That you will have bidding competition. The size of eBay tends to guarantee that you will. Nonetheless, you will find plenty of auctions where the expected competition does not materialize. You can often pick up valuable goods for even less than the minimum price you anticipated.

That your bidding competition will be tough, knowledgeable competitors. In fact, not everyone takes the time to bone up on eBay bidding, and your competitors may do some dumb things.

That your competitors who have already made competitive bids will also be there in the last few minutes of the auction. In fact, most bidders cannot appear at the finale of every auction they enter. Some of your competition might be missing during those last few minutes.

In conclusion, there are no guarantees, but nonetheless, there are opportunities to buy at significant savings.

Strategies

What is your strategy for making purchases on eBay? For most people it will be one of the following five purposes:

1. Buying goods (e.g., camera equipment) for less money than elsewhere. This is a *money-saving* strategy.

2. Buying from a large selection of goods (e.g., offbeat brands). This is a *consumer-buying* strategy.

3. Buying goods not otherwise available conveniently (e.g., old items). This is a *time-saving* strategy.

4. Buying for resale (e.g., buy at or below wholesale and sell retail). This is a *profit* strategy.

5. Having fun (e.g., last-minute bidding). This is an *emotional* strategy.

Some buy on eBay to save money, some to get a bigger selection, some to save time, some to make profit, and some to have fun. These are general strategies. Each eBay category may have its own special strategies, but with tens of thousands of categories, this book cannot cover all. Thus, I don't provide strategies for buying any particular category of merchandise, but the general strategies ought to work well in most cases.

Save Money

I can't speak for anyone else, but I can tell you my general strategies for buying on eBay.

- New items: These must sell at 40–55 percent of list price (i.e., a 45–60 percent discount). If you can't get the merchandise at such low prices on eBay, you should buy it at a discount store; it's less risky. You know the discount store, you know where it is, and the discount store usually provides a liberal return policy. Buying from an eBay seller, you usually don't get the same assurances.

- Factory-refurbished items: These are almost the same as new goods if they come in a factory-sealed box with a warranty. I will pay almost as much for these goods as for new goods (i.e., discounted price) under two conditions. First, the refurbished items are not generally available at retail. If they are, the price should be significantly lower than new goods. The scarcity of factory-refurbished goods makes them almost as valuable as new goods (i.e., new goods sold with a deep price discount). Second, the item is soon to be obsolete (within a few years). For example, a hard drive will last for ten years in a home office. You will use it for only three before you buy a bigger one. What difference does it make if you buy a factory-refurbished one instead of a new one?

- Used items in excellent condition: These must sell at 35 percent of list price (i.e., a 65 percent discount). When anyone can buy an item new at a discount store for 60 percent of list price, used items even in excellent condition usually aren't worth as much as one would think. Most people given the choice between buying a new item at 60 percent of list and a used item at 40–60 percent of list will choose the new item. Realistically, the market value for most used goods is normally below 40 percent of list (i.e., more than a 60 percent discount).

I won't pay more than the above guidelines indicate. That's my strategy. Of course, there are plenty of situations on eBay that do not meet my general guidelines. Often one brand leads the field in a category, and everyone wants it (e.g., Marantz for high-end stereo components). Items with the hot brand name often sell on eBay for what you might pay for them in a discount store, or even higher. This doesn't make sense, but it happens. You won't find me making such a purchase on eBay. However, I live in a metro area of seven million people with scores of specialty discount stores. Naturally, I would feel differently if I lived in a place where the nearest specialty discount store was 250 miles away.

For Sellers

I don't think my guidelines are unusually strict. If you paid full retail for an item when anyone could get it at a discount store for 60 percent of list price, you took an immediate 40 percent loss. Even if the item is still sealed-box-new, you won't make up your loss by selling on eBay. You will take an additional loss, in most cases, or you won't attract any bidders

Some used goods are rare but in high demand. They can go at surprisingly high prices relative to their original list price (e.g., used Leica film cameras). For such goods, if I needed them, I would certainly bend my guidelines. But generally speaking, you can say that my strategy for buying on eBay is to pay less than I would pay elsewhere.

Not a Collector

Note that I'm not a collector. I'm a money-saver. Collectors tend to be time-savers.

Get a Bigger Selection

Many people live in rural areas where their local retailers don't offer the range of choices they would have in metro areas. They can find a wider range of choices on eBay. Catalog sales have thrived on this reality for over a century. Indeed, catalog sales remain high even in metro areas where people are too busy to shop or the specialty discount store is miles away on the other side of town. Keep in mind that a significant amount of the merchandise people sell on eBay is new. It's not all old stuff. The strategy here is to get a large selection. Low price isn't as important for this consumer strategy as it is for the money-saving strategy outlined above.

Save Time

There are two aspects of saving time: (1) saving yourself a long search for a hard-to-find item and (2) simple convenience.

Saving Big Time

You have an old Shure microphone you bought ten years ago. Now you want an exact match for a special event at which your singing group will perform. But Shure doesn't make that model any longer. Where do you get it? You can hang out at the local rock band store or the audio equipment store hoping that a duplicate will turn up in the used equipment department. But eBay will offer a wider choice of used goods than is available locally, and it provides you with a good opportunity to find what you're looking for.

For this type of item, you have to price it at what it's worth to you, or you may waste a lot of your time. In other words, don't use your guidelines for money-saving purchases. This is a time-saving purchase. Will you really turn down a high price on eBay and continue to look for a cheaper price? For instance, suppose the Shure microphone listed for $150 ten years ago. Today, even in excellent condition, theoretically it should be worth about ten cents on the dollar (i.e., 10 percent of original list price). If you find one at 70 percent of list value ($105) on eBay, how much longer are you going to look around to find one cheaper? In fact, good microphones don't necessarily deteriorate if maintained properly and used properly, and the list price on a comparable new microphone today might be $250. So, as a practical matter, what you think *should* be the price (about $15) and what you are willing to pay (you want the duplicate) will probably be different. Keep in mind that eBay may be the only place where you can find this item without a lot of time-consuming searching in several nearby towns or cities. So, the strategy here is saving time. It's quick and easy to find it on eBay (if it's there).

Collectors

Many collectors fall into this category. They delight in finding something on eBay that they might never find in a decade of searching locally, and they will pay a price for an item that has no logical relationship to its original list price. The Beanie Baby phenomenon makes a good example. Collectors were willing to spend a lot for rare Beanie Babies on eBay to make their collections more complete because chances of happening across such a Beanie Baby locally were not good.

Convenience

And then there are those of us who look at eBay as a convenience machine. Why spend the time to drive to a faraway store to pick up an item you need but don't have to have immediately? Even if you don't save money buying it on eBay, at least it's delivered to your front door. I've been buying on eBay since 1998—a lot of new stuff for home and business. So far I have not had anything damaged in shipment.

Yes, you see it online. You get your PayPal to pay for it. And it magically appears at your front door. Not a bad shopping experience.

Make Profit

This is strictly a business strategy. For buying, you need to buy low, just as with the money-saving strategy, and sell at a profit. For arbitrage, you need to have the confidence that you can sell immediately at a higher price.

Retail

If you can buy new goods at or below wholesale on eBay and resell at retail (e.g., in your physical store), you can make a profit. However, presumably the risk of buying on eBay is higher than buying from a distributor. Thus, the price of new goods on eBay will normally have to be significantly lower than wholesale to justify the risk. Thus, the profit strategy is virtually identical to the money-saving strategy.

The exception is for goods in high demand that may be temporarily unavailable from distributors or manufacturers. If you can buy such goods on eBay, even for a premium above wholesale, and resell at retail (or even above retail), you can make a profit that you otherwise wouldn't be able to make. Here the strategy is to get the merchandise; but it's not that simple. You still have to get the goods at a low enough price to make a reasonable profit selling at retail. But be cautious. When the temporary shortage of goods passes, retail prices will fall quickly.

It's a little different for used goods. Some retailers enjoy a healthy market for used goods but cannot find enough inventory to buy for resale (e.g., antique dealers). However, eBay provides them with a major source of used goods that they can depend on for acquiring inventory. Here the strategy is to build up your used inventory; but you still have to get the goods at a discount deep enough to enable you to resell the goods and make a reasonable profit.

Arbitrage

Arbitrage is buying in one market and selling immediately in another market where the price is a little higher. In other words, if you can buy something on eBay and sell it immediately at a higher price somewhere else (another market that's not as efficient, either online or offline), you can make a small profit. Certainly, other online auctions do not operate as efficiently as eBay; that is, they do not have the volume to determine a stable price for a particular item. Perhaps you can engage in arbitrage between such auctions and eBay. If you can be sure of selling something immediately for a higher price in another market, buy it on eBay where it's likely to sell cheaper, and then resell it in the other market.

Arbitrage is a stock market technique. It does not work as well for the more erratic and less efficient goods market. The transfer of stocks is immediate. The cost of transfer for stocks is small. On the other hand, the transfer of goods usually takes time. The cost of transfer for goods involves shipping and sometimes sales tax and other costs. Nonetheless, where prices are out of sync enough and an immediate resale is assured, you can use arbitrage to realize narrow profit margins.

Arbitrage Is Not Retail

Buying at low prices on eBay and selling at retail is not the same as arbitrage. If you can buy at wholesale prices or below on eBay, which is quite possible, then you can sell at retail offline without having to sell immediately. There's more profit in a retail sale, so you don't have to make an immediate sale to minimize your holding costs.

Arbitrage can work two ways for you with eBay. First, you can buy elsewhere and sell on eBay, or you can buy on eBay and sell elsewhere. The principle is simply that the resale must be certain, immediate, and profitable.

An example is baseball caps with official major league team insignias, about $8–$16 per cap at retail stores. If you can find a closeout purchase (in the closeout market) for $0.50 per cap and resell the caps easily to end users on eBay for $3 per cap, that's a retail operation. If you can resell the caps easily on eBay to sports distributors for $1.50 each (minimum order seven cartons—1,008 caps), that's more like arbitrage (between the closeout market and the wholesale market). The sale to the sports distributors is certain because they normally pay at least $4 per cap and would rather pay only $1.50, and the caps are always in demand. After all, the caps have the official major league team insignias.

In the example of selling to the distributors, you would not want to take delivery of the caps. You would want to make the resales to the distributors so quickly that you could have your seller ship directly to your buyers (distributors). In other words, you would be strictly a middleman.

For arbitrage, the buying strategy is to buy low, but it must be coupled with a resale plan that can be carried out immediately. In other words, the price you anticipate for the resale determines the upper limit for which you can buy the goods and still make a small profit on the immediate resale. With arbitrage you have to be careful. Because the profits are usually small, you can't afford to make a mistake.

I might also point out that arbitrage requires large transactions, often significant amounts of capital, and extensive knowledge of the markets. The profit is small, so the transaction must be large to make the deal worthwhile. And unless you have excellent knowledge of the markets in which you deal, arbitrage is financially suicidal.

Have Fun

Online auctions can be fun. They're like a game. It's perfectly legitimate to pursue participation just for the fun of it. Don't forget, though, that legally an auction is not a game. It forms a legal contract between the seller and the high bidder. If you are the high bidder, you are legally obligated to buy the item. If you're not willing to complete the contract (i.e., pay for the item), don't play the game. Read Chapters 7 and 8 carefully.

Tactics

Naturally, your tactics will be different for different strategies. If you want to save money or make money, you will behave differently than if you just want to save time or have fun.

Tactics are things you can do to reach the goals implicit in your strategies. Once you have taken some time to develop your eBay strategies, you will have a clearer idea of what you want to accomplish on eBay. From what you read in this book and your own experience, you will come up with things you can do to reach your objectives.

Mixed Strategies

Many people have mixed strategies. I'm a money-saver. But I'm starting to appreciate the convenience factor. I keep both in mind when I choose my tactics.

Research

Nothing beats research as a tactic. If you want to use the money-making strategy, you have to know the list prices of the items you bid on. Then you can apply my percentage guidelines to estimate your high bid prices, or you can invent your own percentage guidelines. You can get list prices at manufacturers' websites, in online catalogs, printed catalogs, local stores, and the like.

You also need to know what identical or similar items have sold for on eBay in the past. You can click on *Completed Items* on the left side of a list of eBay auctions and view the completed transactions going back three weeks (with the highest bids displayed). eBay will eventually extend this research archive to four or five weeks. Andale (*http://andale.com*) offers a research service that covers six months of back auctions. With enough of these transactions, you can estimate the maximum bidders will bid for an item.

Completed Items

You cannot see the Completed Items link until you've narrowed your search by making an entry in the search input (in the upper left) and clicking on the Search button.

Know your offline markets too. It's silly to pay more for something on eBay when you can buy it with less risk locally (but see the Convenience subsection earlier). And that is the case for many items. eBay is not 100 percent effective in providing the lowest prices for all merchandise.

Check out the seller. Check his or her feedback. Check his or her other eBay auctions. If the seller has a commerce website, check that. You never know what you might find out that will help you in your bidding.

Popular Items

For popular items you can try http://www.worthguide.com to get guidance on auction values.

Without research, not only will you be prone to making significant mistakes, but you will have a difficult time gauging your success. Do your homework.

Research at Andale

For a modest fee, Andale, an auction management service covered in Chapter 17, provides an eBay research service based on past eBay sales.

Buy It Now

This is a simple tactic and one I've come to use more every week. This is strictly convenience. Use *Buy It Now*, eBay's fixed price sales program. The *Buy It Now* program has been very successful for eBay sellers. As a buyer, take advantage of it if you seek convenience. You can make an immediate purchase and have the item delivered within a few days.

Sellers Be Careful

You might think that convenience is worth a higher price. To some extent that's true. But people still shop on eBay because they can find bargain prices. If *Buy It Now* prices cease to be bargain prices, it seems to me that eBay's fixed price program will no longer be successful. Convenience is great, but low prices are a primary consideration for many buyers.

The Kill

If a seller does not follow the best practices outlined in this book, he or she will generally receive fewer bids for an item and will get a lower final bid. Look for sellers who have made one or more of the following mistakes in their eBay listing:

- Misspelling in the auction title
- Placement in the wrong category
- No photograph
- A poor photograph
- Too little information about the item
- Unreadable information
- Unreasonable terms
- An unfriendly presentation

When you find such an auction, you may be able to acquire an item at a bargain price. You have to know the item you are buying well enough to feel confident in your purchase, because the seller may not provide you or other bidders with the information or confidence you need. In other words, you have to have greater product knowledge than the bidders who will ignore this auction. You're like a vulture moving in for the kill on a crippled seller. Enjoy!

The Refresh

The Refresh is not only a tactic but a necessity. As you reach the final few minutes of an auction, you must keep informed of the bidding. To do so you refresh (reload) the auction webpage by clicking on the refresh button on your Web browser. This is the only way you can determine the latest high bid. The high bid amount for an auction in a list of auctions on eBay is hopelessly out of date—perhaps by hours. Keep this in mind when planning your last-minute tactics, and don't rely on the list of auctions for up-to-date bid information.

The Scare

This is a tactic to scare away potential bidders because they think the bidding is too intense. Suppose you will bid as much as $85 on an item that currently reflects a high bid of $23. The high bidder has bid $52 (but you don't know this figure). If you bid $24, eBay raises the high bidder to $25 (automatic bidding or proxy bidding; see the Bay Way later). You are now the second-highest bidder. There are three bids.

You bid again, this time $26; eBay raises the high bidder to $27. You bid again, this time $28; consequently, eBay raises the high bidder to $29. Now there are seven bids.

You can continue this procedure until you find the high bid. By the time you finally outbid the high bidder with a bid of $53, there will be 30 bids. That looks like a lot of activity, and eBay provides no way to analyze the auction except by looking at the number of bidders. Many bargain-hunting potential bidders will not take the trouble to look beyond the number of bids and will not bother to bid because of the apparent intensity of the bidding.

This tactic works best for standard items for which it is easy to establish a value. Potential bidders know the item and search for a bargain price. The bidding intensity will likely scare them away because they think the price will go too high.

Bidding intensity, however, attracts the curiosity of many bidders, particularly regarding nonstandard items for which it is difficult to estimate market value. Bidders may be curious to see what the intensity is all about. Therefore, this tactic may backfire for non-standard items. The intensive bidding makes the items seem hot and attracts bidders rather than scares them off. Thus, this tactic works best for standard items such as new merchandise with well-known brand names.

Legal?

Is this tactic in violation of eBay rules? No. However, if you are assisting the seller (or if you are the seller operating under a different alias) by using this tactic as a means to artificially inflate the bidding, it is not only against eBay rules but is illegal in many states.

The Pass

Some items are just popular. Normally, new items sell for under the discount store price on eBay. But for a few popular items, the high bid often exceeds the discount store price. Why buy the item from a distant seller on eBay that you don't know? Pass. Buy it at your local discount store instead.

The Bay Way

Set your highest price, and walk away. eBay has it set up so that you'll win the auction if your high price is higher than any other bid; but the eBay system will only set your bid one increment higher than the second-highest bid. What a deal! With this tactic, you don't have to be at your computer in the final minutes of the auction. You only have to bid once. You will pay only one increment higher than the second-highest bidder. This automatic bidding (proxy bidding) is built into the eBay system.

Suppose the highest bid is $22, and you bid $46. eBay will now show you as being the highest bidder at $23. Another bidder comes along and bids $24. eBay will automatically make you the highest bidder at $25. And so it goes. The only way someone can outbid you is by bidding more than $46.

This tactic works when you are sure of yourself and sure of the value range. You know about how much the item will sell for, and you know definitely what you will pay for it. If the value range is lower than you will pay, you should win the bid in most instances. If the value range is higher than you're willing to pay, there will be some auctions, but not many, where you will have the highest bid. Take a shot at it; it doesn't take long to make one bid.

The Game

This is a nonfinancial tactic that enables you to enjoy the fun strategy mentioned above. Because bidding on eBay can be fun, you can play it as a game. The goal is to win the bidding, but the primary goal is not necessarily to win with the lowest winning bid possible. It's to win without an excessively high bid but have some fun doing it, that is, have some fun bidding.

In reality, when you bid in the final minutes of the auction, you might switch into game mode whether you intend to or not. The excitement of the final minutes may lead you to bid more than the high limit you set for yourself. Hopefully, however, you won't get excited enough to win at any cost. That could lead to a severe financial hangover.

If there is intense bidding in the final minutes and you're having fun, it's worth a few extra dollars to win. Go for it. The auction game is great fun to play.

Don't, under any circumstances, bid on auctions that you don't intend to complete when you're the high bidder. You will end up getting kicked off eBay and lose what will almost certainly turn out to be a lifelong asset, eBay membership.

The Smoke Out

You use the Smoke Out before you use the Bay Way; it gives you a better idea of what the winning bid might be. Sometime well before the auction ends, you attempt to smoke out the price range of the final bidding. This is especially important when you have trouble estimating the value of the item.

Suppose you have a vague idea that the item might be worth about $120. You need it and don't have time to find it elsewhere. The current high bid is $42. When the final minutes of the auction come, you'll be across town on a business appointment. You don't have a snipe program (see the Snipe subsection later), so you'll make your final bid a few hours before the end of the auction.

This tactic requires that you bid in modest increments (e.g., $5) until you have the high bid (assuming it's under $120). Do this early in the auction. Then wait to see if anyone outbids you. If not, you may have reached the range of value for the item. Unfortunately, you won't know for sure until the end of the auction. But if someone outbids you immediately, it shows that you haven't reached the range of value.

Suppose you bid up in $5 increments to $75 to become the high bidder with three days to go. Two and a half days go by, and no one outbids you. That may indicate a value range lower than the $120 you anticipated. For your final bid you might want to try $85.

On the other hand, suppose you do the same, but within a day someone outbids you. You again bid up in $5 increments to $95 to become the high bidder. Another day and a half goes by, and no one outbids you. Now, you might want to try $105 for your final bid.

In both of these cases, you try to smoke out the value range because you're not sure what the value is. If you know what the value range is, you don't have to use the Smoke Out. In both of these cases, you make a higher bid at the end because you won't be around for the finale. You hope the higher bid will be enough to win in your absence.

Even if you will be present for the bidding in the last minutes, the Smoke Out can be a valuable tactic if you're not sure of the value range. It can help you anticipate the value range. For instance, if you're prepared to pay $120 and the value range turns out to be $90–$100, smoking out the value range early will give you confidence in the final bidding because you're psychologically prepared to pay a higher price than the value range indicates.

If you smoke out the value range and it turns out to be over $120, however, it gives you more information with which to further develop your tactics. You can drop out of the bidding and save what otherwise would be wasted time. Or, you can rethink your estimate of value. You may decide that a value range over $120 is not unreasonable. In that case, you'll be psychologically prepared to bid higher and stay in the game.

Obviously, the Smoke Out is not a perfect tactic. But it can help you in many circumstances. It gives you another way to gather information to prepare yourself before the final minutes of the auction.

The Snipe

The pure sniper never appears before the final minutes or seconds. Then he or she places the winning bid out of the blue at the last possible moment.

I make a bid of $40 to purchase an fiber optic patch panel for my charter school's new network. It cost $500 at retail. Such items normally sell on eBay, when available, for less than $100. I was ready to pay $125 or more. I placed my bid six days before the end of the auction. No one else bid. I decided not to make another bid but was eager to get this piece of network equipment. So, just for kicks, I watched the end of the auction. Wouldn't you know it? Someone bid $41 in the last 10 seconds of the auction and bought "my" patch panel to my chagrin. That's a pure snipe. And it's perfectly legal.

With Software

Many snipers use special software to do their sniping. You can buy it on eBay at various auctions. The software places a winning bid at a certain time before the auction ends, say 30 seconds before. In the software setup for the Snipe, you can put an upper limit on the bid so that you don't spend more than you want to.

Using the software seems like an almost foolproof way to win an auction. When you think about it, however, it doesn't do any more for you than the Bay Way, except it might come as a surprise to other bidders. In other words, using snipe software, you can't change your tactic at the last minute, and the software is not infallible.

If you set the software to make a bid in the last 10 seconds before the end of the auction and eBay takes 30seconds before accepting the bid, you're out of luck. There are times during the week (e.g., Saturday evening) when eBay will take 15, 30, or 45 seconds to crank out webpages. So, you might set the software to make a bid 60 seconds before the end of the auction. If eBay happens to be working fast at that time, you've given your bidding competitors plenty of time to place higher bids within the last 60 seconds.

Without Software

If you don't use software to snipe, you need to be at your computer ready to roll during the final moments. You don't know whether your last-minute bid will work because you don't know what the highest bid will be. You do know that you need to make a bid higher than the current highest bid, but you don't know how much higher you have to bid to win because of the way the eBay proxy system works. Consequently, the Snipe is theoretically a one-shot tactic. Maybe it'll work. Maybe it won't. That is, even if your snipe bid is higher than the highest bid showing, someone who has made a proxy bid higher than your snipe bid will win the auction.

However, you can combine the Snipe with the Smoke Out for an effective last-minute tactic. Perhaps we should call it the Last-Minute Smoke Out and Snipe. Give yourself a few minutes. You smoke out the value range in a hurry by making a series of quick bids. Once you find the value range, you have to decide what your last-moment bid will be and how long it will take to submit it (based on eBay's current operational speed).

No Smoke

If there is spirited bidding but there appears to be no proxy bidding, you won't have to do a Smoke Out. You can watch and then do a last-second Snipe.

Unfortunately, eBay runs at different speeds at different times. Weekend evenings seem to be extra busy, and eBay may take up to a half-minute to deliver each new webpage, although eBay does a better job today of handling traffic than it did a few years ago. When you try to snipe where timing is crucial, a lag time can frustrate you. You will have to test the response, estimate the lag time, and make your bids accordingly. For instance, suppose you test the response time and it seems to be about 20 seconds. You want to snipe within 10 seconds of the close of the auction. Under these circumstances, you need to make your final bid about 30 seconds before the end of the auction.

Refresh

Remember the Refresh? Refreshing the eBay auction webpage is the only way you can keep up with the bidding. This is not a problem when eBay is fast. When eBay is slow, it compounds your sniping problems.

If you run into competition, you'll find yourself in the middle of a bidding war. The difference between this and a normal bidding war is that as the sniper, you will be a surprise competitor, perhaps disrupting the expectations of the other bidder(s). You will have to be ready to submit additional bids instantly in response to the competing bidders until time runs out.

The perfect Snipe is one that wins with 0 seconds left. With eBay's varying speed and with such precise control normally out of reach, it's difficult to win with 0 seconds left. But you might win with 5 seconds left under normal conditions.

The Double Window

How can you best submit those last-minute bids efficiently and responsively? Use double (or triple) browser windows. Open your browser, go to eBay, and open the auction at which you will bid. Next, for Netscape Navigator, go *File, New, Navigator Window* to create a new and fully functional browser window that is, in effect, a second browser. For Microsoft Internet Explorer, go *File, New, Window.* Now, as Figure 9.1 shows, you have two browser windows (two browsers, in effect) to make quick bids.

Actually, you can make as many browser windows as you want. I usually make about six to prepare for last-moment bidding. You add the bid price as you use each browser window to bid (see Figure 9.1).

Now, when you hurry in the final moments of the auction to compete with other bidders, you can make a bid quickly. After every bid, discard the window you just used, and move on to a fresh browser window (i.e., one prepared ahead of time). This works very effectively. You don't have to go backwards. (It worked more effectively before eBay changed the bidding sequence in the summer of 1999 from ID and password in the first window and price in the second window to the reverse. Apparently eBay did this either to slow down the intensity of the last-minute bidding or to prevent the more knowledgeable bidders from gaining an advantage.)

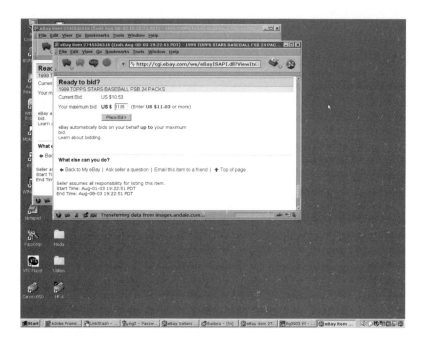

Figure 9.1   Two browser windows set up to bid.

The last few minutes of a hot auction can get very intense, and the
Double Window tactic keeps you in the bidding. Don't worry about
snipers. You can snipe better than any program can, particularly when
eBay is busy and not working at full speed.

Sign In to Save Time

See Chapter 5 for information on signing in. If you sign in and elect
bidding as a sign-in preference, you don't have to enter your ID
and password when you bid. This gives you an advantage in the
final minutes of a hot auction because you can save the time it
takes to enter an ID and password and can respond more quickly
to sniping. Click on the sign-in link above the navigation bar on any
eBay page.

The Goen Technique

This is a tip from inventive reader LeeAnne Goen. She refreshes the *History* page when sniping because it's faster than the auction webpage. It has little text and no graphics. That is, she refreshes the *History* page in one browser, and bids in another browser. She can snipe more effectively this way.

The Ten Cents Difference

In order to make a bid, you must increase the amount of your bid by the requisite eBay increment (see Chapter 5). Presumably, most people submit a bid based on one or more increments. But you don't have to do it that way.

Suppose you bid $28 but eBay proxy bidding automatically preempts you by a bid of $29 by someone who has bid $32. The incremental bid amount is $1. You want to smoke out the high bidder. You bid $30. The eBay proxy bids $31. If you bid $32, you will tie with the high bidder, but the high bidder—being first—will win the auction. If you bid $32.01, you will have the high bid and will win the auction. Thus, it's a good idea to always bid at lease one increment plus a penny. I always bid at least one increment plus 10 cents.

Turn the above scenario around. Suppose you made the high bid at $32.10, and someone else is trying to outbid you in the last moments of an auction. They bid $32. You win by a dime.

Why bother with a few cents? Why not bid an extra dollar instead? Hey, the nickels and dimes add up. Look at the overhead for a buyer (see Chapter 2). You can get nickeled and dimed to impoverishment. Win the bidding by 10 cents and save 90 cents wherever you can.

The Routine Check

This puts the time-saving strategy into action. You will find eBay especially valuable if you can wait. Suppose you need the Shure microphone (in the Save Time subsection example) for a Christmas performance, but it's now August. Perhaps you can't find it today on eBay, but check every week. It'll turn up sooner or later. If you want to be diligent, you can check every three days because there are some three-day auctions. But check at least once a week. It takes just a little time to check the current auctions. When the Shure microphone does appear, keep in mind your strategy and act accordingly.

This is actually a good tactic to use for any merchandise, and I've used it to save money. But it's perhaps most valuable for the time-saving strategy. After all, for the time-saving strategy, there may be no viable alternative to the Routine Check other than going around looking for the merchandise at physical locations, which takes a lot more of your time.

The Multiple-Auction Finesse

Sometimes you bid multiple auctions on the same item that end within a short time of one another. It seems to me this is dumb on the part of a seller. As a seller, you want to give the bidders plenty of opportunity and time to concentrate and bid on each auction. But we've all seen two or three single-item auctions with the same item offered by the same seller end within a short time of each other. I've even seen three or four Dutch auctions, with the same items offered by the same seller, end within 40 seconds of each other. As a bidder, how do you handle this situation?

There are two rules. The first rule is forget the first auction (ends first). The person willing to bid the highest will win that auction. Why be the high bidder if there is more than one auction? The second rule is figure out the most difficult thing to do, and do it. Everyone else will tend to pick easier tactics. If you pick the most difficult tactic, you have a good chance of winning.

The necessity for the Multiple-Auction Finesse, of course, depends on competition. If you don't have competition, you don't need to use the Finesse tactic.

Two Auctions

Because you wll not bid the first auction, what do you do about the second auction? Well, you see the first auction through to the end, even though you don't bid on it. You need to know the winning bid amount. You have a pretty good idea of the value range because you witnessed the end of the first auction. The best tactic is to snipe the second auction. You will have an edge because you set up to snipe the second auction ahead of time. Don't forget the Double Window tactic. Presumably, your competition is now frustrated and busy trying to regroup in the short time between auctions. You experience no frustration. You're ready to wrestle. It seems to me that you have the advantage. In this case, the most significant thing is to plan ahead.

Three Auctions

Bidders have the greatest difficulty regrouping for a second auction right after the final frenzy of the first auction. Again, you watch the first auction to the end. The bidders will tend to take the easiest path to winning a bid by skipping the second auction and bidding the third. That leaves the second auction with no competition or light competition. Because you set up to bid the second auction ahead of time, you have a good chance of winning the bid. The third auction will be a replay of the first, with higher bidding than the second. In this case, the most significant tactic is to bid the second auction.

If you don't win the second auction by some horrible accident of fate, you can easily snipe the third if you set up to bid the third auction ahead of time. Again, don't forget the Double Window tactic.

Why?

The intervals between auctions must be small for the Finesse tactic to work (under two minutes). Why would a seller schedule auctions of the same item this close together? It might be ignorance. It might be the result of a bulk upload of auctions. It might be the result of a hurried entry of auctions. Whatever the reason, it happens more often than you might think.

If the intervals are too long, the bidders can regroup more easily and bid more effectively. Then the Finesse doesn't work.

Dutch Auction Bids

As explained earlier, at a Dutch auction, the high bidder wins but pays only the amount of the lowest successful bid. Suppose the seller auctions five identical items and five bidders bid on one item each. The bidding results in the last few minutes are as follows:

$77

$74

$73

$70

$68

If you bid $69, and no one enters another bid, you will be a winner and buy at $69. But if someone else bids, you may get knocked out of the winner's circle because you hold the last place at the bottom. However, if you bid $74, and no one enters another bid, you will be a winner and buy for a price of $70 (you knocked out the $68 bidder). And if someone else bids, they probably won't knock you out of the winner's circle, and the final low successful bid (the price to you) may still be lower than your bid of $74. Thus, the tactic is to bid in the middle of the pack and hope for a successful low bid that is less than your bid.

Organization

For one auction, you don't need much organization. You can keep everything under control just by following a plan and improvising. However, if you bid on multiple auctions, you need to devise a systematic way of keeping track of your bids.

First, you don't want to bid on multiple separate auctions for the same item. You could become doubly successful (triply successful perhaps) and have to buy more than one item or possibly suffer negative feedback for the items you win but don't buy.

Second, you can't count on eBay's email notification system to keep track for you. While such a system is handy in certain ways, particularly for your after-auction records, it won't help much for successfully bidding on multiple unrelated items and for avoiding costly mistakes. I've bid as many as three different unrelated items at the same time. Even with just three auctions to manage, things start to get out of control without some kind of informal auction management system for bidding.

Summary

Think about what strategy you will follow for bidding on eBay. Then pick and choose your tactics to carry out your strategy. Invent some tactics of your own. There is never a guarantee that you will win an auction, but with a clear strategy and some useful tactics, you will do as well as you can on eBay.

And, remember, the bidder who bids highest wins. If you don't bid the highest, no strategy and no tactic is going to make you the winning bidder.

IV

Selling Strategies

10

Customer Service

It doesn't matter whether you run five auctions a year, five auctions a week, or twenty-five auctions a day, the better you treat your customers, the more bids you will get and the higher the final bids will be. Consequently, this section of the book begins with a chapter on customer service, not with a chapter on auctioning techniques. The Web is an interactive medium that gives you the chance to serve your customers (buyers, bidders) well.

The Occasional Seller

Put yourself in a buyer's shoes. You want to make a bid for $620 on a used telephone system (retails for $1,849) for your small office. The seller represents the system as in excellent condition and wants a money order for the final bid price (no escrow).

You are faced with sending a money order for $620 to someone you don't know. You don't know whether you will receive anything for your money. If you do receive something, you don't know what kind of condition it will be in. Will you make the bid? Try the following four scenarios:

1.   The seller has no history (i.e., no sales or purchases).

2.   The seller has a history of 5 transactions, all rated neutral.

3.   The seller has a history of 7 transactions, all rated positive.

4.   The seller has a history of 153 transactions, 2 rated negative and the remainder rated positive.

How are you going to vote with your $620? Chances are you'll pass on number one, too much of an unknown. Number two looks as though he or she will be trouble of some sort; that's a pass. Number three looks like a reasonable risk. Number four looks like a low risk.

Each of the above sellers will lose a certain percentage of the potential market. Number one will get some bidders, but because of the high price, many potential bidders will pass because the risk is high. Few potential bidders will think it's worth the time and trouble to deal with number two, who obviously isn't making anyone happy. Although number three looks good, the information is a little thin, and some potential bidders will pass. Virtually all potential bidders will feel comfortable with number four; they've probably got more favorable information on number four than they do on many retailers in their own communities.

The point here is that your reputation is important as a seller, and your reputation depends on your customer service. It doesn't matter whether you sell occasionally or sell regularly. Make your customers happy, and you'll build a good reputation. A good reputation will bring more bids. More bids will bring a higher price.

Now, *as the seller*, what can you do to improve customer service for the auction of the used telephone system? Here are four options:

1. Accept a credit card (or PayPal).

2. Offer to put the transaction in escrow.

3. Provide a warranty.

4. Throw in a gift certificate for a book at Borders on how to install and operate a small office telephone system.

If you accept a credit card, a person dissatisfied with the transaction can do a charge-back on the credit card transaction. That provides a buyer with a potential remedy. That will increase your bids. (PayPal has almost become an acceptable substitute for accepting credit cards.) If you offer to put the transaction in escrow, it makes everyone feel more comfortable because it lowers the risk. You'll get more bids. If you provide a warranty, it doesn't necessarily lower the risk, but it makes everyone feel more comfortable, and you'll get more bids. Even the book will broaden the appeal of the auctioned item. Consequently, with a little customer service, you increase your potential for making more money. The four customer services listed above are a few among many you can offer, and even if you are an occasional seller you can offer them.

Credit Cards

About 90 percent of buyers on eBay use credit cards where sellers accept them. Debit cards via MasterCard and Visa are now a part of the credit card system, for all practical purposes, and many people with only checking accounts can therefore "charge" just like people with credit cards. (I was sent a MasterCard debit card by my bank without requesting it. I use it now much more than I use my credit cards.)

Perhaps the best, but most common, customer service you can provide is accepting credit cards. There are dozens more ways to get merchant accounts for Web ecommerce in 2004 than there were a few years ago. Get yourself a merchant account, and start accepting credit cards.

If you are an occasional seller, you need to read about PayPal in Chapter 16. PayPal makes a reasonable substitute for a credit card merchant account.

What can you do generally as an occasional seller to increase customer service? Respond to communications (e.g., email) promptly. Be prepared to ship promptly the item you sell. Think of yourself as a seller, and exercise common sense. Follow some of the suggestions in the remainder of this book in regard to providing convenience for potential bidders.

The Part-Time eBay Business

If you have a part-time business on eBay auctioning merchandise at retail, pay close attention to customer service. Some of the things you can do follow:

- Follow the guidelines in this book for running your auctions and conducting your eBay business.

- Promptly respond to communications from potential bidders and customers.

- Organize a responsive follow-up system to track your customers through the transaction process. Read about auction management services in Chapter 17.

- Run your shipping operation in a professional manner.

- Accept payment in as many ways as possible.

- Provide guarantees where practical.

- Listen to your customers.

If you summarize the above list, it boils down to one idea. Get organized! Don't take selling on eBay lightly. Even selling just a few items a week can get out of control before you know it, if you're not prepared. If things do get out of control, you will have some unhappy high bidders and other unhappy eBay members; that does not bode well for success on eBay.

You can't conduct a part-time eBay business haphazardly and expect it to be as successful as possible. If you take it seriously and provide good customer service, your business may grow into something to which you can eventually devote your full time and energy; then you can quit your job!

Independent Contractors

If you have a full-time job and you are trying to supplement your income by selling on eBay, you may find it difficult to provide the customer service you need to maximize your success. Hiring employees to do some of the work is out of the question. Just the paperwork to employ a person is too demanding. One way to improve your customer service, when you don't have the time, is to hire independent contractors.

Shipping is a good example of something you can *outsource* (have done for you by another business). Some small businesses specialize in shipping merchandise for customers. Shipping is a chore. Have a shipping company do it for you. That will leave you time to spend on other customer service activities that you can do better, more efficiently, more quickly, or more easily. Obviously, the shipping company is an independent contractor.

Not so obvious is having a friend, neighbor, or acquaintance do your shipping for you as an independent contractor (e.g., out of his or her garage). Potentially, this can be a better service for you at less expense while providing more convenience. However, you need to consult the part of the tax laws that defines the difference between employees and independent contractors to make sure you can't be deemed by the IRS or state agencies to have an employee. Essentially, you will have to hand over your merchandise with a mailing label and let the shipping person do the rest. You can't exercise control. But this could be good part-time work for a stay-at-home spouse or someone who wants an extra part-time job for evenings or weekends.

If you don't follow the tax laws (and the labor guidelines of other governmental agencies), no one will ever catch you, right? Actually, that may not be the case. You'll get reported by the person you contracted with. Potentially, it will happen a couple of ways. First, the IRS will get after the person for not paying income taxes, and the person will say that he or she thought you were withholding taxes (a lie, but that won't stop the IRS from coming after you). Second, the person will file for unemployment benefits after you stop doing business with him. Third, the person will file for workmen's compensation after getting injured in his own garage with his own equipment while doing your shipping. So, it pays to make sure that you really establish an independent contractor's relationship with the person you contract with to do the shipping.

The details of this particular relationship are beyond the scope of this book, but it pays to research it thoroughly. You need to research it because outsourcing via independent contracting can be a very practicable and cost-effective way for you to do business, and it will become even more viable in the future as more people work at home. See *eBay Business the Smart Way* (AMACOM 2003).

Fulfillment

Filling the order (the sale from the auction) is one of the most important functions you will provide as part of your customer service. Fulfillment means processing the order and getting the merchandise shipped in a timely manner. You need to have a speedy procedure to handle fulfillment. Today people expect things they have purchased to arrive quickly. You are not excluded from this expectation just because you don't have a website storefront or a physical retail location.

If you have a part-time retail business on eBay, you can't wait until the weekend to do your shipping. You have to ship as soon as payment is secured, or you will have some irritated customers. If you can't do the shipping part of the fulfillment every day, find someone to do it for you.

Drop Shipping

One clever way to do your fulfillment is drop shipping. Drop shipping means having your wholesaler ship the merchandise directly to your customer. Many wholesalers are set up to do this. Today, to be competitive many wholesalers give quick shipping service. Hence, drop shipping can solve your fulfillment problem at the same time that it eliminates your inventory warehousing problem. The only questions are, How much does it cost?, and Can you do it more cost-effectively yourself?

Don't use drop shipping and then forget about the fulfillment service to your customers. It's your responsibility to make sure your customers get good fulfillment service via your drop shipping arrangements. That means you have to follow up with customer satisfaction surveys or otherwise test the quality of service that your customers are receiving. You'll always hear from customers if the quality of your service is bad. But if your service (via the drop shipper) is just mediocre, you may not get the complaints that alert you that something is wrong.

Therefore, you have to stay alert and keep testing to ascertain the quality of your drop shipper's service to your customers.

The drop shipper is no different from an independent contractor in regard to quality. The difference is that you can usually check up on a local independent contractor more easily than you can a faraway wholesaler. As a result, you have to use other techniques to check up on the drop shipper.

If You're Small

If you're small, doesn't it mean that you can get away with not worrying about fast fulfillment and other customer service? The answer is yes, if you don't want to get bigger. But if you want to develop a good business or expand your business, you have to provide good customer service today regardless of the size of your business.

The Full-Time eBay Business

If you operate a full-time business that conducts business on eBay, you will be expected to provide excellent customer service because there is too much Web commerce that does provide first-rate customer service. From dealing with Amazon.com and the like, people's expectations are high. If you do not provide such service, you will be an ongoing irritant to your customers, hardly an enviable position considering the eBay feedback system.

With a Website

If you sell at retail full-time on eBay as a business or if you are a retailer who sells a fair amount on eBay but who has a physical location too, you might seriously consider operating an ecommerce website. The question is, What is an ecommerce website? The following are some characteristics:

- Website catalog with inventory for sale

- Transaction system that takes orders, arranges payments, arranges shipping, and hands off the order to the fulfillment process

- Set up to receive payment in a variety of ways

- Organized to provide easy ways for people to communicate in regard to their orders or otherwise

- Attractive website with easy-to-use navigation

Perhaps the best ecommerce website of all is Amazon.com. The story of Amazon is one of pure customer service. The Amazon website may not win any awards for aesthetics or for technical flamboyance. But it sure creates an easy, interesting, and convenient experience to buy a book online (or other consumer items).

If you do have an ecommerce website that functions intelligently, you can weave it into your eBay business. Here are some things you can do:

Include a link to your *About Me* webpage in your eBay auction ads. In *About Me* you can include a link to your ecommerce website to generate extra business.

Link to your eBay auctions from your ecommerce website to generate extra business.

Refer winning bidders in your eBay auctions to your website for routine, reliable, and convenient transaction processing.

Extend your customer service activities at your ecommerce website to your eBay winning bidders.

In other words, if you are a successful Web retailer with an ecommerce website, you probably already offer competent customer service. Why not extend it to your eBay customers too?

Without a Website

Having said all that, the fault in the plan to operate an ecommerce website is that you will have to market extensively to draw any traffic to the website. If you're thinking of starting an ecommerce website, however, you might consider a more cost-effective alternative. You are better off, in my opinion, to forego establishing an ecommerce website and focus your attention on other eBay-related sales mechanisms such as eBay Stores which do not require a huge amount of marketing.

Communications

If you do not operate an ecommerce website, you have to ask yourself how you can provide comparable services. The first reaction you might have is that you can communicate by telephone, snail mail, and email.

It seems to me the telephone may not work well. For instance, does someone whose only contact with you is via the Web, and possibly email, really want to start talking with you on the phone? Here are some reasons that it may not work well:

Customer doesn't like to pay for long-distance phone calls. (Who does?)

Customer isn't available to talk on the phone during business hours.

Customer doesn't like to talk on the phone.

Customer wants a written record of entire transaction process.

You can handle a few of these things if you are to provide telephone ordering. You can get an 800 number so that the customer doesn't have to pay for the long-distance call. You can extend your business hours to cover evenings. Both are somewhat expensive, but your business volume may warrant such practices. And, after all, everyone talked on the phone before the Internet came into use.

What about snail mail? Too slow. That leaves email as a primary means of communicating with customers. And that leaves you with the question, How can you provide customer service by email? The customer came to you (on eBay) via the Internet, not via email.

There is no simple answer to this question. Email is a capable, powerful, and even flexible means of communication. Certainly, you can use email efficiently to conduct business. Indeed, it's just people talking to people, but not in real time. What are some techniques you can use with email communication?

Send a form(canned) email, like a form letter. This is very important for handling various routine matters with standard form emails.

Attach a file (e.g., word processor file) to an email message.

Transfer lots of text into an email message via copy and paste.

Put links to websites into an email message.

Set up auto-responders to send automatic replies to certain email informational requests.

You will find that using email fits nicely into Web business practices.

Auction Management Services

Another way to provide customer services without a website is to use auction management services (see Chapter 17 for more details). Not only do these relatively new services provide you with enhanced customer communications and other services, but they also provide you with many of the ecommerce services provided on ecommerce websites with traditional ecommerce software. In other words, auction management services bring ecommerce services to your eBay selling activities. This is a legitimate breakthrough and provides a solid basis for operating without an ecommerce website.

A Little Bit More

As a retail seller, exceed expectations. Go the extra mile. Do a little bit more than you said you would. For instance, communication is so important. As soon as a buyer's check clears and you ship the merchandise, send an email notifying the buyer that the merchandise has been sent. It's not required, but it will be appreciated. If you are well organized, you can do it easily.

Guarantee

There's nothing like a good old-fashioned guarantee. Why not offer one to your eBay customers? Many national retailers do. Sure it will cost something, but it will also give potential bidders the confidence to become actual bidders. And the more bidders, the higher the price. The guarantee works well for many retail sellers on eBay.

Packaging

Bidders probably don't expect much from occasional sellers. But from retailers on eBay, they expect a professional job of presentation and packaging. That means an item needs to be cleaned and shined and then carefully packaged for shipment. If you don't do this, you will not maximize your retail business on eBay.

Goods That Don't Work

Many sellers sell merchandise in "as is" condition with no representation that the item will function or with a disclosure that the item does not function. Presumably such goods sell at low purchase prices because they are not in working condition. Clearly, eBay is an appropriate place to sell such goods, and buyers obtain such goods for parts or with the expectation that they can be repaired. However, if you're a retailer, you will do well to avoid such goods and only sell goods that function properly. Let someone else sell merchandise that doesn't work.

The Gift

Don't overlook the gift program that eBay operates. For $1 you can add a gift icon to your auction listing. Presumably you will reserve the use of this program for items that will make good gifts (almost anything) for the occasion. You have your choice of many icons representing different occasions, such as St. Patrick's Day, Mother's Day, and weddings. The items will be located in a special gift section as well as in the normal auction category.

The gift! Macy's, Neiman Marcus, Marshall Field's, Hudson's, and Nordstrom's. Does this ring a bell? Yes! Offer gift wrapping. Offer to enclose a card. Offer to ship direct to the gift recipient with some documentation sent to the buyer that the item was shipped in a timely manner. Offer a gift service. That's a nice touch for customer service.

Payment

The acceptance of payment in convenient ways for buyers is an important customer service. For eBay, the more ways you accept payment, the better for your customers (bidders). Because this is so important, it is treated separately in its own chapter, Chapter 15.

Response Times

As you know, if you sell much on eBay, there are deadbeat high bidders (bidders who never pay).

Get After Those Buyers

To protect yourself, you must deal with each buyer systematically. Depending on your eBay selling experience, you may want to give deadlines for responses. For instance, you may want to send a form email to winning bidders informing them that they have won, requesting payment, and setting a deadline for a reply (e.g., three days). If you don't hear from them via email in three days, you automatically send another email requesting a response within three days. If there's no response to the second email within three days, you might send a last, more strongly worded email. Most sellers seem to quit at three requests. Then it's time to relist the item or offer it to the second-highest bidder (and be sure to report negative feedback on the deadbeat buyer).

Is this customer service? Sure it is. You give every buyer a reasonable chance to perform because you're a reasonable person. This seems like common sense, but you'd be surprised at the number of sellers who have a short fuse and relist an item (or sell to another) when they haven't heard from a buyer within two or three days.

The Other Side of the Story

As the winning bidder you're ecstatic. You just won. It's something of an ego trip, particularly when the bidding was heated and you feel you got a good price anyway. Then you have to wait three days for the seller to contact you. This is a big no-no on the part of the seller.

As a seller, you need to contact the winning bidder(s) as soon as possible after the close of the auction, certainly no more than one day later and ideally in less than three hours. This is essential customer service. You've got a hot prospect who's ready to pay. All you have to do is arrange payment. Don't dally. As the transaction cools down, your chances of completing it (and getting paid) start to diminish. Be prompt in your communication to winning bidders.

Shipping and Handling

If you simply charge for shipping, then you have to wait until after the auction to quote a charge (depending on how far away the buyer lives). The buyer remains uncertain about what the charge will be until he or she receives a quote. If you quote a *shipping* charge in the auction ad and collect it, the buyer may be angry when the actual shipping charge turns out to be less.

One way to get around this frustration is to charge for *shipping and handling*. No one knows what handling is. It probably should be covered in your overhead. Yet, many people charge it. My policy is to quote a shipping and handling charge in the auction ad. That gives the buyer certainty. My shipping and handling charge is enough to cover shipping anywhere in the US, but no more. If the actual shipping charge to a place close to where I live is less than the shipping and handling charge, the buyer has no grounds for complaint. This is less trouble for both parties.

Some people make their profit on shipping and handling. They charge a lower price for the item and a high price for shipping and handling. So long as the charge is stated in the auction ad, buyers have little grounds for complaint. Still, this practice is irritating to buyers and not recommended.

If you state no shipping or handling price in the auction ad, you'd better be ready to justify the charge. Otherwise you may get into a shouting match with the buyer.

Look at Zonalyzer (*http://zonalyzer.com*) for a program that you can embed in your auction ad, which enables bidders to chose and calculate certain shipping costs.

Packaging

Package well to minimize your shipping problems. Most people over-package perhaps. I've never received an item damaged that I've bought on eBay. But it's better to overpackage than to have to deal with damaged goods, collect insurance, and other nasty details.

Plastic Bag

Put the items you send in plastic bags to protect against moisture, unless there's a compelling reason not to do so. You never know when the package will get drenched in a rain storm. When it goes out the door, it's out of your control. eBay sellers in arid climates (i.e., the West) are the most likely to forget to do this. Rain does not enter into their daily equation. But when you ship everywhere, you need to keep rain and snow in mind.

Naturally, eBay is a fertile ground for selling packaging materials. Consequently, you do not have to look beyond eBay auctions to find materials you need to package well at good prices. Also ask your shipper (e.g., FedEx) what is provided free in the way of shipping materials (e.g., containers). The following are also sources of packaging materials and containers:

Bubblefast, *http://www.bubblefast.com*

OfficeMax, *http://www.officemax.com*

ShippingSupply.com, *http://www.shippingsupply.com*

Staples, *http://www.staples.com*

Uline, *http://uline.com*

UPS Store (previously Mail Boxes Etc), *http://www.theupsstore.com*

iShip (*http://iship.com*), a subsidiary of UPS, offers an online shipping comparison website. You can use it to compare shipping costs by several different shippers. The UPS Stores also use it.

Free Packaging

Some shippers supply free packages for customers. The Postal Service is the leader offering a wide range of free packages. Go to *http://supplies.usps.gov* in order to see what they have.

Also try the eBay Shipping Center for links to shipping supplies. Go *Services, Shipping Center.* And learn more about shipping at eBay too. Go, *Site Map, Selling Tools, Shipping Education Center.*

If It Doesn't Get There

What if you send it, and it doesn't get there? Who is responsible, the buyer or seller (you)? One way is to put the responsibility on the buyer and offer the buyer the opportunity to buy insurance. But what if the buyer doesn't buy insurance and it doesn't get there? Who is responsible, the buyer or seller (you)? Clearly, the buyer is responsible because that's the way you set up your sales requirements. This is terrible customer service, however, and you had better figure out another way to handle the missing package.

One way is to self-insure. If a package isn't delivered, you simply send another at your cost. Don't worry about getting and paying for insurance. Another way is to require mandatory insurance and require that the buyer pay for it. A third way is to use shippers that provide a minimal level of insurance (e.g., $100, UPS) at no extra cost. Whatever your solution, don't overlook this aspect of doing business on eBay. And don't put the buyer in a losing situation.

Shippers

Any analysis of the different ways to ship that includes current costs would be instantly outdated. So, I will leave you to figure that out for yourself. Keep in mind the following, however, in evaluating shippers:

Convenience How convenient is it for you to use a particular shipper? This is different for everybody. The shipper itself may offer different convenience options. How much paperwork does the shipper require?

Size and Weight What are the maximums? How do the maximums relate to what you need to ship?

Cost How much does it cost? Is it a flat fee or a fee based on distance?

Included? What does the shipping service include? Pickup? Insurance? Package tracking? Guaranteed delivery?

Reliability How reliable is the shipper? I believe FedEx is at one end of the spectrum and the Postal Service is at the other end. How far apart are they?

Customer Service A shipper's website where one can monitor shipping reliably 24 × 7 may be important for your customers.

Shipping is currently very competitive and changes continually. Keep up to date on the options available to you. The less hassle your shipper causes, the more smoothly your fulfillment operation will function.

There are other reliable shippers, but most people use one of the following:

Airborne Express, *http://www.airborne-express.com*

DHL, *http://www.dhl-usa.com/index*

Federal Express, aka FedEx, *http://fedex.com/us*

Federal Express Ground, Home Delivery

United Parcel Service, aka UPS, *http://ups.com*

US Postal Service, aka Post Office, *http://usps.com*

For large items you may need to ship by bus (*http://www.greyhound.com*) or truck (*http://freightquote.com*). Go *Services, Buying and Selling Tools, Freight Resource Center* for assistance with trucking.

Postage

Postage meters are a must for those who use the Postal Service and have a busy fullfillment operation. Or, you might try instead one of the Web postage services; you can print out postage on your computer printer.

Ascom Hasler, *http://www.haslerinc.com*

Endicia, *http://www.endicia.com*

> **Stamps.com,** *http://stamps.com*
>
> **Pelouze,** *http://pelouze.com*
>
> **Pitney Bowes,** *http://www.pitneybowes.com*
>
> **Pitney Works,** *http://www.pitneyworks.com*
>
> **Postal Service,** *http://www.usps.com*

The Whole Thing

What about a company that will do the whole fulfillment chore for you? That is, all the packaging and shipping. Unbelievably, for a reasonable flat fee, paDepot (*http://padepot.com*) in Allentown, Pennsylvania, will do it for you. In fact, it will even warehouse your inventory. Although there are other services that do this for corporate customers, paDepot does it for small businesses. Compare paDepot's service to Craters & Freighters mentioned under the title Where the Gold Is later in this chapter.

Communication

Communication is the lubricant of the eBay mechanism. If you can stay in communication with the other party, you can usually work out almost any difficulties. Treat communication as a customer service.

Communication is time-consuming. Hope that you don't have to do anything but the routine communications (form emails) for every buyer. But when problems arise that need special treatment (special communication), and they do occasionally, be ready to spring into action and exchange email messages.

Take the initiative in your initial email to winning bidders. Provide them with full information. Invite them to communicate with you if there are any problems. Be ready to handle those communications in a timely and efficient manner. The better organized and more systematic you are in handling your auctions and winning bidders, the fewer the problems and the less need for communications.

How to Get Organized

How do you get organized? That's a question you have to answer within the scope of your skills and knowledge or the skills and knowledge of your employees. Some ideas follow, but you know far better than I what's best for you.

Database Manager

Desktop database managers such as Corel Paradox, FileMaker, and Microsoft Access are fabulous and powerful programs. You will find them easy to use. They offer great potential, and you will find them very handy for keeping track of your inventory, auctions, and transactions.

Database Auction Management System

There's nothing better than a compelling project with which to cut your teeth on a new program. You can learn quickly and get better organized in the process. Learn some general database principles, usually available in books on the various leading programs, and forge ahead to build a custom application for yourself using one of the desktop database managers.

The best approach is to build one table into which you enter all your basic data as well as your follow-up data. When the table is open in front of you, you can easily and quickly go directly to the appropriate fields (column cells) and input data, delete data, or change data. You can cover a lot of territory in a short time. Or, a data entry and maintenance employee can do a lot of work in a short time.

Eventually, you may find yourself graduating to greater functionality by creating related tables (relational database) and doing all sorts of clever database things. But starting out with one easy-to-build table is an easy step to take, and a productive one. See Appendix IV in *eBay Business the Smart Way* for more information.

Auction Management Service

This database auction management idea is a great one. But it's already obsolete. Today eBay itself offers very capable auction management services at a low price, and a dozen other companies offer a full range of auction management services at low prices. All these services base their programming on the use of internal databases. You don't have to reinvent the wheel. Take advantage of one of these relatively new services, and leave the creation of database auction management to someone else. Read more about these auction management services—used via the Web—in Chapter 17.

Spreadsheet

A spreadsheet such as Excel or Lotus 1-2-3 can help you account for your transactions. What you should know is that you often use the database capabilities of the spreadsheet program rather than the calculation capabilities. Why not use a database manager instead?

I don't recommend the use of a spreadsheet unless you are a spreadsheet expert and don't know or don't want to know how to use a database manager. eBay attempted to devise a spreadsheet solution to the bulk upload situation (Master Lister) and finally backed off. Spreadsheets are great for calculations but not so adroit for accounting systems.

On Paper

Does anyone still use paper? Ultimately, pushing paper is not as productive as pumping digits. But sometimes the best move is one that's comfortable for you. A total paper system to handle Web commerce is insanity. But a hybrid system (paper–digital) makes sense. The goal is to get as close to 100 percent digital as is practical. Nonetheless, you don't have to get there immediately. Work toward that goal at a comfortable pace while still using some of your paper practices.

PowerSellers

The eBay PowerSellers program is for people who do a lot of retail auctions on eBay. It provides certain customer service benefits to you as an eBay customer. For example, as a PowerSeller, you can display the PowerSellers logo, which identifies you, in effect, as a high-volume eBay retailer.

This is likely to instill more confidence and trust in you by bidders than you would otherwise receive.

The program has monthly minimum sales requirements and several levels of participation based on sales. This program has evolved into something quite valuable for eBay retailers. Check it out at *Services, PowerSeller Program*.

This is not a small program. eBay has over 70,000 PowerSellers. eBay recently increased the benefits for PowerSellers and now provides $500 fraud insurance to the customers of PowerSellers, coop advertising up to $8,000 per quarter, and other marketing programs. It has also arranged health insurance. This program for successful sellers gives some permanent sales structure to eBay and is beginning to resemble a well-oiled selling machine. It's certainly something to aspire to if you're a high-volume eBay seller. Your PowerSellers logo shows that you are doing business successfully on eBay and therefore implies that you provide acceptable customer service.

Amazon.com

If you want to maximize customer service at your website, study Amazon. Everything at Amazon is aimed at making it easy for customers to make purchasing decisions about books (and other merchandise) and then to easily purchase them. And sometimes at a discount! Navigation is easy. Searching is easy. Information access is easy. And ordering requires only one click.

One click does everything! It puts the book in your shopping basket and checks you out automatically. If you order another book within two hours, Amazon makes sure that both books (or more) are shipped together, if possible, to save shipping costs. It doesn't get any easier than one click.

This didn't happen haphazardly. The Amazon founder, his wife, and a few employees spent a year designing and testing their website system before they opened on the Web for business. That means they spent a year on customer service before they took their first customer. (They could have easily opened in a month with off-the-shelf software.)

Try Lands' End (*http://www.landsend.com*), which enables you to try on clothes at its website via *My Virtual Model* (a model of yourself). Now that's customer service!

Ironically Speaking

Sears, the king of catalogs, discontinued its massive catalog just a few years before the Internet caught on in the early 1990s. It had the residual experience and expertise to quickly become a top Web department store like Amazon.com but lacked the vision. Recently the moribund Sears bought Lands' End to get back in the game. Will we see the Sears catalog again on the Web someday?

Do you have the control to do these kinds of things on eBay? Certainly not. Nonetheless, you can develop your own brand of customer service within the eBay setting. In fact, eBay has established many customer service devices for sellers to use. Just learning and using all of them will put you ahead of the pack. In addition, the auction management services are replete with customer service devices. Just using *all* the modules of one of these services will put you ahead of the pack.

Benchmarks of Customer Service

Of the Web we will know in 2020, probably only about 5 percent has been invented yet. Invent something you can do to improve your customer service on eBay (and be sure to let me know).

Even if you are an occasional seller, you need to provide good customer service. You have your own set of interests. The things you sell over the years will reflect those interests. The people you sell them to will tend to have similar interests. Despite the huge number of people using eBay, you may run across some of the same people in your eBay auctioning activities from time to time, if not regularly. Your reputation will count for something with such people.

So, to conclude, the following is offered as a baseline list of Web customer service benchmarks for eBay auctions:

- Easily readable text in auction ads
- Robust information on products for sale
- Guarantees
- Clear instructions on transaction procedures
- Multiple payment methods
- Quick service

- Professional fulfillment procedures
- Prompt communications

Don't feel comfortable with this list. It's a good beginning, but it's not enough. If the above is all you have, some of your competitors are already ahead of you. But if you meet all the benchmarks above, you're ahead of most of your competitors.

Where the Gold Is

In every gold strike (California, Colorado, Alaska), it never seems to be the miners who get rich. It's the store owners in the gold-mining towns that spring up who make the money. Similarly, you might consider providing services to eBay retailers. I know of an antique dealer in the Bay Area who provides the following package of services to other antique dealers she knows:

1. Puts their antiques up for auction on eBay

2. Conducts the auction and communicates with bidders

3. Receives the purchase payment

4. Ships the antiques

All an antique dealer has to do is stop by and leave the antique off at her office. She gets a percentage of the selling price. In other words, she does not only the fulfillment but also the auctioning.

See Chapter 22 under the subtitle Consignment for more coverage on consignment selling and potential franchise opportunites as well as eBay's Trading Assistant program. Think up customer services you can perform for serious eBay sellers, and make a business out of it.

For example, check out My EZsale (*http://myezsale.com*), an information service for eBay sellers (and other online retailers), and Craters & Freighters (*http://cratersandfreighters.com*) with shipping from 60 locations nationally.

Summary

Customer service is the essence of selling on the Web, whether it's an ecommerce website or a series of auctions on eBay. As a seller, customer service should be in the front of your consciousness at all times. If a securities analyst on Wall Street can get together with a Web programmer and invent Amazon.com, you can probably come up with a few new ideas yourself for providing better customer service in regard to your eBay auctions.

11

Handling Images

Digital photographs sell merchandise. eBay enables you to embed images in your eBay auction ad. This is a wonderful opportunity to show what you're selling. People like to see the things they contemplate buying.

Photographs may seem unimportant for some products. For instance, how do you show software or other seemingly intangible products? It's simple. You show the box. Even showing the box will help you sell. In fact, showing the box or showing manufacturers' photographs and drawings will help you sell used products as well as new products.

Where the merchandise is used, blemished, scratched, or otherwise damaged, however slightly, a good close-up photograph of the item will provide potential bidders with the information they need to make a bidding decision. The more disclosure you make, the less trouble you will have from buyers. A photograph is often the best way to disclose exactly what you're selling.

Surprisingly often, a photograph assists a seller to make more accurate disclosure. If you advertise one model but show another in a photograph, some knowledgeable potential bidders will set you straight. It's not unusual at all for a potential bidder to be more knowledgeable than a seller in regard to an item, and you see sellers being set straight routinely. Better to learn about your mistake before the auction is finished than after.

Photography Tips

Product photography is something of an art, but you're not taking pictures for the Buick brochure, so don't worry about it too much. Do, however, take the little bit of extra time to ensure that your photographs are appealing.

Here are some things you can do:

1. Photograph in color. Does anyone use B&W anymore?

2. Use diffused outdoor light—lightly overcast day or in the shadow of your house—if practical. If you shoot outdoors on a sunny day, you may need a flash to fill in the shadows.

3. Use a flash indoors. Diffuse the flash with a translucent cover (e.g., a piece of white plastic garbage bag taped over), or bounce the flash off the ceiling, to avoid glare. It's even better to use flood lights if you have them. Use three. Use one each to point at the item from the left and right about 45 degrees offset from center. Use the third to backlight the item (out of sight), if practical.

4. With film, avoid using light bulbs, fluoresent lights, or halogen lights. Your photographs may have a color cast to them (yellow or blue). Many digital cameras, however, will automatically change the white balance to adjust to the light, and using such light sources should work fine so long as you don't mix them. Try inexpensive halogen work lights that you can find at your hardware store.

5. Use a plain, dull (not shiny), pastel one-color background. Cloth backgrounds (e.g., sheets and tablecloths) work well.

6. For large items, shoot against an appealing background. For instance, shoot cars in a residential neighborhood, not on an asphalt parking lot.

7. Get as close to the item as possible. Use a closeup lens, if appropriate. But be careful of overexposure from a flash.

8. Fill the frame when you shoot. The image of your item will be larger and higher quality. If you use a digital camera, use the highest resolution setting (minimum of 640×480).

9. With film, take multiple photographs with different settings. Give yourself a choice so you won't have to shoot over.

10. Use a tripod, and focus carefully.

Take multiple photographs for items that deserve multiple photographs in your auction ad (e.g., vehicles). Don't forget to take photographs of blemishes and defects that bidders will want to see.

Close Up

Film cameras usually require a close-up (i.e., macro) lens to get close enough to small things to get good photographs. Most digital cameras, however, do not require a special close-up lens for shooting small items; you can get good photographs of small items easily.

Digitizing Photographs

You have your choice of ways to digitize photographs so you can use them on eBay.

Kodak Photo CD

You can take photographs with a 35mm camera and send them for processing via Kodak Photo CD at virtually any photo finisher. It costs something for the CD plus one roll of film developed (you get thumbnail prints and negatives too), but the CD can hold 100 images (4 rolls of 24, or almost 3 rolls of 36). You get back high-quality digital images (photographs) in six sizes each; but only the two smallest (or the third smallest, if you crop it) are suitable for eBay. The quality of Photo CD is much higher than you need for your eBay ad, but it's one method of digitizing your photographs.

Kodak Picture CD

Kodak Picture CD (available at almost all photo finishers) costs less and gives you less than Photo CD. But Picture CD is really all you need. It provides you with a JPEG image file you can use on the Web, but only in one large size. You will need to use an image editor to reduce the size.

AOL You've Got Pictures

AOL features its You've Got Pictures service wherein you can have a copy of your photographs posted on the Web when you get your film developed (*http://www.kodak.com/US/en/consumer/aol*). This is the old Kodak PhotoNet service and continues to be affiliated with Kodak. It's a good way to digitize your photographs. You can download them from where they appear on the Web. Go to the URL to get complete instructions.

Removes a Step

As you will read later, you need to upload your digital photographs to the Web in order to use them for an eBay auction. With this service, you do not have to upload the photographs to the Web yourself, thus eliminating a step. Kodak does it for you. Again, you use this service through photofinishers.

Scanner

You can digitize the photographs (prints) with a flatbed scanner. Such scanners are now inexpensive (under $60), and the quality is adequate for eBay. This is an excellent way for you to convert your snapshots into digital photographs. Glossy prints scan better than matte.

Scan your photographs at the highest resolution possible for your scanner, usually better than 700 dots per inch (dpi). Although computer monitors typically display at about 92 dpi (the standard is 72 dpi), you would not be happy with photographs scanned at 92 dpi or even 300 dpi. Consider 600 dpi a minimum for scanning images.

Not Just Photographs

You can also use a scanner to make images of documents, flat art, photographs printed in publications, and the like. Scanners work just like copy machines.

You can also go to a place like Kinko's to get a photograph scanned, but it's expensive.

Another alternative is to use a film scanner. A film scanner for 35mm film costs at least $250. You actually put the film negative or positive (slide) in the scanner, and the scanner makes a high-quality scan. This quality is higher than a consumer flatbed scanner and beyond the quality you need for eBay.

For all of these methods, the film must be developed. You need prints for the flatbed scanner and Kinko's, and negatives or slides for the film scanner.

Digital Camera

Inexpensive digital cameras are not known for their high quality in comparison to film cameras, but they're perfectly adequate for eBay photos. If you do a lot of eBay auctions, using a digital camera is the least expensive, quickest, and most convenient way to create digital photographs. Just shoot the photographs and load them into your computer. It couldn't be easier.

A 1-megapixel digital camera (under $100) provides adequate quality for most purposes. If you sell antique Japanese prints and want to capture the subtle colors, don't use an inexpensive digital camera. Use one with at least a 3-megapixel image ($200+). But most products do not require such quality, and a 1-megapixel digital camera does just fine. With a 2-megapixel camera, you can take high-quality photographs (if you know how) of almost anything for eBay auctions. So, you don't need an expensive digital camera to produce even high quality photographs for your eBay auction ads.

Make sure that any digital camera you buy has the capability of taking close-ups. This is a feature you will use a lot. Fortunately, unlike film cameras, most digital cameras do have close-up capability without a special lens.

If you buy a digital camera used (e.g., on eBay), make sure you get the manual, software, and a USB cable (for connecting to your computer). Otherwise, you might spend a lot of time and money acquiring such items; and you will need them.

Avoid older digital cameras that don't use a USB cable to connect to your computer. They are likely to be troublesome.

Camcorder

Many digital camcorders and some analog camcorders (oddly enough) have the capability of taking digital snapshots (one frame at a time). Consult your owner's manual. If you can get such snapshots into your computer (via whatever means the manufacturer provides), you will have digital photographs you can use for eBay.

Size

Don't make your photographs large. Seldom is a photograph larger than 500 × 375 pixels justified for an eBay ad. Make it smaller. Digital images larger than 400 × 300 aren't needed and take longer to download. Large photographs make your eBay ad photographs slow to appear, perhaps even slowing the download of your entire ad. They also may interfere with your auction webpage. However, don't think by recommending 400 x 300 that I'm saying you should enlarge smaller photographs to that size. If you have smaller photographs, use them in their smaller size. Digital photographs don't enlarge well.

Typically, adequate digital cameras use at least a 640 × 480 pixel format, and you don't want to use anything smaller. This is quite large. Since digital camera formats and the Picture CD format do not provide a proper size, you will have to shrink your digital photographs. One way to do it is via the image markup, but this doesn't change the download time. Another way to do it is to reduce the size of the image with an image editing program (covered in Chapter 19) to make the image file smaller to download.

Image Markup

Regardless of the actual size of the digital photograph, you can set the size that it will show on eBay in the image markup. Suppose the image is 640 × 480 pixels. You want to shrink it to 400 × 300. Use the image markup:

```
<img src=" [URL] " width="400" height="300">
```

The size of the digital photograph remains the same, but the browser reduces the image shown in the webpage (the ad) to 400 × 300. This does not reduce the download time but saves you the task of image editing. This is not a recommended procedure, primarily because it causes an unnecessarily long download time. Note that when you do shrink a photograph, you need to maintain the aspect ratio (the ratio of the width to the height), or your photograph will become distorted.

Photo Editing

You can use an image editing program such as Adobe PhotoShop to decrease the size of the image before you use it. PhotoShop is a well-known, high-end program, but hundreds of inexpensive photo editing programs can resize digital photographs and also do much more. Such programs are usually bundled with digital cameras, scanners, new PCs, and even other software. Most will enable you to easily change the contrast, brightness, and sharpness. In other words, these programs act like a digital darkroom. You can make better photographs than you took. Whether you want to go to all that trouble is a personal matter, but if you have to change the size, it's usually little additional trouble to at least sharpen your photographs. You can see the photograph change as you make the adjustments. Chapter 19 covers image editing.

Format

All digital images must be in the GIF (.gif), JPEG (.jpg), or PNG (.png) format. Most digital photographs are in the JPEG format. The photo editing programs enable you to make conversions to other formats.

Tools and Services

Interesting photography tools and services are starting to pop up. You may find some of them useful.

The Boxes

Several vendors offer lighted boxes inside which you can shoot great product photographs. These range in price from $90 to $4,000, and some come with a digital camera included.

EZCube, *http://store.yahoo.com/greenbatteries-store*

Cloud Dome, *http://www.clouddome.com*

Coloreal eBox, *http://www.ortery.com*

MK Digital Direct, *http://www.mkdigitaldirect.com*

Why would you pay so much for a box? Well, if you have small expensive items to sell, the higher quality photographs and the efficiency will eventually pay for a box. You can, of course, build a box yourself with flat-white walls and lights inside. But some of these boxes have features that you might find it difficult to duplicate easily with a do-it-yourself project.

Outsourcing

Outsourcing means having someone else take your photographs. Auction 123 (*http://www.auction123.com*) will shoot your vehicle photographs for a modest fee and provide you with a nice presentation for your eBay Motors auction ad. It's a useful service called Dealer Assist and is available to everyone. If you're looking for extra work, Auction 123 is looking for franchisees and photographers.

Captions

A photograph without a caption is not as informative. You can use software called PhotoTags (*http://www.photags.com*) to easily create captions affixed to your product photographs. It also acts as a photograph catalog, which will even do a search on the caption words. Slick! It's particularly slick for high volume sales where efficiency is important for routine photography and image handling.

Making Photographs Available

You store digital photographs on your hard disk. When you want to make them available to others via the Internet, you have to upload them to a hard disk that's on the Internet such as a host Internet Service Provider's (ISP's) hard disk.

Storing Photographs

The reason you must store a photograph on a hard disk on the Internet is that it gives it a URL.

Website

Suppose you store your photographs at your website (*www.yourwebsite.com*). Your root folder (directory) at your website is:

```
/clients/yours/public_html
```

You can create a handy folder named *photos* just to store your photographs:

```
/clients/yours/public_html/photos
```

Suppose you need a photograph named *item41.gif* (in your auction ad at eBay) that you have stored on your website in the *photos* folder. The image markup in the ad will look as follows:

```
<img src="http:// www.yourwebsite.com/
photos/item41.gif">
```

Thus, your image stored on your website will appear magically in your eBay ad. (See Chapter 18 for ideas about using a Web authoring program to create your image markups.)

If you need help with creating folders and determining what the URL of your images will be, consult your host ISP. In particular, America Online (AOL) provides space for you to store files.

ISP Account

If you don't have a website, you may be able to store your photographs on your dial-up ISP's hard disk in the space reserved for you. Your ISP reserves space for your email messages. Most ISPs also enable you to use such space for webpages too. If you can put up a webpage, you can store photographs. Suppose your Web address is *http://www.isp.com/ ~yours*. You can create a folder named *photos* and upload all your photographs for eBay auction ads to that directory. The image markup will be:

```
<img src="http:// www.isp.com/~yours/
images/item41.gif">
```

If you need help with creating folders and determining what the URL of your photographs will be, consult your dial-up ISP. Or, your ISP may have instructions published online. Many ISPs do.

ISPs

If your dial-up and your host ISPs are the same, you have a combined dial-up plus host account.

Special Services

There are a number of Web services that cater to auction users. They will store your photographs for auction ads for free or for a fee. Go to their websites to get instructions:

- Auctionimage, *http://www.auctionimage.com*

- AuctionEnhancer, *http://www.auctionenhancer.com*

- FreePicHosting, *http://www.freepichosting.com*

- Imagehost, *http://www.imagehost.com*

- ImageHosting, *http://www.imagehosting.com*

- PennyThings, *http://www.pennythings.com*

- Picturetrail, *http://www.picturetrail.com*

- PixHost, *http://www.pixhost.com*

- Pongo's, *http://www.pongo.com*

- Webshots, *http://auctions.webshots.com*

These are not the only places you can store your photographs. eBay itself will allow you to store one photograph per auction without charge. ISPs like AOL and MSN offer photograph storing services. And most of the auction management services include photograph storage too.

Make sure when you sign up with one of these services that you know how to upload your photographs to the service (to their website). Also make sure you know exactly what the URL of your image will be once you have uploaded the image. Many of these services also provide scanning and other image services.

Check Chapter 21 for a list of free websites where presumably you can store images in addition to creating a website.

eBay Picture Service

You don't have to use an outside service for storage. You can use the eBay Picture Service (*http://pages.ebay.com/help/basics/pictureservices.html*). The first photograph per auction is free. After that, it costs you a nominal fee. You don't have to do anything special. This service is integrated into the auction listing process. This is a convenient service that you will want to try. eBay automatically deletes your photographs after your auction ends.

Uploading Photographs

To upload your photographs to your storage place (website), you use the File Transfer Protocol (FTP). Consequently, you will need an FTP client to upload the images. There are many freeware and shareware FTP clients available. Try *http://www.cnet.com* and look for *downloads*.

I upload with WS_FTP, which is easy to use. It enables you to show a directory (folder) on your own hard disk on the left and a directory on the hard disk of your website on the right. After getting online, you simply highlight the file(s) on the left and click on the arrow pointing right to make the upload. You can also download by highlighting the files on the right and clicking on the arrow pointing to the left (see Figure 11.1).

Get WS_FTP at *http://www.ipswitch.com/_ebay/index.html*. This URL also provides special instructions for eBay users. Other FTP clients include:

- CuteFTP (*http://www.cuteftp.com*)
- Fetch (for Mac—*http://fetchsoftworks.com*)
- FTP Voyager (*http://www.ftpvoyager.com*)

Pulling In Photographs

Through the magic of links, you can pull media into your eBay auction ad from other servers on the Internet. This is a little different from a link to another webpage. A link to another webpage will take you to that webpage. But a media markup will bring the media into the eBay auction ad in the auction listing (which is a webpage). The media can be images, sound clips, or even video clips (see Figure 11.2).

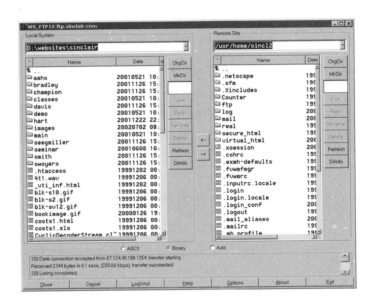

Figure 11.1   WS_FTP uploading files to a website.

But we are concerned primarily with digital photographs. Store the photographs at your website, in your ISP account storage space, or at one of the Web services that offer to store photographs. Then pull it into your eBay auction ad with the HTML image markup.

```
<img src="http://isp.com/~yours/photos/
image1.jpg">
```

Making It Happen

So, you've stored your photograph where it's accessible on the Web. You have its correct URL. What do you do next?

At eBay

When you access the *Sell Your Item* form in the Sell section to enter your eBay auction ad, be ready to enter the URL of your image. The URL will start with *http://*.

If you don't add the URL at the time you enter the other information for your auction, you can add it later. If you add it later, however, the photograph will be tacked onto the bottom of the ad and will look like an add-on.

In the Template

In the template featured in Chapter 12, you add the URL of the photograph into the template. You then enter the entire template in the *Description* for the auction ad (i.e., at *Sell Your Item*). You do not enter the URL of the photograph into the *Picture URL* for the eBay auction ad when you use a template; just leave the *Picture URL* blank. The template places the photograph in a special place. The whole point of using a template is to create an attractive auction ad with the photograph well integrated (see Figure 11.2).

Other People's Photographs

Other people may have photographs you can use. It's not difficult to get them and use them. But then there's the question of permission.

Manufacturers

More specifically, you can use photographs from manufacturers' websites; simply right-click on the photograph. You will see the file name of the photograph, and you can also save the photograph to your own hard disk. Once you have saved it, you can use it as if it's one of your own; that is, you can upload it to your Web photograph storage place.

Another way you can use it is to look at the Source for the webpage (Go *View, Source* in either the Netscape browser or the Microsoft browser) after right-clicking on the photograph to get the image file name (see Figure 11.3).

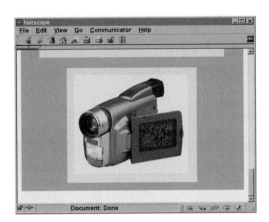

Figure 11.2   Photograph in auction ad made with template.

The source will show you the URL of the photograph. (Sometimes the URL is incomplete because it is a relative reference, and you will have to try to figure out the complete URL. This level of analysis is beyond the scope of this book, but this method is worth mentioning for readers who know HTML.) Once you have the correct and complete URL, you don't need to download the photograph and you don't need to store it at your Web photograph storage place; you only need to use it where it is. That is, you use the URL of the manufacturer's photograph at the manufacturer's website by putting the manufacturer's URL in the *Picture URL* in your eBay auction ad (i.e., *Sell Your Item*).

Now it's one thing to say you *can* use these techniques, but the fact that you can doesn't mean you should. In fact, you must consider everything on the Web to be copyrighted. If you use other people's copyrighted materials without permission, you are liable for copyright infringement. So, before you download a photograph or logo from a manufacturer's website into your eBay auction ad, you might first consider getting permission from the webmaster at the manufacturer's website.

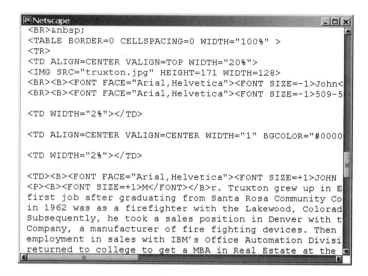

Figure 11.3   The source shows the entire webpage in HTML.

Unfortunately, this is impractical, and many eBay sellers download and use manufacturers' logos, product literature, photographs, and other intellectual property for their eBay ads with impunity. A different approach is to provide a link to a manufacturer's website where bidders can find complete information on products and photographs too. This is a better practice.

eBay Sellers

You can also use the photographs taken by other eBay sellers. You can download or pull them in the same way as you do for manufacturers' photographs. Of course, such sellers are likely to be your competitors, and your pilfering is likely to upset them. It's not a good practice.

Nonetheless, I have always taken a mellow view of this. If someone wants to steal a seller's photographs, who is he to stand in their way? Like many sellers, he is likely to have pilfered photographs and logos from manufacturers. It seems a little hypocritical to get irritated at a fellow eBay member for doing the same to him. Oh, and I might add that there are lots of sellers who disagree with me about this.

If this irritates you, you can probably find a JavaScript script somewhere on the Web that will prevent people from stealing your photographs out of your auction ad. The JavaScript script goes inside the image markup.

Graphics

A digital photograph is just a digital color graphic. You can use any color graphic just as if it were a digital photograph. Consequently, you may want to use a drawing or other art form rather than a photograph. Whatever graphic you use, however, you must first convert it to a GIF, JPEG, or PNG file format. Photographs are always best, but if you can't find a photograph or can't take one, a color graphic may be better than nothing.

Summary

A digital color photograph helps sell merchandise on eBay. It is well worth going to the trouble of taking one, developing it, digitizing it, editing it, and using it in your eBay ad. If you use a digital camera, you can skip developing it and digitizing it. The seemingly toughest part of the procedure, image editing, is really quite easy, and it's a step you need to take just to resize or crop your photograph, if nothing else (see Chapter 19).

Once the digital photograph is ready, it's just a matter of posting it via FTP on a website and referencing its URL in your eBay auction ad—a pretty simple process, and a pretty powerful means of advertising. Of course, it's even more simple to use eBay to store your photographs.

Creating Your eBay Auction Ad

eBay provides you with a webpage space (call it an "auction ad") with which you can do almost anything to advertise the item for your auction. Take advantage of this great opportunity. This is your chance to create some interest in your offering that will bring in a higher final bid.

eBay Advertising

Every medium has its own unique characteristics. The Web is an information medium. You can publish unlimited information on the

Web at a small cost. It's not a medium like television where every time slot commands a premium price and where advertising is relatively expensive. Take advantage of the Web's strength and publish plenty of information on the item you auction.

Keep in mind that the Web (and eBay) is not a retail store where a customer can walk in, examine the merchandise, and talk to sales clerks. What you publish is what the customer gets. Your eBay auction advertisement has to create interest, then inform, and finally, close the sale.

An eBay ad has two parts: the one-line title that goes in the listing and the webpage section that is part of the auction page. This chapter considers the one-line title at the end of the chapter, but let's start with the ad itself.

The First Goal

The first objective of the ad is to create interest. A little hype is OK here, so long as you can back up the hype with facts a little farther down the page. The top of the ad should always include:

1. The specific identification of the item being auctioned

2. Condition of the item

3. One or two major benefits of the item to potential bidders

Put your strongest benefits here. You may get only one chance to hook the bidder/reader. Give it your best shot at the top of the ad.

Clearly and specifically identify the item being sold here. Otherwise you will frustrate and anger potential bidders. Even worse, it may create a lot of unnecessary, undesirable, and time-consuming communication for you. If the item is a model XMT-5001 camcorder, not a model XMT-5011, you'd better get it right.

The condition of the item is important and should be stated at the top of the ad. New, mint, and excellent condition are prime selling points. Don't neglect to put them in up front. However, many people can't afford to buy a new product of the type you're selling. They look for bargains where the product is *in good working order but has a few cosmetic blemishes* (and other such descriptions). Express the condition as a prime feature, and you will draw potential bidders regardless of what the condition is.

Determine one or two major selling points that will draw the interest of the most likely bidders. Don't try to tell the whole story here. You have plenty of room later. Just mention one or two benefits to hook potential bidders.

Hook them into bidding? No. Your objective with the hype at the top of the ad is not to get them to make a bid. It's to get them to read more about your offering, that is, to get them to acquire enough facts on which to base a confident decision to bid.

> Poor: ActionCatcher camcorder with picture stabilization, flicker reduction, digital zoom, review/retake functions, and random editing.

> Better: ActionCatcher camcorder XMT-5001, new, all automatic features, perfect for intermediate users and even novices.

What's wrong with the information in the first example? Nothing. But it's too much information, and it doesn't seem directly tied to benefits. There's plenty of space to mention such information below. Action-Catcher has many different models of camcorders ranging in price from $300 to many thousands of dollars. Which model is it?

What's right with the second example? It mentions that the item is new and clearly identifies exactly what's for sale. Then it adds a little hype. It's probably not going to interest expert users, but then they won't buy the XMT-5001 anyway. It's not for experts. Novice and intermediate videographers will be likely to read more.

The Second Goal

The second part of the ad has two parts, the product information and the purchasing information.

Product Information

Now that you've hooked bidders into reading, provide them with the facts. The hype is over. Leave the hype to the television folks who only have a few seconds to hook potential buyers. And keep in mind that a television ad attempts to hook potential buyers into what? Into going to a local store to make a purchase, a local store where the potential buyer will interact with a sales clerk. On eBay there is no sales clerk. There's only your ad. Consequently, for the main body of your eBay ad, it's your job to supply the facts and benefits to enable the potential bidder to make a decision to bid (to buy).

On eBay, there's no limit on the ad. This circumstance requires facts. Provide as much factual data on the item for sale as you can find. Don't assume that anyone knows anything about the item. If you do, you'll be cutting out a significant percentage of your potential market.

What do you publish? Don't reinvent the wheel. A good place to start looking for information is the manufacturer's information and specifications. Get them off the box. Get them off the manufacturer's website. Get them out of the user's manual. Put in a link to the manufacturer's information and specification sheets on the manufacturer's website.

Hype, Information, and Specifications

The manufacturer's information and specifications usually contain some hype. Is that OK? Sure it is. So long as the ad is essentially informative, a little hype woven in is to be expected. Just a little hype, though. Overly hyped information loses credibility with potential bidders. Instead, they want facts and benefits.

A link to a manufacturer's website by itself is not enough. Such a link can cut your ad from seven paragraphs to one perhaps, but you still need a paragraph or two to keep readers involved in your ad. If you use a link, make sure it is a link directly to the specific webpage at the manufacturer's website that has the relevant information.

Express your personal enthusiasm for the item. If you have a positive opinion of the item, express it in terms of benefits to bidders. Honest opinions, even coming from the seller, are valuable. If you have a negative opinion of the item, don't say anything. Let the manufacturer speak for you. If the item is a lemon product, even if new, you better warn the bidders, albeit mildly. If you don't and you sell a lot of stuff on eBay, you may negatively affect your reputation. eBay is not a dumping ground for lemon products. If you treat it that way, you may adversely affect your reputation and fail to achieve your long-term commercial objectives on eBay. Lemons can be sold honestly, albeit at lower prices, with happy sellers and buyers, but only with disclosure up front.

Don't make the ad too long. You could put the full text of three magazine reviews on the product in your ad, but that would be too much in most cases. Link to them instead. Beyond 1,000 or 2,000 words, you're bound to start losing people. However, it's different for every product. Bidders probably don't need 2,000 words about an office file cabinet. But if you're selling a $19,000 timeshare at a Steamboat Springs, Colorado, ski resort, 2,000 words may not be enough.

Losing Your Market

I was looking for a new camcorder on eBay. One person was selling two or three each week of the model I had decided to buy. He provided a generous amount of information (all the text from the manufacturer's website), enough to inspire a decision. He was selling the same model over and over again for an ongoing average price of about $550. I got ready to make my initial bid.

I reviewed what was being auctioned one last time. Surprisingly, I discovered another person selling the identical camcorder (also new). This person had posted very sparse information on the camcorder, only four sentences and few specifications. As a result, he had attracted few bidders. I put in my bid at this person's auction, won the bidding, and got the new camcorder for $450. The same day the other person sold three more identical camcorders at his Dutch auction for $550; the bids were $550, $600, and $600.

The moral of the story is that if you're a seller, it pays to provide plenty of information. If you're a buyer, it pays to look for the lazy sellers.

Purchasing Information

To build the bidder's confidence in purchasing from you, you must give complete information on how the transaction can be closed. How can the buyer pay? The more ways, the better. But whatever the acceptable payment methods, state them clearly. Don't forget shipping and handling. State specific amounts for such expenses up front.

Payment Methods

You will sell more if you accept credit cards (or PayPal). Do you know that you can take checks via the Web or via telephone? This is not popular yet, but it could be someday, and it's easy for you to do. See Chapter 15.

This is a golden opportunity to put in a link to your *About Me* webpage on eBay where presumably you have a lot of information about yourself or your eBay business. For some reason, a lot of sellers who should be doing this don't. You shouldn't miss this opportunity; it doesn't cost anything extra. However, don't put in a link to your website. eBay not longer allows it from your auction ad.

An alternative to operating a website for your business is to have an eBay store. You will certainly want to put in a link to your eBay store. eBay will automatically put a link (red price tag) to your eBay store after your name in your auction listing.

Promote Yourself and Your Other Auctions

Promoting yourself works best after you have accumulated some proof that you're trustworthy. That is, as soon as you've built up some positive feedback, you can state, "Check my feedback." Make your self-promotion modest and factual. Do it, but don't overdo it. Also, use your auction ad to promote your other eBay auctions. You can put in a link in your auction ad to the eBay list of your other auctions.

The Third Goal

Ask for the order; that is, ask people to make a bid. Don't make a statement like "The lucky winning bidder will enjoy the CleanCut Estate Mower for many years." Rather say something like "Make a bid now. I think you'll be satisfied with the quality of this mower if you're the winning bidder, and I appreciate your interest in my auction." What you say doesn't have to be long or elaborate, but do ask for the bid.

Unique Products

Certain products do not lend themselves neatly to the preceding format, which is designed essentially for mass-produced goods with which many potential bidders will be familiar. Unique products and custom products require more explanation. Not only that, but in many cases, it may be appropriate and worthwhile to provide information expressed in a creative way.

Suppose you want to sell printing press prints of Van Gogh's self portrait. This is a well-known, inexpensive, mass-produced item that you find in college book stores for $15. Information about this work of art will help sell it, but the information isn't absolutely necessary. People will buy it because they like the way it looks, and it's low cost.

However, suppose you want to sell numbered (limited edition), handmade lithograph prints by an emerging new artist for $450 each. Providing voluminous information on the artist and the work of art as well as favorable art reviews and the like will definitely help sell the prints. And if you can present this information in an attractive, unusual, and elegant way, you will realize even more sales.

Potential bidders who are looking for unique products will take the time to review a creative presentation of relevant information. It's difficult to imagine someone who is only interested in comparing camcorder specifications prior to purchasing, instead, taking the time to read a lengthy creative presentation about a camcorder. But a limited edition print by an emerging new artist catches the imagination and requires a lot of information to make a sale.

Presenting the Ad

What's the goal for your presentation of the ad? The same as for the ad itself. You want potential bidders to read the entire ad. The best way to do so is to make it easily readable.

Text

Text is your most important medium. Remember, the Web is an informational medium. The most efficient way to convey the requisite information to potential bidders in most cases is via words.

The following subsections outline the format for the text. The penalty for neglecting to follow these guidelines is shrinkage of your potential market. Each guideline you fail to follow will shrink your market more. At some point, there will be no market left, and potential bidders will ignore your auction. In addition, if you do a sloppy job of publishing your ad, you detract from your credibility as a seller.

Grammar

Write the ad well. Check your spelling. Don't use acronyms or abbreviations; at least half the bidders won't know what those mean. Even if you use what you think are commonly understood acronyms having to do with the product or procedures on eBay, you will lose a lot of bidders, and you will never know it. Use good grammar and complete sentences. You are not writing a classified ad for which you pay by the word. Write something that's readable.

Don't be afraid to make mistakes. We all make spelling and grammatical mistakes. These are understandable and forgivable. What is irritating is the intentional cutting of corners (abbreviations, acronyms, incomplete sentences, all-lowercase, all caps, etc.) that makes reading more difficult for everyone and often makes the text itself virtually incomprehensible.

Paragraphs

Divide your text into paragraphs. It astounds me that some people put 1,500 words of information in their ad, all in one paragraph. That makes the text very difficult to read and comprehend. For example:

The ActionCatcher XMT-5001 camcorder with LCD color monitor. MSRP is $1,399. Features include: Built-in still camera with 140,000 pixels. LCD color monitor with 290-degree screen rotation for high- and low-angle viewing. Quick 44X Zoom with close-up focus. Picture stabilizing that differentiates between intentional and unintentional camera movements. Six-head mechanism for precision recording. Built-in head cleaner. Automatic system for recording, including auto focus, white balance, and auto exposure. Flicker reduction, flying erase head, and random editing. Floodlight built in that automatically turns on or off as needed. Review and retake functions with indicators for remaining tape time and remaining battery time. Remote control, editing, and dubbing. Image transfer and recording software. Special effects and titling. Languages: English, French, Spanish, and German. Fog and ND filters. Mic input. S-Cable output. Lens cover, dew sensor, 3-way power supply. New, sealed in box.

You can easily divide the above paragraph into separate paragraphs by using the HTML paragraph markup *<p>* at the beginning of each paragraph:

```
The ActionCatcher XMT-5001 camcorder with
LCD color monitor. MSRP is $1,399. Features
include:<p>Built-in still camera with
140,000 pixels.<p>LCD color monitor with
290-degree screen rotation for high- and
low-angle viewing.<p>Quick 44X Zoom with
close-up focus.<p>Picture stabilizing that
differentiates between intentional and
unintentional camera movements.<p>Six-head
mechanism for precision
recording.<p>Built-in head
cleaner.<p>Automatic system for recording,
including auto focus, white balance, and
auto exposure.<p>Flicker reduction, flying
erase head, and random
editing.<p>Floodlight built in that
automatically turns on or off as
needed.<p>Review and retake functions with
indicators for remaining tape time and
remaining battery time.<p>Remote control,
editing, and dubbing.<p>Image transfer and
recording software.<p>Special effects and
titling.<p>Languages: English, French,
Spanish, and German.<p>Fog and ND
filters.<p>Mic input.<p>S-Cable
output.<p>Lens cover, dew sensor, 3-way
power supply.<p>New, sealed in box.
```

After you do so, the presentation will be more readable in a Web browser:

The ActionCatcher XMT-5001 camcorder with LCD color monitor. MSRP is $1,399. Features include:

Built-in still camera with 140,000 pixels.

LCD color monitor with 290-degree screen rotation for high- and low-angle viewing.

Quick 44X Zoom with close-up focus.

Picture stabilizing that differentiates between intentional and unintentional camera movements.

Six-head mechanism for precision recording.

Built-in head cleaner.

Automatic system for recording, including auto focus, white balance, and auto exposure.

Flicker reduction, flying erase head, and random editing.

Floodlight built in that automatically turns on or off as needed.

Review and retake functions with indicators for remaining tape time and remaining battery time.

Remote control, editing, and dubbing.

Image transfer and recording software.

Special effects and titling.

Languages: English, French, Spanish, and German.

Fog and ND filters.

Mic input.

S-Cable output.

Lens cover, dew sensor, 3-way power supply.

New, sealed in box.

Note: To make the above list of paragraphs conform to HTML best practices, you will need to add the closing paragraph markup *</p>* at the end of each paragraph.

Although the above presentation is not as attractive as it can be with additional HTML coding (it needs bullets), it is definitely more readable than a solid block of text. Anyone can add the *<p>* markup without knowing HTML.

To add bullets, you must use more HTML markups. The *<ul>* and *<li>* markups are simple but not as simple as just *<p>*.

```
The ActionCatcher XMT-5001 camcorder with
LCD color monitor. MSRP is $1,399. Features
include:

<ul>

<li><p>Built-in still camera with 140,000
pixels.</p>

<li><p>LCD color monitor with 290-degree
screen rotation for high- and low-angle
viewing.</p>

<li><p>Quick 44X Zoom with close-up
focus.</p>

<li><p>Picture stabilizing that
differentiates between intentional and
unintentional camera movements.</p>

<li><p>Six-head mechanism for precision
recording.</p>

<li><p>Built-in head cleaner.</p>

<li><p>Automatic system for recording,
including auto focus, white balance, and
auto exposure.</p>

<li><p>Flicker reduction, flying erase
head, and random editing.</p>
```

```
<li><p>Floodlight built in that
automatically turns on or off as needed.</
p>

<li><p>Review and retake functions with
indicators for remaining tape time and
remaining battery time.</p>

<li><p>Remote control, editing, and
dubbing.</p>

<li><p>Image transfer and recording
software.</p>

<li><p>Special effects and titling.</p>

<li><p>Languages: English, French,
Spanish, and German.</p>

<li><p>Fog and ND filters.</p>

<li><p>Mic input.</p>

<li><p>S-Cable output.</p>

<li><p>Lens cover, dew sensor, 3-way power
supply.</p>

<li><p>New, sealed in box.</p>

</ul>
```

When the browser displays the code immediately above, it will have bullets, as shown in Figure 12.1.

Copy Writing

What are we talking about here? We're talking about writing copy. Copywriters write copy. Some of the best copywriters working for large manufacturers, advertising agencies, and catalog companies make a lot of money just writing compelling copy correlating product features to consumer benefits. You can't expect to be a skilled copywriter without study and practice, but part of being a copywriter is writing clearly and in an organized manner. You can strive to do that much.

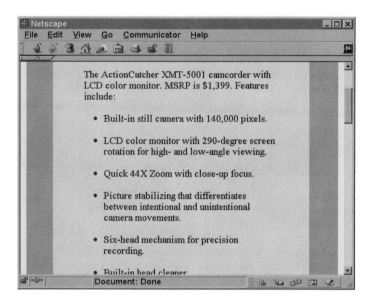

Figure 12.1   A bulleted list looks better than an unbulleted list for the presentation of this camcorder.

Read *Writing That Works*, Roman & Raphaelson, HarperResource, 2000, a small book that will improve your copy writing in a few pages.

Typesetting

The choice of fonts is quite simple. Use the browser defaults.

PC: Times New Roman, serif; Arial, sanserif; and Courier New, monospaced

Mac: Times, serif; Helvetica, sanserif; and Courier, monospaced

If you don't do anything, the text will appear in the browser default serif. This is your best choice. It's readable. It may be boring, because you see it all the time on the Web; but you're not trying to win a typesetting contest. You want your text to be readable above all else. Times New Roman and Times are easy to read on the screen.

If you use any font except the browser defaults, for the font to work, the viewer will have to have the font installed on his or her computer. Chances of that may not be good. Therefore, your choices are limited to the fonts mentioned above.

Follow these eight standard typesetting guidelines:

1. Use italics for emphasis, not bold. Bold type is difficult to read through quickly. The use of bold for emphasis is appropriate only for warnings for equipment-threatening or life-threatening situations and for similar uses.

2. Make your lines between 9 and 11 words wide. This provides optimal reading. Wider lines are difficult to read. Narrower lines are difficult to read without special typesetting treatment (e.g., smaller type).

3. Avoid small type. Use at least 12-point type. Reading on a monitor is difficult enough. Don't make it worse. Space is not limited. (Note: 12-point type is the Web browser default, so you don't have to do anything in regard to specifying the type size.)

4. Avoid large type for text. Oversize type is difficult to read quickly.

5. Avoid huge type for headings. Headings are great, but keep their size modest. Use bold type.

6. Avoid centered text. Centered text is difficult to read. Make all text left justified.

7. Avoid *all caps*. People cannot read all caps quickly. You don't need all caps for headings; you can use a larger-size font and bold.

8. Don't use all lowercase. It's difficult to read.

These rules are simple but nonetheless necessary for a professional look and readable text.

Layout

The width of the browser maximized is too wide for text. You need to narrow the text column to an easily readable size. There are a number of ways to accomplish this with HTML. If you don't use a template, you will have to learn a way to narrow the text column. The following code provides you two ways.

First Method

```
<table width="450"
cellpadding="10"><tr><td>

[your text paragraphs]

</td></tr></table>
```

This is the best way to ensure an accurate size of text column. This keeps the column 450 pixels wide. You can adjust the pixel dimension according to your needs, but don't go over 550 pixels or your presentation may not be as readable as it needs to be.

Second Method

```
<dl><dl><dl>

<dd> [your text paragraphs]

</dl></dl></dl>
```

This shrinks the width of the column by expanding the left margin but is not an absolute measurement. Therefore, the column will expand and contract depending on the size of the browser window.

Each of your paragraphs should be marked with the *<p> </p>* markups. For example:

```
<p>The vase has a miniature hand painting
covering most of its midsection. The
painting has bright colors, which have not
faded, indicating that the vase has been
well cared for over the years. This is a
vase that museums would love to have.</p>
```

This is the proper way to do paragraphs. Avoid fancy and complex text layouts. Simple is best. Don't try to win a design contest. Just make it readable.

Color

Color is a dangerous thing for webpages if not controlled carefully and properly.

Background Color

Some people change the background color of their ad using the *<body bgcolor="...">* markup. The result is that no one can read the auction information and make a bid. eBay is not going to stop you from shooting yourself in the foot this way.

Don't interfere with eBay's color scheme. Don't use the *<body bgcolor="...">* markup. The eBay auction section, both above and below your ad, together with your ad, comprises one webpage. If you change eBay's color scheme, you make it difficult for bidders to understand what's going on. In many cases, the eBay information will be unreadable if you change the background color.

Ad Background Color

To change the background color just for your ad without affecting the eBay color scheme, use the *<table>* markup. This means putting your entire ad in an HTML table. Use the first layout scheme mentioned above in the Layout subsection and add background color:

```
<table width="450" cellpadding="10"
bgcolor="#99ffff">
```

This will confine the background color to your ad, and the eBay auction listing color scheme will remain the same, as it should.

Color Combinations

There is nothing wrong with having your own color scheme in your ad. In fact, it can be quite attractive, if properly designed. Remember, it's readability you seek. There must be contrast between the background color and the text (foreground) color. The text default color is black, and you need a light background to go with it to make it readable. Here are some readable possibilities:

Black on white (default)

Black on light blue, light turquoise, light green, or cream

Browser-Safe Colors

Always use browser-safe colors. Not all colors appear the same in all browsers except the browser-safe colors. The browser-safe colors have the following pairs of hex numbers in them:

00, 33, 66, 99, cc, ff

Thus, the color #00ccff is browser-safe. The color #01ccff is not browser-safe. The hex numbers correspond to RGB numbers (see Table 12.1).

Table 12.1 Hex Numbers and RGB Numbers for Browser-Safe Colors

Hex #	RGB #
00	000
33	051
66	102
99	153
cc	204
ff	255

Color Numbers

Browsers use hex numbers. Image editing programs use RGB numbers (and in some cases hex numbers too). RGB stands for red, green, blue. RGB numbers are easier for people to understand. Total dark is 000, and total light is 255. Thus, 000,000,000 is black; 255,255,255 is white; 255,000,000 is red; 000,255,000 is green; and 000,000,255 is blue.

Recommendation

For a useful collection of browser-safe colors that makes good background colors for reading, see Table 12.2. Unless you have experience as a webpage developer, stick with the default black type. Use a light green (#ccffcc), light turquoise (#ccffff), light rose (#ffcccc), cream (#ffffcc), or another light browser-safe background color.

Table 12.2 Light Browser-Safe Colors That Provide a Good Background for Reading with Black Text (colors named by author, not official Netscape or Microsoft names)

Color	Hex #	RGB #
Cream	ffffcc	255,255,204
Tan	cccc99	204,204,153
Flesh	ffcc99	255,204,153
Light Grey	cccccc	204,204,204
Medium Grey	999999	153,153,153
Light Rose	ffcccc	255,204,204
Dark Rose	cc9999	204,153,153
Light Green	ccffcc	204,255,204
Fatigue Green	99cc99	153,204,153
Light Mauve	ffccff	255,204,255
Mauve	cc99cc	204,153,204
Light Purple	ccccff	204,204,255
Purple	9999cc	153,153,204
Light Turquoise	ccffff	204,255,255
Turquoise	99cccc	153,204,204
Light Blue	99ccff	153,204,255

Or, experiment to see what you like, always keeping readability in mind. Naturally, certain colors are more appropriate for some things than others, and maintaining good taste is always important. You don't want to get out of sync with your bidders.

Links

eBay offers you a wonderful opportunity to put links in your portion of your auction webpage. A link markup looks like this:

```
<a href=" [URL] "> [text] </a>
```

What are the possibilities? The possibilities are limitless, but you need to limit them to what's relevant to your auction. The purpose of an ad is not "show and tell." It's to sell the item being auctioned.

eBay Link Policy

Regardless of what this book says, you need to occasionally consult the eBay link policies in the *Sellers Guide* on eBay. eBay used to allow you to link to your website from your auction ad. That's no longer permitted. And the link rules are getting so complicated that you almost need a lawyer to decipher them. eBay evolves, and as it does, so does its policies. The thrust of the link policies is that eBay doesn't want you to link to your ecommerce website if it sells the same merchandise that you sell on eBay at the same or lower prices than you sell on eBay.

Your Website

You can't include a link to your ecommerce website in your auction ad. But can you include your website URL not as a link? It's unclear. eBay seems to consider a URL as a "static link," whatever that is? Thus publishing the URL of your ecommerce website is apparently not permitted. Perhaps it will become more clear in the future. If permitted, you should include the URL of your website in every ad. If you have an ecommerce website, it's your chance to market your other merchandise. A person may not bid on your item being auctioned but nonetheless may buy something at your website. If you do not have a commerce website where you sell merchandise, then this idea is not relevant.

eBay Store

If you have an eBay store, link to it in your auction ad. How do you get the URL? Go to your eBay store and look in the URL window near the top of your browser. Highlight and copy the URL displayed there. Paste it into your auction ad in a link markup.

About Me

If you're more than an occasional seller, link to your *About Me* page on eBay. Your *About Me* page needs to present full information about you and your eBay business. It will enhance your credibility as a seller. And eBay permits you to put a link to your ecommerce website from your *About Me* page.

Manufacturer's Website

If you do not have (or do not want to type) the manufacturer's information on the product being auctioned, you might find it on the manufacturer's website. If so, you can create a link from your ad to the place in the manufacturer's website where the information and specifications are posted. This relieves you of a lot of work in processing information for many products. But, in any event, you still need to put a short paragraph about the product in your ad.

Review Website

If a Web magazine or other entity has favorably reviewed the product being sold, put in a link to the review. Don't copy the review and include it in your ad. That's a copyright infringement and may make your ad too long for casual reading. A link gets people who want to learn more directly to the review, and you don't have to get permission to publish the review.

Email

You might find it appropriate to provide an email link in your auction ad. This is a link that automatically pops up a potential bidder's email client with your email address already entered on the *To:* line. Although this provides a convenience to your potential bidders who want to contact you, it also has a tendency to clutter your auction ad with too many links. Experienced bidders know they can find your email address at the top of the auction in the eBay portion of the auction webpage.

To add an email link, use the code that follows:

```
<a href="mailto:emailaddress">text</a>
```

Here's how I like to do it:

```
<a
href="mailto:jt@sinclair.com">jt@sinclair.
com</a>
```

This not only pops up an email client but also displays the email address (text) as a link.

Auction List

You can put in a link to a list of your current auctions on eBay (see Chapter 18). Again, this is a convenience to potential bidders, particularly if the other items you auction on eBay are similar to the item featured in your auction ad. However, experienced bidders know that they can find this link at the top of the auction in the eBay portion of the auction webpage. To put it in your auction ad may add unnecessary and unattractive clutter.

This is not a rigid rule, however, and you may want to experiment with cross-linking to your other auctions. Rather than putting in a link to your list of eBay auctions, try putting in links to your specific eBay auctions that are somehow relevant to the item being promoted by your auction ad.

Media

You can link to Web media too. This is a mixed blessing, as is explained in the media subsections that follow. Media links use different markups too.

Spanning the Web

It's one thing to go to another website via a link. That's easy to understand and easy to do with the link markup mentioned above. In addition, you can also bring media, such as images and sound clips, into your ad (webpage). Such media doesn't have to be the same place as your ad at eBay. It can be anywhere on the Internet. Media is only a URL away. Thus, you can span the Web to retrieve your media. You can retrieve any media for which you have a URL, although the unauthorized use of someone else's media is a copyright infringement.

Photographs

Photographs sell merchandise. Always use them. They will increase the number of buyers bidding on your item and are thereby likely to increase the high bid amount. You take the photograph. Then you digitize it into a GIF or JPEG format file. Finally, you make the file available at a place on the Web (a URL). You can retrieve it (pull it into your auction ad) with the image markup:

```
<img src=" [URL] ">
```

The *src* is the *URL* of the image file. See Chapter 11 for a detailed overview of using photographs in your eBay auction ad.

Use your business logo if you have one. It needs to be a digital image just like a digital photograph. It will add credibility to your ad. Use the logos of manufacturers, if you dare. They are trademarks, and you may be liable for violating owners' trademark rights, although I suppose that you can get away with this most of the time. Many sellers seem to do so.

Other Media

You can use other media in a webpage too. How about audio, digital video, Flash, animated GIFs, or clip art? These are seldom justified, although your ad can incorporate them just like digital photographs. (Again, the eBay link policies don't seem to cover this type of media. Better check the latest version of the policies before you use such media.)

Dancing digital doodads can be very distracting. They diminish the impact of the text information that sells the item being auctioned. They brand you as a Web amateur. Don't use them unless they directly relate to what you sell and unless they add to the information on the product.

Consider the Bidders

Remember, unless you are running multiple auctions, you may have a tendency to fancy up your one auction page. This can prove disastrous. What you think is *cool* and attractive may be a reading impediment to potential bidders. Serious bidders survey the offerings before they bid. Often it's long, hard work. The faster and easier a potential bidder can glean the information from your auction ad, the happier he or she is and the more credibility you have as the seller. Potential bidders often read through dozens and dozens of auction offerings before they make a decision to bid. Before they make the decision, they invariably return to a few of the auction offerings to narrow the field. They make their decisions to bid based on adequate information, price, and the urgency of their need. They don't base their decisions on the coolness of your ad.

However, don't let me spoil your afternoon. If you want to run a cool auction ad because you're a would-be website developer without a website, lavish your attention on your ad. It's great fun. But in your quest to make your ad cool, don't forget to make it readable too.

Using an eBay Ad Template

If you have done some Web development, you will have no trouble creating your own ad. If not, and you want to learn, buy a basic book on HTML (see also the HTML tutorial in Appendix IV). You can learn to do your own ads quickly and easily. Otherwise, use ad templates.

What Is an Ad Template?

An eBay auction webpage is an ordinary webpage constructed with HTML. A webpage is an ASCII document, a plain text document. You mark up the plain text with simple markups that tell the browser how to display the text, incorporate media, and make links (hyperlinks). It's a simple, straightforward system.

An ad template is an HTML document, a template webpage. All the markups already exist. You just put in the text, and your ad is done. You're ready to go.

Using a Template

Using a template is easy. You just fill in the blanks. The template shows the blanks with the comment markup:

```
<!-- [instructions] -->
```

This markup provides instructions to you and has no other purpose. It does not show up in the webpage. By looking for this markup in the template, you will find the places where you need to enter text or URLs.

Sample Template

I created the following template for eBay auctions. Note that it has a comment line before and after every input.

```
<table bgcolor="#99cccc"
width="100%"><tr><td>
```

```
<br>
<table bgcolor="#ccffff" width="520"
align="center"><tr><td>

<table width="400" align="center"><tr><td>

<br> <br>

<!-- add your short description of the item
BELOW this line to replace the xxx BELOW --
>

<center><h3>xxx</h3></center>

<!-- add your short description of the item
ABOVE this line to replace the xxx ABOVE --
>

<br>

<!-- add your text for your ad BELOW this
line to replace the xxx BELOW -->

xxx

<!-- add your text for your ad ABOVE this
line to replace the xxx ABOVE -->

<br>

<!-- add your shipping charge to replace
the xxx in the paragraph BELOW this line --
>

<p>High Bidder pays $xxx.00 shipping and
handling delivered anywhere in 48 states.
Higher outside the lower 48 states.</p>

<!-- add your shipping charge to replace
the xxx in the paragraph ABOVE this line --
>

<!-- add your boilerplate text BELOW this
line to replace the xxx BELOW -->

<p><b>Terms: </b>xxx</p>
```

```
<!-- add your boilerplate text ABOVE this
line to replace the xxx ABOVE -->

<br> <br>

</td></tr></table>

<br>

<table bgcolor="#ccffff" cellpadding="20"
align="center" border="0"><tr><td
align="center" valign="middle">

<!-- Put the URL of the photograph to
replace the xxx BELOW this line-->

<img src="xxx" border=0>

<!-- Put the URL of the photograph to
replace the xxx ABOVE this line-->

</td></tr></table>

<br>

</td></tr></table>
```

The first *xxx* to replace is for the short description of your item for auction. The second *xxx* to replace is for the text of your ad. The third *xxx* to replace is the shipping and handling charges. The fourth *xxx* to replace is the boilerplate. What is boilerplate? It's what you want to appear in every ad regardless of what you're auctioning. And the last *xxx* to replace is the URL of the digital photograph of the auctioned item.

You create your text in your word processor. Then you copy and paste it into the template. Save the template itself as a new file (e.g., *ad1.html*). Next test it; look at it with your browser. If it's OK, you're ready to go to the next step. If not, go back and adjust it.

When you're ready, go to eBay. Enter the ad into the proper input that's part of setting up an auction (see Chapter 6). You simply open *ad1.html* and copy and paste the contents into the eBay input. It will appear on eBay just as it did in your browser.

Item for Auction

The first thing in the ad is a short description of the item for auction. This should match the one-line title of the auction, but it need not be as short. However, don't make it too long either.

```
ActionCatcher camcorder XMT-5001, new, all
automatic features, perfect for novices and
intermediate users
```

This will appear in bold as a heading.

Body of Text

The body of the text is your opportunity to act as a salesperson. Give complete information. Anticipate questions, and provide the information that will answer the questions before they are asked.

```
xxxxxxxxxxxxxxxxxxxxxxxxxxxxxxxxxxxxxxxxxx
xxxxxxxxxxxxxxxxxxxxxxxxxxxxxxxxxxxxxxxxxx
xxxxxxxxxxxxxxxxxxxxxxxxxxxxxxxxxxxxxxxxxx
xxxxxxxxxxxxxxxxxxxxxxxxxxxxxxx

xxxxxxxxxxxxxxxxxxxxxxxxxxxxxxxxxxxxxxxxxx
xxxxxxxxxxxxxxxxxxxxxxxxxxxxxxxxxxxxxxxxxx
xxxxxxxxxxxxxxxxxxxxxxxxxxxxxxxxxxxxxxxxxx
xxxxxxxxxxxxxxxxxxxxxxxxxxxxxxxxxxxxxxxxxx
xxxxxx

xxxxxxxxxxxxxxxxxxxxxxxxxxxxxxxxxxxxxxxxxx
xxxxxxxxxxxxxxxxxxxxxxxxxxxxxxxxxxxxxxxxxx
xxxxxxxxxxxxxxxxxxxxxxxxxxxxxxxxxxxxxxxxxx
xxxxxxxxxxxxxxxxxxxxxx
```

Boilerplate

The boilerplate is the administrative information you put in each ad. It covers procedures and policies.

> We accept VISA, MC, money orders, checks,
> and PayPal. Michigan residents add 8.25%
> sales tax or send a copy of valid resale
> certificate. Customers from outside the
> United States are welcome. We ship anywhere
> in the world. High bidder must pay within
> 10 days of auction or the transaction is
> canceled. We will post positive feedback on
> all finished transactions if the bidder
> posts feedback. Please check out our other
> auctions too. Bid now please, and thanks
> for your bid! Camcorders for All, Inc.

Photograph Link

This is the URL of your digital photograph. It must be a complete URL.

```
http://www.camcordersforall.com/photos/
cam5001.gif
```

Changing Colors

In the template the general background color is #99cccc, a medium shade of turquoise. The other background color is #ccffff, a light shade of turquoise. These background colors provide a neutral, unobtrusive appearance that does not detract from your information. Yet, they give your presentation a neat and professional look. If you want to change the colors, go through the template, find the numbers, and substitute your own hex numbers (colors). The subsection Color earlier in this chapter shows you how to use hex numbers.

Doing a Little HTML

You will notice that if you paste four paragraphs of text from your word processor into the body of the template, the paragraphs will merge together as one paragraph (browser view). You will have to add the HTML paragraph markups in your text.

```
<p>xxxxxxxxxxxxxxxxxxxxxxxxxxxxxxxxxxxxxxxx
xxxxxxxxxxxxxxxxxxxxxxxxxxxxxxxxxxxxxxxx
xxxxxxxxxxxxxxxxxxxxxxxxxxxxxxxxxxxxxxxx
xxxxxxxxxxxxxxxxxxxxxxxxxxxxxxxxxxx</p>

<p>xxxxxxxxxxxxxxxxxxxxxxxxxxxxxxxxxxxxxxxx
xxxxxxxxxxxxxxxxxxxxxxxxxxxxxxxxxxxxxxxx
xxxxxxxxxxxxxxxxxxxxxxxxxxxxxxxxxxxxxxxx
xxxxxxxxxxxxxxxxxxxxxxxxxxxxxxxxxxxxxxxx
xxxxxxxxx</p>

<p>xxxxxxxxxxxxxxxxxxxxxxxxxxxxxxxxxxxxxxxx
xxxxxxxxxxxxxxxxxxxxxxxxxxxxxxxxxxxxxxxx
xxxxxxxxxxxxxxxxxxxxxxxxxxxxxxxxxxxxxxxx
xxxxxxxxxxxxxxxxxxxxxxxxx</p>
```

This will display three paragraphs instead of one.

Definition

Note that the template starts with the *<table>* markup and ends with the *</table>* markup. The entire ad is inside an HTML table. The table defines the ad. It doesn't look like a table because we're just using the HTML table function for layout purposes, not to create an actual table.

The Ad

Voila! The ad completed using the template looks custom made. Note how the template adjusted the ad to the amount of the text and the size of the photograph (see Figures 12.2 and 12.3). With a template the design, layout, and typesetting are predetermined. You need only create the content that goes into the ad. Using any method of creating an auction ad, you still have to create the content; that is, you always have to write the ad and obtain or take the photograph.

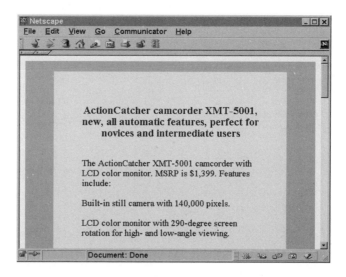

Figure 12.2   Top of eBay ad made with template.

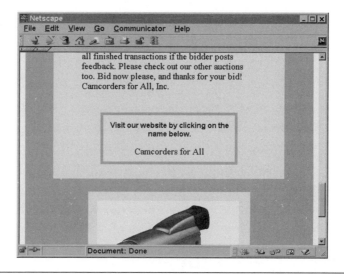

Figure 12.3   Bottom of eBay ad made with template. Note that a link to your website is no longer permitted, but a link to *About Me* is **OK**.

Shortcut

A shortcut for creating your own auction ads is to use a Web authoring program instead of hand coding in HTML. See Chapter 18 for further information.

Alternatives

eBay now gives you a choice of themes (templates) to use for your eBay listing ad. Pick a theme that fits your item, and eBay will automatically generate a nice auction ad for you, free! You can do this when you provide the input for your auction listing on eBay.

Auction management services also provide ad templates (themes) for your auction ads. Your choices are usually greater than what eBay offers, and such templates are easy to use.

At the time I wrote the First Edition, readers needed templates, because templates weren't readily available. Now templates (themes) are available from a number of sources and most are easier to use than mine. Still, reading this chapter will give you a much better idea of how to put together an attractive auction listing ad.

For the templates available on my website, you don't have to worry about HTML. You just replace the *xxx* (via copy and paste) with the appropriate text wherever you see the *xxx* in the webpage. Go to *http://bookcenter.com* for many more of my templates.

You do not necessarily have to use the template in this chapter or ones from other sources. You can design your own; you can find a Web developer to design a template for you; or you can simply alter whatever templates you can find on eBay to suit your own purposes better.

The One-Line Title

Finally, at the end of the chapter we get to the beginning of the auction webpage, the one-line title. This is the one-line heading that eBay uses both as a heading (title) for the auction webpage and for the auction's listing on the page with the list of auctions. This line cannot be more than 45 characters long. The one-line title should:

- Include keywords for searches

- Clearly identify the item

- Be easy to read

- Avoid using punctuation or symbols

- Not include extreme adjectives such as *awesome*

Searches

Some people search through the lists of items for sale on eBay. Most probably use the eBay categories to narrow the search first, then the search engine. Putting an item in two categories, if appropriate, gives you extra marketplace exposure, but it also costs more. People use keywords to search. If you're looking for a camcorder, life is simple. *Camcorder* is the keyword. The search result will be a list of camcorders for auction.

Word Order

The brand name, if it is important, should come first. The product should come second. The model identification should come third. Condition, if new or mint, should come last; if not new or mint, the condition should not be included in the title.

```
ActionCatcher camcorder XMT-5001 new
```

A potential bidder probably searches on *camcorder*. He or she looks for known brands and known models. For an unbranded item, the most compelling characteristic of the product should come first. Use your judgment. Always put the most important feature a potential bidder might look for first.

```
Eighteenth-century vase with miniature
```

A potential bidder probably searches on *vase*. He or she is already in the Antiques section, so there's no need to include the word *antique*. *Eighteenth-century* immediately categorizes the vase, although a more specific description would be better. Mentioning *miniature* indicates the vase has hand-painted art.

The line must be easy to read and specifically identify the item for auction. Review the one-line title for the camcorder:

```
ActionCatcher camcorder XMT-5001 new
```

ActionCatcher is a well-recognized name. (Actually, it's a fictitious name. Imagine that it's a well-known brand.) The fact that the camcorder is new, not used, is important enough to include. People looking for camcorders will find this item easily. Do not jazz up your title. It just makes it more difficult to read. Don't use exclamation marks or all caps to draw attention to it. It will be more difficult to read and more frustrating for a reader (potential bidder). Remember, an average reader looks at two or three lines a second.

Some products are more difficult to write titles for than others. For instance, if you are auctioning a microphone, you have a keyword problem. People will search both on *microphone* and on *mic*, so you have to include both in your title:

```
Shure dynamic microphone mic SM58
```

Each product has its own characteristics and jargon that you must consider. For instance, some people will even use *mike* for microphone.

If the item is new, always include that fact at the end of the line. New items command a premium price. Many people look for new items.

Sermon on the Title

I have always instructed that you should make your titles according to normal typesetting rules. No bold. No all caps. No highlight. No jazzed up characters. Most other eBay authors disagree with me. And eBay statistics show that these typesetting treatments that I have warned against actually get more sales. Don't believe it.

First, eBay charges more for these treatments. They have a vested interest in publishing any statistics that support higher fees. Second, there are simply too many variables to take simple statistics like this seriously. For instance, aggressive sellers who make their living on eBay are more willing to pay extra for these treatments. But they do a lot of other things to increase sales that other sellers do not do. Is it the treatments or the other things they do that increase sales? Third, every eBay category is different. The bold, all caps, and highlights actually work in some situations.

For instance, when people are window shopping—they don't know what they want to buy—the bold, all caps, and hightlights might draw attention to an item. People aren't skimming the list. They read each title to see what might interest them.

When people know what they want, they look for it by skimming the titles. Bold, all caps, and highlights just make skimming more difficult. When people want a camcorder they often know the specifications of what they want, particularly what brand and model. Thus, in the camcorder category they will skim for brand name and model or perhaps a specification choice such as analog or digital. The more readable the title, the easier and faster it is to skim. It's the less readable titles that potential bidders are the least likely to read. Consequently, using bold, all caps, and highlights has just the opposite effect of that intended.

Now, there are no absolute rules for eBay selling, especially when there are 16 million items in 27,000 categories. But I believe that using good typesetting for titles is a more productive (profitable) general rule for sellers than using difficult-to-read typesetting in an ineffective attempt to draw attention to a product.

At the End, the Beginning

The reason this section comes at the end of the chapter instead of the beginning is that it's the last thing you write. After you have thought through and have written your ad, you will usually have a better idea of what the title should say. Think about the keywords you will use. Think about exactly what potential bidders will be looking for. Then write the title.

Many sellers do a good job of writing one-line titles for their auctions. Consequently, good examples are not scarce. Nonetheless, there are plenty of bad examples too, so write with care.

Purpose

The purpose of the title is not to hook people. It's to identify items for which some potential bidders are looking. If I'm not looking for a camcorder to buy, no matter what your title says, it won't interest me. If I am looking for a camcorder, you don't have to hook me to take a look. You just have to identify your item in such a way that I can find it easily (i.e., read it easily) on a list or via a search. Once I take a look at your ad, that's your opportunity to hook me on the particular product you have up for auction.

Summary

Your ad in your eBay auction listing provides you an opportunity to include all the information you need to sell one item effectively. Don't miss this opportunity. Present the information clearly and attractively. Don't overdo it with a lot of webpage frills. Above all, the information must be easily readable on the screen. And don't forget the photograph; photographs help sell merchandise on eBay.

13

Conducting Auctions

Auctioning items one at a time may be fun and profitable, but it's no way to make a living, unless each item has a high price and a large profit. Most people who make a living on eBay make money by running multiple, simultaneous auctions, the more the better. Some retailers are running hundreds of auctions a week. So, for those who want to use eBay more productively, this chapter covers the handling of multiple auctions. For people who will run only one auction at a time, this chapter will also cover general auctioning strategies.

General Auction Techniques

Although the general techniques this chapter covers below appear to pertain primarily to individual auctions, these techniques also apply to multiple auctions. Successful multiple auctions are always a collection of individual auctions that work well.

Timing

You do not enter an auction when it is convenient for you if you want to generate the most bidding action. You enter an auction so that it ends at a time when the most potential bidders will be online to pay attention to it. Consequently, if you think the most potential bidders will be online between 5 PM and 9 PM on Saturday evening, start your auction so that's when it ends.

This is easy to do because the auction will end at the exact time you entered it, either three days, five days, seven days, or ten days later. In other words, if you want a three-day auction to end Saturday at 7:30 PM, enter it at 7:30 PM on Wednesday evening.

Needless to say, there are complications. For instance, 7:30 PM where? There is a three-hour difference between New York and Los Angeles. There is an eight-hour difference between London and Los Angeles. Keep in mind, too, that eBay runs on Pacific Standard Time (PST), that is, the time in San Jose, California, where eBay headquarters is located (see Table 13.1).

As you can see in Table 13.1, eBay uses military time. And why not? It's unambiguous time; that is, it numbers each hour of the day uniquely. Thus, from the table, 19:00 hours (eBay time) is 7:00 PM Pacific time, 10:00 PM Eastern Standard Time (EST), and 3:00 AM Britain time.

Table 13.1   eBay Time and US, Japan, and Britain Time Zones

Japan	Hawaii	eBay	Pacific	Mountain	Central	Eastern	Britain
5:00	10:00	**0:00**	**12:00**	1:00	2:00	3:00	8:00
6:00	11:00	1:00	1:00	2:00	3:00	4:00	9:00
7:00	**12:00**	2:00	2:00	3:00	4:00	5:00	10:00
8:00	1:00	3:00	3:00	4:00	5:00	6:00	11:00
9:00	2:00	4:00	4:00	5:00	6:00	7:00	**12:00**
10:00	3:00	5:00	5:00	6:00	7:00	8:00	1:00
11:00	4:00	6:00	6:00	7:00	8:00	9:00	2:00
12:00	5:00	7:00	7:00	8:00	9:00	10:00	3:00
1:00	6:00	8:00	8:00	9:00	10:00	11:00	4:00
2:00	7:00	9:00	9:00	10:00	11:00	**12:00**	5:00
3:00	8:00	10:00	10:00	11:00	**12:00**	1:00	6:00
4:00	9:00	11:00	11:00	**12:00**	1:00	2:00	7:00
5:00	10:00	**12:00**	12:00	1:00	2:00	3:00	8:00
6:00	11:00	13:00	1:00	2:00	3:00	4:00	9:00
7:00	**12:00**	14:00	2:00	3:00	4:00	5:00	10:00
8:00	1:00	15:00	3:00	4:00	5:00	6:00	11:00
9:00	2:00	16:00	4:00	5:00	6:00	7:00	**12:00**
10:00	3:00	17:00	5:00	6:00	7:00	8:00	1:00
11:00	4:00	18:00	6:00	7:00	8:00	9:00	2:00
12:00	5:00	19:00	7:00	8:00	9:00	10:00	3:00
1:00	6:00	20:00	8:00	9:00	10:00	11:00	4:00
2:00	7:00	21:00	9:00	10:00	11:00	**12:00**	5:00
3:00	8:00	22:00	10:00	11:00	**12:00**	1:00	6:00
4:00	9:00	23:00	11:00	**12:00**	1:00	2:00	7:00

Greenwich Mean Time

PST is Greenwich Mean Time (GMT) less eight hours. GMT is a standard reference that you can use to calculate the difference in hours between a place (time zone) and PST. Consequently, if you know that PST is –8 and EST is –5, you know there's a three-hour difference that you need to consider.

Now, what if you are selling cases of Dr. Pepstop's Anti-Insomnia Elixir? The middle of the night might be a good time to have your auction end. Therefore, you have to enter it in the middle of the night.

Or, suppose you want to sell Arizona cacti (souvenir of the Old West) to Europeans. You might want to enter your three-day auction at about 11 AM PST on Wednesday. That puts the ending after dinner Saturday evening in Europe.

To set your computer clock, or your regular watch or clock, go *eBay Official Time* on the eBay Site Map accessed via the *Site Map* link over the navigation bar.

System Maintenance

The eBay website system has evolved to the point where it is up and running 24-7. After all, it's international now, and going down for maintenance one night a week affects countries during the day on the other side of the world. Nonetheless, you may find some night that eBay is down for maintenance. This is not a time to enter auctions. Such maintenance would be announced. If you have trouble posting new auctions during the night on eBay, check the announcements. Go *Community, News, System Announcements*.

Best Times

Most eBay sellers will tell you that evenings and the weekends, particularly the weekends when people are home from work, are the best times to have an auction come to a close. Are there any good times of the month? Most offline retailers will tell you that sales are good around paycheck times. However, on eBay that phenomenon may not hold up. After all, someone can be the winning bidder on eBay and not have to buy a money order or write a check for several days after the end of the auction. Therefore, several days before payday (first and fifteenth) might work well in theory. And several days after payday may be prime selling time too.

Best Time of Year

What about time of year? Avoid holidays? Too many people traveling, right? But what about all those people who aren't traveling and who stay home looking for something to do? I remember, while on vacation, rushing to use someone's PC to make my final bid on an item. This leads me to think that holidays might be OK for eBay auction action.

But tax time in April is always a tough time for most offline retailers. It's probably not a good time to auction your item on eBay either. The Christmas season, of course, is prime time to sell merchandise, especially an item that makes a good gift (just about anything). For the mail-order catalogs, the Christmas season starts in September or October. The closer to Christmas, the more success you'll likely have on eBay.

The Right Time

In truth, the right time depends on the item and the circumstances. A dozen authors can voice a dozen different opinions and you might even be able to get general statistics from eBay, but in the end each item has its own set of potential bidders that may or may not follow the normal bidding patterns in regard to timing.

Who's There?

In reality, there is no one there in the final minutes of many auctions no matter when the auctions end. People make their bids earlier and forget about it. There is no last-minute frenzy. In such cases, the time the auction ends is irrelevant. All the theory, speculation, and observations of authors and other cognoscenti are for naught. There are definitely some auctions, however, that do have a lot of action in the last minutes.

Statistics

eBay Magazine, now defunct, published useful sales statistics on eBay auctions. There is no other reliable source that I know of other than eBay itself which publishes general statistics at its annual conference in June. However, for a monthly fee you can access statistics kept by Andale, an auction management service. Such statistics are specific to individual products and can be very useful. Try the Andale Research (see Chapter 17).

Convenience

The bottom line is that your best bet for timing may be an evening on the weekend with a seven-day auction. But that's a busy, and sometimes frustrating, time for everyone because eBay is so active. It may bring you the most bids, but the additional bids may produce negligible results on items that are not "hot." For many items, catering to your own convenience rather than to the perceived convenience of the potential bidders may bring a final bid almost as high. And if your convenience means more to you than the highest possible bid, enter your auction when it's convenient for you.

Multiple Auctions

Some people have run multiple auctions (same item) instead of a Dutch auction. That's not a bad idea. It gets bidders fired up. If they don't win the first auction, they still have more chances left. Where I've seen it done, however, it was obvious that the seller conveniently entered the auctions one after another within a short time. Consequently, the auctions end very close together, usually within two minutes of each other. That does not allow enough time for losing bidders to regroup for a renewed bidding effort. As a result, the second and third items often have fewer bidders and often go for less than the first item. It is important to give bidders some breathing room. Multiple auctions for the same item should be spaced at least five minutes apart.

How Long?

The answer to How long should an auction be? is another question: What's the purpose? If your primary purpose is advertising, the longest auction (ten-day auction) is for you. You're up the longest time for the least trouble and get the most exposure for the dollar.

What if you want to get the most bidders? The theory goes that the ten-day auction is the best because your auction is up longer and attracts more potential bidders. Hey! Enter your auction at 7:30 PM Wednesday evening and get exposure on two Saturdays. What a deal! This definitely appeals to a certain group of potential bidders, bidders with patience.

Another class of bidders, however, those without patience, will more likely bid on an auction with a shorter deadline. Whether because of circumstances or personal character, they can't wait. A ten-day auction goes well beyond their horizon. That's why *Buy It Now* has become popular.

The nice thing about the ten-day auction is that you rope in the patient bidders for the first seven days and the impatient bidders for the last three days and get the best of both worlds. That's why the ten-day auction makes good sense.

But what about you? You may not want to wait ten days. You need the money right now. Or, you've got to get the stuff out of the garage right now before it drives you nuts. Or, your landlord just gave you a ten-day notice, and you can't take your nine-foot wooden giraffe with you to your next apartment, which has only eight-foot ceilings. There are lots of legitimate reasons to do shorter auctions, but most of them have to do with your wants, needs, or convenience rather than the quest to generate the most bids.

A general rule is that the more popular the item, the shorter the auction. In other words, a popular item (e.g., a recognized brand) will bring plenty of bidders in a short time. An obscure item needs all the time it can get to attract bidders. For instance, suppose you're selling a currently popular portable Sony television in the $150 price range. You will attract many bidders if the offering is reasonable. But, if you're selling an antique wooden soup spoon manufactured in Houghton, Michigan, you may have to wait longer than three days for a significant number of bidders to materialize.

Seller Control

In a real sense, a bidder's situation is out of his or her control. There are other uncontrolled competitive bidders with whom a bidder is sometimes funneled into a short bidding frenzy. In contrast, a seller has complete control over the setup of the auction. eBay's liberal policy of *anything goes* in the auction page provides a seller with a great opportunity to skillfully promote his or her item. As Chapter 12 explains in detail, everything you do properly works to attract more potential bidders (e.g., readable text). Everything you do improperly works to reduce the number of potential bidders (e.g., background colors that make text unreadable). Consequently, it pays to learn something about writing copy, advertising, typesetting, using HTML, and editing digital photographs if you're going to be a regular seller on eBay.

And never forget your reputation, which is also in your control. Would you send a money order for $750 to a seller who had obvious problems getting along with bidders and may even have cheated a few people? Would you send a money order for $750 to a seller who had made all his or her bidders happy?

Pricing

Presumably, your objective is to get the highest possible bid. To do so, you usually have to inspire some competitive bidding. How do you price your auction?

Low Minimum with a Reserve

The thing to keep in mind is that in the end, a bidder will bid only so much for an item. The price you set at the beginning has little effect on this reality. Low prices probably attract rookie eBay bidders, but rookies soon catch on that a low price in the beginning does not necessarily mean a low price at the end of the auction. Once rookie bidders realize their initial misconceptions, they look for signs that a seller is being reasonable.

A reserve, until it is met, is a hidden minimum allowable bid and doesn't tell bidders anything simply because it is hidden. If you use a reserve, bidders don't know whether you're for real or just another unreasonable seller. Many bidders will not bid on an auction with a reserve. Many auctions do not get any bidders. The low minimum adds an aura of unreality that may not be inviting to potential bidders. It's perhaps better to send a strong signal that you're for real. See High Minimum Bid (next section).

When does it make sense to use a low minimum bid and a reserve? When you want to test the market. You're not sure of the probable high bid, and you want the market (the bidders) to decide for you. If you set a high reserve, you won't sell the item and won't learn anything. But if you set a low reserve and get bids over the reserve, you may get a strong indication of the market value. You can use that knowledge in your next auction.

High Minimum Bid Without a Reserve

If you want to maximize the high bid, do your homework. Research what identical or similar items have sold for in past auctions. Chances are you're not going to get a bid that's higher. So, set your auction with a minimum bid (no reserve) that attracts potential bidders. It must be high enough to live with should there be an abnormally low number of bidders and an abnormally low winning bid. It should be low enough to lure potential bidders to make a bid. It sends a message that you're serious about selling the item.

Being realistic about selling something is tough. You buy an item for 20 percent off list, use it once and decide it's not for you (although it's a popular item), and put it up for auction on eBay at 30 percent off list. You're an unreasonable seller because many people can buy the item for 35 percent off list at a discount store. To sell it on eBay new will probably require a price of 45 percent off list, but it's not new (maybe *like new*).

People selling items at retail on eBay are realistic about their prices. They have to be, or they couldn't stay in business. You compete with them. Thus, unrealistic pricing just wastes your time.

Research the market first. If you're not happy with the potential high bid, sell your item some other way. Or don't sell it.

Plenty of Stuff Not for Sale

I have plenty of small expensive high-quality stuff in the garage that I won't sell. It seems more rational to keep it, with the thought that I might need it again someday, than to sell it for the low price I know it will bring on eBay or anywhere else. However, one has more incentive to get rid of the large expensive stuff that takes up a lot of space.

Your main goal is to convey the message to people that you're a reasonable seller. They can buy from you at a market price and deal with a reasonable person to complete the transaction. Everyone is looking for a steal. Everyone finds one occasionally. But most of the time people pay the market price for merchandise, and that's something they're willing to do. You can usually find the eBay market price in your research.

Your auction setup, your advertising, your reputation, and the services you offer bidders all work to convey a message to potential bidders. That message should spell *reasonable*. The high minimum bid that's still lower than the market price is a good way to attract bidders because it seems reasonable.

The Market

Keep in mind that you don't decide price. The market does. For eBay, the market is eBay auctions; that is, eBay auctions for identical or similar items determine the market value of an item. It really doesn't matter what the price of an item *should* be. It doesn't matter what I think it should be according to my magic formulas expressed in this book. It really doesn't matter what you think the price should be. And it really doesn't matter what the price would be in a St. Louis flea market. The only thing that matters is what the market value is on eBay. Knowing and using accurate market values is the best selling technique you can use.

Research

Thus, the most important procedure you can use as a selling strategy is research. Research the market value of the item you want to sell. Use past eBay auctions to do an appraisal. Use offline data. Use list price as a reference for items that aren't very old. Use whatever reliable information you can find. At *http://www.worthguide.com* you can find auction data on some popular items. Using an accurate market price is all-important.

To use the eBay archives, go to a category. Narrow the search for an item by placing a word(s) in the search function. On the lefthand side a link *Completed Items* will appear. Click on the link to access the archives of completed auctions. This is an excellent means of doing your value research.

As mentioned before, Andale (see Chapter 17) has an excellent research system at a reasonable price that enables you to do very sophisticated price researching.

Anomalies

Despite the fact that eBay has a high volume of both auctions and bidders and is a rational market, there will always be eBay market anomalies. How do you explain commonly available items selling auction after auction for 10 percent more than people would have to pay for them in a discount store? How do you explain a first-rate branded item selling new for as little as 70 percent off list price (30% of list price)? These anomalies happen by chance or due to some undiscernible force in the marketplace. Anomalies create the risk that no matter how careful your research, you won't get the high bid for your item that you aim for. Or, perhaps, you will get more for your item than anticipated.

Regional

I see so many auctions where the seller has put something cute for the Location entry in the auction listing. Don't short change yourself, be serious. Disclose where you're located. Many bidders search the auctions for just their locale to save shipping money or shipping time or to avoid sales tax. If your Location entry is a non-sequitur, they'll bypass your listing.

Case Study

As it turns out, while I was writing this Third Edition, I needed to sell my professional 35 mm film camera on eBay. So, I decided to make a case study out of the project.

An Olympus OM-4 Ti and four professional OM lenses were to be auctioned. My research on eBay (reviewing the Completed Items archive) indicated that these were worth about $1,350 on eBay if each item were auctioned separately. (Unfortunately, I couldn't get direct comparables on the camera body and one of the lenses, so I used similar models. That turned out to be a considerable mistake.) Selling the items separately is more work than selling all in one package, and I anticipated that a package would sell for less. Since I wasn't looking for extra work, I decided to sell the camera and lenses as a package with a reserve of $985 hoping that bidders would get close to the aggregate $1,350 value for the components.

I took many photographs and selected four photographs of the camera body and three photographs of each lens for a total of 16 photographs to include in the auction ad. This may seem like a lot, but this is a big-ticket auction that requires generous photographs to maximize the sale price. My equipment was in "like new" condition, and the photographs demonstrated that fact. I even took care to enhance the photographs with image editing software to sharpen them a bit.

Next I wrote my auction ad text taking some care to make it useful to potential bidders. I'm not a copywriter (an advertising specialty) and cannot easily write compelling catalog text. But I can and did provide complete and accurate information on the merchandise to be sold. I also put in a link to an archive on the Olympus website (the camera is no longer manufactured) where bidders could get detailed information and specifications.

Buyers want to know why you are selling. This is a great chance for sellers to dream up any story that might help sell the item, and buyers know it. Nonetheless, buyers still want an explanation.

In my case, the real explanation was that I seldom used this camera. Although an excellent professional camera, it was too cumbersome to get out and use. I had discovered that digital point-and-shoot cameras are not only more convenient to use but that in my hands they take better photographs. I had become very enthusiastic about digital photography. The explanation in my auction ad, however, did not convey this enthusiasm. It stated simply that:

"Am selling because I use a point-and-shoot camera and never seem to have the extra time to get out this camera with all its lenses to use it."

The word "digital" did not appear anywhere in the auction ad.

Now I was ready to post the auction ad on eBay. I wanted to do a ten-day ad because that would catch more potential bidders. But it was Saturday when I contemplated this strategy, and a ten-day ad would finish on a Tuesday, not optimal. I could wait until the next Wednesday to post a ten-day ad to finish on a Saturday, but if I posted immediately, the auction would end on Memorial Day Saturday. Is that a good weekend to end an eBay auction? Many people go somewhere that weekend and aren't at home to bid on eBay. It might not be optimal. On the other hand, a long weekend is often a relaxed time for people when they might find the time to do some casual shopping on eBay.

To further complicate my situation, my wife was anticipating a possible business trip to Houston. If that fell into place, the whole family would accompany her, and we would leave shortly after Memorial Day weekend. Naturally, that would interfere with selling the camera and lenses on eBay after Memorial Day, and I anticipated using the money from the auction to buy a new digital camera that I could use in Houston.

This goes to show that the optimal situation for an eBay auction may not fit your schedule. When selling on eBay, sometimes life gets in the way. I opted to run a seven-day auction that ended the Saturday evening (about 5:00 PST) before Memorial Day weekend.

The first day five bidders bid my camera package up to $1,024 where the bidding stayed for most of the week. They were all experienced bidders with many transactions to their credit. Thus, the prospects of getting near the $1,350 goal looked good.

I had two people email me during the week saying that they wanted to buy the camera immediately. One offered to pay "substantially" more than the current bid; the other offered $2,000. I turned them both down explaining that an off-auction sale would violate eBay rules but at the same time encouraged them both to continue bidding. I got the idea that they weren't very knowledgeable bidders and that nothing would come of their interest in the auction.

Saturday morning, I checked, and the bids were up to a surprising $1,425. That was encouraging, and I figured that the bidding might even go a little higher. I missed the finale, however, and didn't know the result until I read the eBay email notification about two hours after the end of the auction. The final bid was $2,185. The buyer paid me via PayPal within two hours.

This was a rather substantial mistake, but I was lucky. I had obviously done a poor appraisal of two of the items for lack of comparables. I should have found direct comparables somewhere else since they weren't available in the eBay archives (Completed Items). Had it been a slow week for Olympus camera buyers, I might have sold the camera set for $1,000, apparently less than half what it was worth.

The moral of this story is that if you're a seller, make your value research (appraisal) precise. Get current comparable sales data somewhere other than eBay if you can't find it on eBay. If you're a buyer, look for dumb sellers like me who haven't done their homework and hope that not many other buyers make the same "find."

Package Value?

Another miscalculation in this case may have been my perception that the camera and lenses separately would sell for more than the package. There may have been some extra value in offering a set of camera equipment rather than individual components. This is a tough judgment call. Sometimes packages are worth more, and sometimes they're not.

Dutch Auctions

Selling in quantity makes sense sometimes, but not all the time. A Dutch auction offers something special.

Special Attraction

For instance, if you have a dozen new outboard motors (list $10,000 each) to sell at a high auction price (40 percent off list— i.e., 60 percent of list price), an eBay Dutch auction is probably not your best bet. But if you want to sell the outboard motors at a rock-bottom price (e.g., 70 percent off list—i.e., 30 percent of list price), a Dutch auction might work well.

A Dutch auction should offer something special to bidders so that it attracts enough bidders to be successful—that is, the auction sells the multiple items. If there is nothing special about the offer, you are better off selling the items in separate auctions over a span of time that enables the eBay market to absorb the offering.

Storefront

Sellers also use Dutch auctions in a special way. They use them as storefronts. What about a Dutch auction that offers 30 Agfa film packs every week at a minimum bid of $10.95 each but always sells only about a dozen? This is not an auction. This is, in essence, a storefront on eBay. The price is always $10.95. The Dutch auction is run every week. It's a store where you stop in to buy an Agfa film pack (ten rolls) whenever you need to take some photographs.

This offers you a real opportunity to sell large quantities at a fixed price. Always offer more items than the eBay market can absorb so that the price never goes up with competitive bidding. The special attraction of your Dutch auction is the low price for which you sell your items, and you don't want the price to go up even temporarily.

With eBay's relatively new fixed price option (*Buy It Now*), the Dutch auction used as a storefront is no longer as important as it once was. In addition, you now have the option of opening an actual store on eBay.

Featured Auctions

For a substantial extra fee, you can have your auction featured. For $99.95 you can have your auction featured on eBay. For $19.95 you can have your auction featured in its category. The featured auction appears in the *Browse* section on eBay or at the top of its category. It also appears in the regular auction listings in bold.

Is it worth it? Probably not for most items. When potential bidders look for something specific, they probably don't look in the featured sections. Impulse items, however, may sell well in the featured sections. Many people visiting the featured sections are just out browsing around looking for something, anything, to buy.

If an item is difficult to search for (difficult to identify with keywords) and it's on a listing with a huge number of auctions, the featured section may be your best shot at selling it. If you are selling to novice eBay users, many of whom do not know how to search effectively, you might have some luck with the featured sections. And if you are selling a popular consumer item, you may sell well in the featured sections too.

Never

As a buyer I never look at the featured section. Why? Because the featured items are selected by their sellers who pay money to get them featured. They are not selected by some objective panel that chooses outstanding offerings to alert bidders. The featured items (top of the listings) are repeated in the general listings (below). If I look at the featured listings, I end up reading them twice. Why bother? I always skip the featured section, and I believe many buyers do likewise. On the other hand, if buyers don't know what they're looking for, they might read the featured section.

But, again, I am in disagreement with other authors and eBay about this. eBay furnishes self-serving statistics indicating that featured items sell better. I am skeptical. I don't think putting your item in the featured section is cost-effective in most cases.

Changing Auctions

You can always change your auction ad (*Description*). The change will appear tacked on the bottom of your auction ad. However, don't make changes that will upset bidders. You may get nasty email. For instance, don't auction a Cadillac Seville and then change it to a Mercury Tracer near the end of the auction.

Check the Buyer

You don't have to sell to anyone you don't want to sell to. If you don't like the buyer, don't sell to him or her. Not selling to someone, though, has its consequences. For instance, suppose you check out the high bidder at your auction, and he has a feedback rating of +2 in eight transactions (i.e., five positive and three negative). You decide you don't want to do business with this guy. You refuse. On one hand, you may be saving yourself a lot of trouble. On the other hand, you may get negative feedback from the jilted high bidder. Sure, you can explain the feedback. But do you want to go through that process?

If you don't want to sell to someone, make sure you tell him or her before the auction is over, not after.

Notify High Bidder and Set Deadline

As the seller, don't ever leave things ambiguous. Notify the high bidder (buyer) what to do and when to do it in complete detail. If the buyer doesn't meet deadlines, send reminders via email. Many people seem to agree, if you don't get any reaction from the buyer after two reminders (the initial email message plus two reminder messages reasonably spaced), consider the auction canceled. Perhaps you can sell to the second-highest bidder.

It's even better to announce a payment deadline in your auction ad (i.e., prior to the completion of the auction). That way a buyer has little grounds for claiming that your deadline is unreasonable.

Don't Flood the Market

Need to auction something, but there is a current auction offering an identical item? No reason to flood the market. Wait until the current auction is close to completion and then put your identical item up for auction.

Follow-Up

Chapter 10 on customer service covers follow-up for your auctions, and this chapter will not repeat such information except to say that systematic follow-up is an important part of your auctioning activity. There is a special type of follow-up, however, that can add retail sales.

If you have additional items to sell, you can use the auction follow-up to cross sell; that is, advertise your other items. The more similar the other items are to the item purchased, the more effective such advertising will be.

Database Techniques

You can enter multiple auctions in eBay by hand, but it's tedious and takes a lot of time. The more auctions you create, the more you have to keep track of. Pretty quickly things get out of control.

Multiple Individual Auctions

Although databases and other tools enable you to handle multiple auctions with efficiency and profit, you cannot forget that each

individual auction must stand on its own and use the general techniques for auctions outlined earlier.

There's no reason to suffer such a demanding routine. A desktop database can make your life easier. What should you include in your database? That's a matter of personal style and organization. Whatever
works for you. You need to build your own system based on your particular situation. My book *eBay Business the Smart Way* provides an
outline for constructing your own database system.

As a practical matter, you will want to give serious consideration to
using an auction management service rather than using a database
program to create your own system. Why reinvent the wheel?

Summary

Conduct your auctions intelligently. eBay does not require you to be a
genius to do well. Just knowing how eBay works and observing eBay
practices will give you a good idea of how you can make your auctions
effective.

When your auction frequency reaches a certain level, you're not a
casual seller any longer. You're an eBay retailer. As such, you will
probably find, sooner or later, that a desktop database or better yet an
auction manangemet service is a good way to keep track of your retail
operation. In addition, it enables you to upload multiple auctions at
once on eBay. Chapters 14 and 17 explain this in more detail.

14

Handling Multiple Auctions

To manually enter individual auction listings in the eBay forms is fine for a few auctions. Many sellers, however, run dozens or even hundreds of auctions each weeks. Entering them all in the eBay form would take hours. There must be a quicker way. And indeed there is.

eBay first enabled bulk uploads of auctions via a strange system, essentially using an HTML template. The procedure did not accommodate the direct use of a database. I had to devise, use, and write about a contorted database-mail-merge procedure for using this eBay function. The database component made things much easier.

299

Then came the eBay software, Master Lister, for making the procedure easier. The flaw was that the procedure itself didn't change. eBay simply offered software. Before Master Lister you were on your own. Master Lister at least made things easier but did not enable the use of a database.

In the meanwhile, the auction management services came on the scene and evolved into very useful tools. You no longer had to devise your own procedure or use the hobbled Master Lister. Most auction management services took care of your auctions regardless of the number, and who cares how they did it. (Hint: they did it with databases.)

It wasn't until Turbo Lister was introduced in late 2002 that eBay brought its bulk upload function into the 20th Century. That is, you can use a database with Turbo Lister if you need to. And Turbo Lister is a reasonable database application by itself.

Moving on into the 21st Century, Turbo Lister is too little too late. The leading auction management services offer such comprehensive digital accounting for your high-volume auction business that it's crazy not to use such a service. See Chapter 17. But eBay has also supplemented Turbo Lister with other software services to make it more competitive with the auction management services.

Consequently what was a very long chapter on database use in the last edition of this book is now a short chapter. Thank goodness.

Databases

The advantage of a database is that you can see large groups of information all at once in a table on one screen. Presumably each table row is an item, and you can see 40 or 50 rows at a time. This makes it easy to make data entries quickly and efficiently.

Indeed, TurboLister and its competing software from the auction management services are set up like database entry forms to enable the quick and efficient entry of data. The data in this case is the requisite information for eBay auction listings including auction descriptions (auction ads). Once you have entered the data, Turbo Lister will upload it for you. You don't have to sit at your computer and upload each auction individually. Do we still need to consider using other database software such as Microsoft Access?

The answer is yes and no. If you already use a database system for something else, TurboLister will enable you to integrate such a system into your auction management system with simple and straightforward techniques. If you don't have and don't need another database system for your business, one of the auction management services will provide you what you need.

Some reasons why you might want to use your own database application:

1. You built a custom system a few years ago, and it still works great. Comment: You might check the auction management services to see what you're missing. It just might inspire you to switch.

2. You use a typical sales and inventory control system (with a database core) for your physical store, and you want to integrate that accounting with your auction management. Comment: This is a good strategy. However, you might want to watch the auction management services as they evolve. Someday you might be able to use one of them to manage your offline store as well as your online auctions.

3. You use ecommerce software (with a database core) for your ecommerce website, and you want to integrate that data with your auction management. Comment: This is a good strategy. However, you might want to consider the auction management services. You can use some of them on your website in place of your current ecommerce software thus serving a dual purpose.

4. You use the system I published in the first two editions of this book, and you're afraid if you change anything, you'll be out of control. Comment: That's possible. It was a very contorted system due to eBay requirements but necessary for efficiency at the time. It's outdated now. And it's time to switch to a more comprehensive and easier-to-use auction management service.

If you think you need a database system aside from the database driven applications offered by the auction management services, see my book *eBay Business the Smart Way* for more information.

More likely, instead, you need to consider using an auction management service to manage your eBay auctions and other processes. At the heart of every auction management service is a database application that maintains the data necessary for effective business and financial management. Such services are terrific software.

The word on the street is that auction management services take all the work out of an eBay business leaving you with only the problem of finding some inventory that you can sell profitably. There's a lot of truth in that.

How Many Auctions?

How many auctions can you run before you need an efficient system? That's a tough question to answer. I ran four auctions once without a system, and it drove me nuts. A paper system can carry you through a certain amount of volume, but probably not enough to make a worthwhile profit. Some eBay members think the fees of the auction management services are burdensome. But if you run a paper system instead, you just substitute a lot of your time for a little bit of money.

The following is one way to look at it:

If you run an eBay retail business, you can't do it efficiently without an auction management service.

Even if you run a sideline eBay business part-time, you need an auction management service.

If you're a regular seller but don't sell as much as a part-time business, you're on the borderline. Maybe you need an auction management service, and maybe you don't. It probably comes down to your working style.

If you're an occasional seller, you can get by with a paper system.

You owe it to yourself to at least investigate what the auction management services can do for you. One interesting aspect of such services is that many are available in modules. You can pick a few services out of a variety offered. In other words, you can use and pay for only what you need.

And what about eBay? Doesn't eBay offer free auction management services? It does offer some free software such as Turbo Lister. But it also offers some auction services for a fee putting it in direct competition with other auction management services. See more on these services in Chapter 17.

Turbo Lister

Turbo Lister is a good example of what software can do for you. It acts as a webpage authoring program (like FrontPage and Composer) and in fact seems to be based on FrontPage. It enables you to create your auction listings (auction ads) offline at your leisure in an easy step by step procedure. It manages and schedule your listings. And it sends your listings to eBay. Because it works offline, the program works fast and you can work without delays. See the first four screens for Turbo Lister in Figures 14.1-4.

(text continues on page 306)

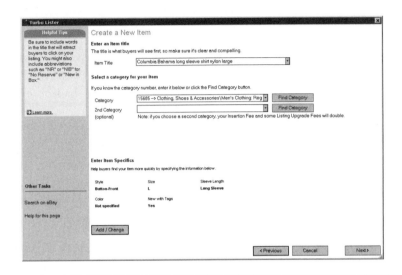

Figure 14.1   Starting screen for eBay Turbo Lister.

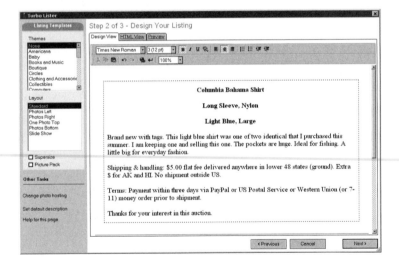

Figure 14.2   Second screen for Turbo Lister.

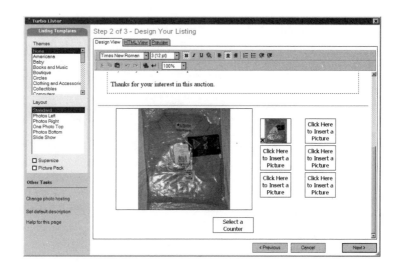

Figure 14.3   Adding a photograph in Turbo Lister.

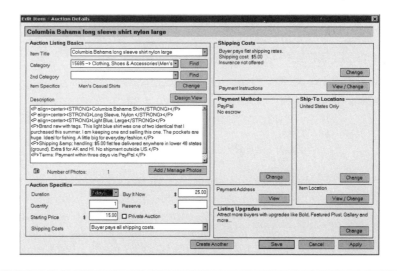

Figure 14.4   Comprehensive screen in Turbo Lister.

Turbo Lister enables you to duplicate listings (handy for similar items) and use other efficiencies. You can rerun and reschedule auctions, which is very useful when you sell a lot of the same inventory again and again. You always have a list of your auctions handy (see Figure 14.5).

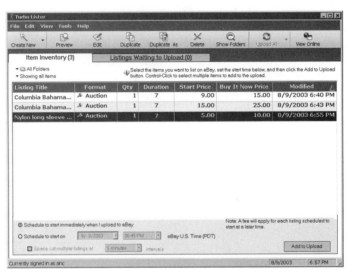

Figure 14.5   Turbo Lister list of auctions.

Turbo Lister also enables you to use eBay's new fashionable auction templates (themes). You have a variety from which to choose. They will give your auctions a professional polish (see Figure 14.6).

A Real Benefit

How is Turbo Lister different than the online process to enter an auction? First, it works faster, particularly faster than a dial-up connection. Second, it's more relaxed. If you're like me, doing data entry work online always seems a little tense, even using broadband. Offline you don't have to worry about making a mistake that's irreversible. There's no pressure to complete anything. You can walk away in the middle of a task, have lunch, and come back and complete the task. It's probably all just a perceptual difference, but nonetheless it seems like a real benefit.

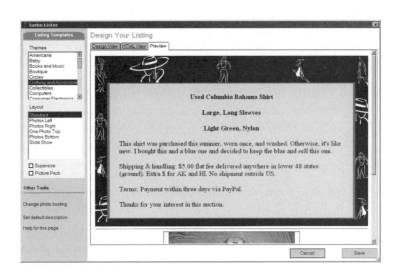

Figure 14.6 An eBay auction listing template (clothing theme).

Database Considerations

Don't overlook the fact that Turbo Lister can import delimited data files. This is a first for eBay and long overdue. You can use almost any program with a database core (e.g., inventory management, order accounting, and the like) that can export a custom data file and thereby integrate it with the eBay listing process via Turbo Lister. This is a real breakthrough for those who are using or want to use sophisticated retail software for their businesses. Again, this makes my old database-mail-merge system obsolete.

Or does it? The fact is that Turbo Lister data entry is still slower than entering data into a multirow, multicolumn database table. Turbo Lister is easier, especially for beginners. But a database solution can be much faster and more efficient for data entry. Consequently, you can applaude Turbo Lister as an efficient tool for its wide scope of capability, but for massive data entry you might want to consider something else. Whatever else you use, Turbo Lister can accommodate it by accepting a delimited data file. Indeed, Turbo Lister can export a delimited data file too.

Auction Management Services

Is Turbo Lister a different process than an auction management service. No. In fact, several of the auction management services that provide all their programming via the Web actually use a desktop program for listing auctions. That is, every other service is online except for the data entry function.

To support data entry, a programmer either has to create a fairly heavy duty but lightweight program that downloads temporarily into your computer or a real heavy weight program that stays in your computer. The compromise that many programmers have found to be practical is a hardy but lightweight listing program that resides on your computer but that can be downloaded and set up automatically in a short time. Thus, if you find yourself a hundred miles from your office without your computer, you can use someone else's computer, download the listing program quickly, and be ready to roll. All you need is your login and password.

You can use Turbo Lister to do that. Turbo Lister is free as are many of the other listing programs offered by the auction management services. Because the listing programs are free, there's no security effort to prevent anyone from stealing them. Try one. It's free.

15

Taking Payment

Taking payment is so important to an eBay seller it deserves a chapter by itself. Why? Because payment is important to buyers. It's important to buyers for three reasons: capability, convenience, and safety. For instance, if a buyer doesn't have a credit card, he or she will not be able to pay if the only means of payment is via credit card. If the only means of payment is by money order and a buyer has to drive ten miles and stand in line to get a money order, the inconvenience will turn many potential bidders into passers (i.e., nonbidders). Of course, any means of payment deemed by a buyer to be unsafe will be likely to be avoided. Safety is a personal perception that varies from buyer to buyer.

Consequently, for sellers to provide adequate customer service, a variety of payment methods must be acceptable. Perhaps you don't have to accept payments by all means possible, but you do need to give buyers some choices.

PayPal has become such an important means of online payment that it has its own chapter, Chapter 16.

Payment Methods

The various payment methods follow. Accept payment as many ways as possible for maximum customer service.

Checks

Checks are the preferred way for Americans to pay. The vote is about 60 percent. Yet, the preferred way to pay online is clearly by credit card. What's going on?

I think the answer is that most buyers and sellers don't know that checks can now be used online as well as over the phone (since 1996). It works as follows:

1. The buyer gives the seller all the information from one of his or her checks via phone or email.

2. The buyer authorizes the seller to write a check for the purchase. The authorization is for a specific amount.

3. The seller inputs the buyer's information into a program such as TurboCheck (*http://www.turbocheck.com*). The seller uses TurboCheck to print the buyer's check using check forms and a computer printer. The seller signs the check on behalf of the buyer and deposits it. (TurboCheck software is inexpensive. The TurboCheck explanations of how online checking works serve

as excellent resources to which you can refer or link your customers. This information helps overcome objections.)

4. The seller waits for the check to clear and then sends merchandise.

The biggest barrier to taking checks via the Web is that buyers have a difficult time understanding how the check-writing procedure works and why it's no more risky than sending a seller a check via snail mail. Therefore, they don't trust the method of payment, particularly if they don't have much reason to trust the seller.

The first two questions that come to mind are:

Seller: "How do I protect myself against a claim of fraud by the buyer?"

Buyer: "How do I protect myself against the seller using the information from my check in a fraudulent way?"

The next two sections of this chapter answer these questions, but it will be a few years before the public embraces the use of checks on the Web. In the meantime, see PayPal in Chapter 16 for another workable means of using your bank account. It appears that PayPal has already preempted check writing via the Internet.

Protection Against the Claim of Fraud by the Buyer

As the seller you can protect yourself against the claim of fraud by the buyer. Simply keep a record of the authorization. The authorization should include the check information plus a statement that the buyer authorizes the seller to write a check for a payment of a certain amount. If you take a check by telephone, you need to make a recording and archive it. If you take a check electronically, you need to archive the electronic text. Either way, should the buyer claim fraud, you can prove otherwise.

Protection Against Fraud by the Seller

As a buyer, every time you write a check, you present the check for a purchase. The seller takes possession. Any seller can use the information on the check to make additional checks and defraud you. Anyone at the drugstore, supermarket, video rental, telephone company, or elsewhere who sees your check has all the information necessary to make additional fraudulent checks. With that in mind, providing check information over the phone or electronically doesn't seem so ominous. Indeed, you have substantial protection against fraudulent checks because the bank will have to credit your account for any fraudulent checks or prove that you provided authorization for them.

What Does an Authorized Check Accomplish?

The most an authorized check accomplishes is reducing the duration of the transaction by the time it takes the check to get from the buyer to the seller via snail mail or FedEx. As the seller you must still wait for the check to clear before you can be sure of sufficient funds to cover it. There are electronic services that will inform you about a buyer's checking account (e.g., whether it has had problems), but they don't provide information about account balances, nor do they guarantee payment.

Try It

If you're a seller, try electronic checks. It could be productive for you. If you want to learn more about it, try the TurboCheck website, which has lots of information. This method has potential, but it will require you to educate buyers regarding how it works.

Miva Merchant Module

Miva Merchant (website ecommerce software) has an add-on module that facilitates accepting checks via TurboCheck. At check-out, it's a choice along with credit cards and other methods. Read more about Miva Merchant and its capabilities in Chapter 21. Note that Merchant also takes add-on modules for eBay operations making it a potential choice for eBay sellers.

Credit Cards

Most online transactions with a seller that accepts credit cards are—guess what?—credit card transactions. This is a very popular means of paying online, although PayPal has become a strong competitor. Thus, if you can obtain a merchant account that enables you to accept credit cards, you can expect to increase your eBay business.

Merchant Accounts

In the past, merchant accounts were difficult to obtain, particularly for mail-order businesses and then for Web commerce. But times have changed. Normal merchant accounts with their relatively low cost (about 2 to 3 percent of a sale) still may be difficult to obtain, but there are many higher-priced easy-to-obtain alternatives available for Web businesses. Research what's available at what price. Establish a track record, and work your way toward eventually getting a normal merchant account, usually from your bank.

What does it take to get a normal merchant account? A good credit rating and a banker who knows you and trusts you. But see PayPal in Chapter 16 for an easy alternative to using merchant accounts.

Money Orders and Cashier's Checks

Money orders and cashier's checks are reasonably safe payment methods. These are pretty secure for sellers to accept. However, they are easy to counterfeit, and it's probably getting easier rather than more difficult to counterfeit them. Fortunately, it's often easier to trace someone who's pulled a counterfeit scam online than it is offline. But that doesn't mean you won't get stuck. Be aware. Be careful. And to be safe, require a specific money order that you can recognize as not being a counterfeit (e.g., a postal money order).

Easy Counterfeit

My bank (huge national bank) issues money orders and cashier's checks that I wouldn't take. They are very plain and are printed on a laser printer. They don't even have a seal or a prominent logo. It looks as if anyone with a computer and a laser printer could easily counterfeit such a money order. However, most money orders are notoriously easy to counterfeit, even ones with complex designs, particularly when ostensibly issued by a nonstandard source (e.g., First International Monetary and Exchange Bank of Escalante). With a misleading bank routing number, a counterfeit money order could take several days (or weeks) to bounce. By then most sellers will have sent the merchandise.

Travelers Checks

Travelers checks are almost identical in concept to money orders and cashier's checks. Be careful of counterfeits (and forgeries). Otherwise there's no reason not to take them. When I return from a long trip, I usually spend my excess travelers checks at the supermarket. But there's no reason I couldn't spend them on eBay too.

Cash on Delivery

Cash on delivery (COD) is a time-honored means of collecting payment for mail-order merchandise (or Web merchandise). The risk to the seller is that the buyer doesn't pay, and the seller gets the merchandise back and gets stuck with high shipping costs too. Consequently, many sellers avoid this means of payment. Nonetheless, for certain markets, it may work well.

International Money Orders

How can you collect payment from abroad? It will take so long for the clearance of foreign checks that international money orders and credit card payments may work best. In addition, your bank may charge a special fee to clear foreign checks. This is a situation you need to research carefully. The potential of a global reach for your business is greater than you think. If you can work out a variety of payment methods to your satisfaction, you may get more business than you ever dreamed. Many retailers ignore this market, leaving it wide open for the more enterprising.

Cash

Never take cash. Taking cash is the best way to get into a knock-down-drag-out fight with a buyer. Cash leaves no record or proof of payment for either party. Cash has a wonderful way of disappearing in transit. It's almost humorous that people resort to using cash when they should know better. Don't be the object of the humor. Just say no.

Sales Tax

Don't forget to collect sales tax for items sold to people in your state (assuming yours is one of the 45 states that has a sales tax). You can find information at *http://www.mtc.gov/txpyrsvs/actualpage.htm* that will give you a start in getting your sales tax license in your state.

Special Payments for the Web

All the means of payment mentioned earlier are traditional. There are also many special means and schemes for making payments via the Web. Most are irrelevant because they are not widely used. One stands out, though, because eBay patrons use it. Indeed, eBay now owns it and has integrated it into the eBay system. It is PayPal, covered in the next chapter.

Escrow

Expensive items should go in escrow. Escrow is not a type of payment. It is a method of ensuring that the merchandise is delivered and payment is made. It's not cheap. But it's safe for the buyer.

Everyone has their tolerance level. Mine is somewhere close to $1,000. Certainly, for anything over $1,000, I would want to set up the transaction in escrow, at least with an unfamiliar seller. Other buyers less affluent than I might have greater tolerances and other buyers more affluent than I may have lesser tolerances, although generally one would expect tolerance to increase with affluence. At some level or another, any buyer with brains is going to want the transaction to go into escrow. As a seller, you need to be ready to agree to requests for escrow transactions at some reasonable level of purchase price.

Summary

The name of the game for eBay sellers is to collect payment via as many means as possible to provide maximum convenience to buyers. This is an important part of customer service. Fortunately, one of the easiest and most popular means of payment, credit cards, is now possible to offer to buyers through a variety of Internet services. And those sellers who do not have credit card merchant accounts can use PayPal instead, probably without losing much business.

16

PayPal

The first edition of this book didn't cover PayPal because PayPal didn't exist when the book was being written. The second edition covered both PayPal, which had grabbed over two million users, and Billpoint which eBay created to compete with PayPal. Billpoint had about one-quarter as many users at that time. Why did eBay buy PayPal? Billpoint was a joint venture between eBay and Wells Fargo Bank, an innovative bank, which would have eventually proven an effective competitor for PayPal. I think the answer is that eBay saw PayPal's

317

potential to become not only a national but international means of exchange for consumer and small business transactions.

Why PayPal and not credit cards? Unfortunately, credit cards are subject to a huge amount of Internet fraud in the Pacific Rim and other places. In Indonesia, it is a rite of passage for college students to pay their tuition with credit card fraud; that is, using credit card numbers scanned from real credit cards or otherwise obtained. In contrast, PayPal has built in verification that minimizes fraud.

PayPal now has 27 million members and offers accounts in 38 countries and exchanges 5 currencies. Let's take a look at how this convenient payment mechanism works.

Verification

Verification is a big deal. PayPal verifies your payment information before it gives you an account. Verification isn't foolproof, but it's an extra step that reduces fraud by a quantum leap.

Credit Cards

If you use a credit card, having the number and the expiration date are enough to use it online. But criminals compile lists of stolen credit card numbers and use them for online fraud. Lately a four-digit CVV2 number printed on the back of a credit card is used for verification. This extra step helps prevent fraud but isn't foolproof. It's new, and criminals will catch on to it quickly. Anyone who has access to your credit card (e.g., waitress) can copy it.

A separate PIN (personal identification number) can verify a credit card user too. But a user has to memorize it (together with a lot of other numbers in life); thus, it is not practical for many users.

Although credit card fraud online or offline is not a huge problem in the US, Europe, and many developed countries, it is a growing problem in some regions of the Far East and elsewhere. Travel bulletins advise travelers not to use their credit cards in Indonesia (and other countries) because their numbers are likely to be stolen (e.g., waitresses) and used fraudulently online, often to purchase merchandise in the US.

The bottom line is that online, credit cards are suspect. Although safe for card holders to use online, credit cards are less safe for sellers to accept online, particularly when the merchandise is to be delivered overseas or to an address different than the billing address for the card.

Computer Vendor's Remorse

A computer vendor in California selling on eBay received an order by email for 12 PCs charged to a credit card in New York but to be shipped to Pakistan. (The transaction was not the result of an eBay auction or a *Buy It Now* sale.) The vendor being no dummy called the card holder to verify that the charge was not fraudulent. A nice conversation with the man on the other end of the phone line indicated that the order was, indeed, legitimate. The vendor shipped the PCs to Pakistan.

A month later the card holder requested a charge-back claiming that he never charged the computers. The vendor called the card holder again and asked what was going on. Yes, the same person at the other end of the phone line denied ever having verified the charge. The vendor reported this to the New York Attorney General who replied that it was the just the vendor's word against the card holder's word and that successful prosecution was unlikely. Therefore, no investigation would be initiated.

The vendor could not report it to eBay because the transaction took place outside the eBay marketplace even though the vendor's business was selling computer equipment exclusively on eBay. Consequently, the vendor took the loss without recourse.

PayPal Verification

When you apply for a PayPal account, your payment information is verified. You can use either a credit card or a bank account to finance your PayPal payments; that is, PayPal charges your credit card or your bank account whenever you pay someone. If you provide information on your credit card, your address is also verified—a significant additional level of verification attractive to sellers.

To make a payment, you must log into PayPal using your password. You send an email (notification) via PayPal to the person or company you want to pay, and PayPal deposits the money in their PayPal account. Thus, both the payer (you) and the payee (the person you pay) must have PayPal accounts. (Any payee involved in a PayPal transaction for the first time can open a PayPal account quickly and easily.)

What's the bottom line for this crazy system? No one can use your PayPal account unless they have your password. It's unlikely a waiter in Indonesia will steal your password regardless of how many times you eat in the restaurant. But the waiter can easily steal your credit card number if you use your credit card to pay for a meal. (Yes, there has been a great revival in the use of travelers checks for those traveling in Indonesia and some other underdeveloped countries.)

So, credit cards have a fatal flaw in the new age of the Internet, and PayPal promises to be the new means of exchange for international consumer and small business commerce.

How It Works

PayPal is the largest Internet payment service after the credit card companies. Once a you get a PayPal account, you can use it just like a credit card to pay for something purchased from any seller that will accept PayPal.

Payments

You make payment by requesting PayPal to transfer funds from your account to the seller's account. PayPal notifies the seller by email that the payment has been made.

PayPal gets the funds you use for payment by debiting your checking account or by charging your credit card. So, to make a payment, you simply log into PayPal at *http://paypal.com*, elect to send a payment, and fill in the webpage form. It's simple to use and has become very popular.

Requests

You can also request that a payment be made to you. PayPal will notify the prospective payer (buyer) that you (the seller, payee) have requested payment. If the payer has a PayPal account, he or she can easily make the payment. If the payer does not have a PayPal account, PayPal instructs him or her how to open an account.

Seller Protection

PayPal has a Seller Protection Program to protect against charge-backs and fraud. It also requires that sellers ship only to confirmed addresses; that is, the payers' addresses that have been verified.

Integration

eBay has integrated PayPal nicely into the eBay auction system. You can:

- Put a PayPal logo in your auction ad indicating that you accept PayPal.
- Invoice your buyer (send a request for payment).
- Use PayPal to pay for shipping with UPS.
- Manage your PayPal records of items sold and of payments made.

eBay and PayPal automatically generate all the necessary documents (primarily email messages) to make all this happen and manage your auctions too. In addition, you can even use PayPal as a sort of a checkout service for your non-eBay transactions.

Accounting

PayPal will even integrate with QuickBooks (accounting software), a handy capability for many.

Not Just for eBay

You can use PayPal to pay anyone. It's not just for use for eBay transactions. You can even use it in other online auctions.

Perhaps most importantly, you can now use it internationally. As mentioned above, PayPal is available in many countries and can exchange money in five currencies. And it will expand by the time you read this book. However, addresses are not yet verified abroad, a serious but presumably temporary shortcoming. The countries currently are:

Anguilla

Argentina

Australia

Austria

Belgium

Brazil

Canada

Chile

China

Costa Rica

Denmark

Dominican Republic

Finland

France

Germany

Greece

Hong Kong

Iceland

India

Ireland

Israel

Italy

Jamaica

Japan

Luxembourg

Mexico

Netherlands

New Zealand

Norway

Portugal

Singapore

South Korea

Spain

Sweden

Switzerland

Taiwan

United Kingdom

This is a good enough selection to get you started in international commerce.

International

You can pay or request payment in whatever currency you desire. The other party can do the same. When the choices of currencies don't match, PayPal will make the exchange at a very low exchange rate. The currently accepted currencies are US Dollars, Canadian Dollars, Euros, Pounds Sterling, and Yen.

What's the bottom line? You can make a payment to anyone in any participating country with a PayPal account easily and instantly, and they can make a payment to you as well. And the payments are safe. This new international system takes all the hassel out of international commerce. Unbelievable!

This alone opens up great new markets and fantastic opportunities for you. Start thinking how you can take advantage of this sudden elimination of international payment bureaucracy.

Cost

A great service, but who pays for it? Buyers get off free. Sellers pay fees similar to credit card merchant account fees. Check the PayPal website for the current fee schedule and figure the fees into your overhead.

Send money or withdraw funds: free.

Receive funds: free for personal accounts and about 3 percent for business (Premier) accounts. Note that personal accounts cannot receive funds generated by a PayPal member's (buyer) credit card.

Special Services

PayPal also offers some special services. The first is a buyer complaint process. You can complain to PayPal about a transaction (about a seller), and PayPal will investigate talking with both the buyer and seller. The second is a money back guarantee program that PayPal offers through certain sellers. Buyers can pay a small fee and get satisfaction insurance. The third is a seller protection program. You have to qualify by doing certain things. It essentially protects you against charge-backs.

How about paying for UPS shipping and printing a shipping label via PayPal? Yes, you can do it. And PayPal will give you a weekly merchant transactions report. PayPal is going wild with new services.

The Bank

As a seller, what happens to your money after someone pays you through PayPal? Well, PayPal holds it in your account. How do you withdraw it? Surprisingly, there are several ways:

1. Direct that the funds be transferred to your bank account.

2. Request a check be sent to you.

3. Shop offline (or online) with a PayPal debit card (MasterCard). PayPal will issue one to you.

4. Get cash out of an ATM (with your PayPal debit card).

5. Shop online with a virtual credit card (MasterCard). This is an innovative arrangement.

6. Pay your bills using PayPal's BillPay.

7. Use PayPal as it was originally designed; that is, make payments online via email, even internationally.

PayPal sure looks like a bank, doesn't it? In fact, you can even deposit money into your PayPal account. PayPal performs the functions of a bank. Internationally, it performs the functions of several banks at once. Remember, you can use PayPal for much more than just your eBay auctions. Hey, your PayPal membership might be a lot more valuable than you thought. And they haven't stopped adding features.

One way to understand PayPal better and to make more effective use of it is to understand it as a bank, albeit a bank with unusual processes. A bank that doesn't charge you $25 for a wire transfer; an email transfer is free.

PayPal Shops

Join PayPal Shops where 27 million PayPal members might stop in. Don't believe it. Nonetheless, if you have an ecommerce website, it can't hurt. To join PayPal Shops you have to sign up for PayPal's money market arrangement (another financial function), which pays a return on any funds in your account. Then your shop and checkout are free. Or, if you have an eBay Store, your PayPal Shop is free. Don't get me wrong. I don't think PayPal Shops are a major retail force on the Internet today, but you never know what tomorrow might bring.

And There's More

Although PayPal remains an easy-to-use service, it is no longer a simple service. It has become a set of multiple financial services and will develop into even more services in the future. Go to the PayPal website soon to study how PayPal works. Then it's worth an occasional visit thereafter to see what's new. Don't neglect keeping up to date on PayPal, or you will miss opportunities for more profit and greater efficiency in managing your financial affairs.

17

Auction Management Services

Wow! Auction management services do it all for you. It doesn't get any better than this. These services take care of your business. eBay takes care of your marketing. You can find someone to do your fulfillment. And all you have to do is find some inventory that you can sell at a profit.

The last two editions of this book took the point of view that most of the software available for eBay auction management was inadequate. In fact, the first two editions offered a database scheme for keeping track of auctions that served multiple purposes. The auction management services were just starting to appear at the time the second edition was written and had not yet reached their potential.

What a difference today! Auction management services—software services delivered via the Web—are now quite robust, and sellers who don't use them will spend much more in lost time than they will save money by not subscribing to them. Even eBay has beefed up its auction management software imitating the excellent services offered by third-parties.

I have no reservations today about recommending that you find an auction management service you like and use it. If you are an occasional seller, you can still keep track with a system on paper. But for routine daily or weekly selling, an auction management service will be your best friend.

Andale

For the purposes of example only, I will illustrate the robust Andale (http://andale.com) auction management service in this chapter. But Andale has plenty of capable competition all of which you need to check out.

The eBay Industry

Growing up around eBay at an accelerating pace is the *eBay Industry*. Thousands of people are now working in one way or another to develop products and services to assist eBay members, primarily sellers, to work faster, easier, and more efficiently. Nowhere is that more evident than in the software business. As you will read in this chapter, there are now not only software programs but also online software services to assist people with their eBay activities. So, this is an appropriate chapter to introduce you to the new eBay Industry. Watch it grow!

What to Do?

Were you to create the perfect auction management program, what would it do? The following are some ideas you might include:

Write Once You should never have to input data into the system a second time.

Inventory Control If you are an eBay retailer, you need to keep track of your inventory.

Product Descriptions Creating attractive eBay auction ads (listing descriptions) should be quick and easy.

Auction Management You need a program to keep track of your auctions.

Customer Communication A special email program that keeps all your eBay email together in one place would make customer communication management more efficient.

Follow-up An automatic follow-up after each auction would save you much time and energy.

Transaction Checkout A transaction checkout just like an ecommerce website would provide convenience for your customers.

Fulfillment A system that accounted for packaging and shipping would save time.

Documentation A system that created all your documentation, most of it automatically when needed, would be helpful.

Accounting Dovetail Transaction accounting software that dovetailed with your general accounting software (e.g., QuickBooks) would save you handling data between programs.

ecommerce Software A system that would coordinate or integrate with your website ecommerce software would be helpful.

Use these ideas, add your own, and judge the numerous auction management services accordingly. Then choose one.

What Is a Service?

A provider delivers its auction management services to you via the Web. That is, you use the software in your browser.

How It Works

It's simple. You go to the auction management service website and log in. Then you can use whatever services you have subscribed to. You use the services through your Web browser. Sure, you have to learn to use each service, but this is simplified by the fact that you always work via the familiar interface of your Web browser.

As long as you remember your login name and password, you can use these services any time from any computer connected to the Internet.

Because you don't necessarily load these services on your computer in the form of resident programs, you don't buy the software. You subscribe to it (i.e., rent it) usually for a reasonable monthly fee.

What Are the Advantages?

We're all used to buying software and using it as much as we like for as long as we like on our computer without further cost. Thus, we need to try and understand the advantages of using software as a service.

1. You never have to update the software. That is done by the provider as soon as the improvement is ready to use. You get the upgrades sooner rather than later.

2. With some services you may not even have to store your data. You can store it on the provider's computer. Presumably the provider does daily backups relieving you of that task and worry.

3. You have unlimited use of the service for a flat monthly fee.

4. The fee per month is low considering the value of the software. When you buy software, sooner or later it becomes obsolete and you have to buy an upgrade. When you subscribe to a software service, it's like paying for software in small installments rather than all at once.

5. You never have to worry about installing the software on your computer or upgrading it.

What it amounts to is carefree use of software at a price that doesn't take a big investment up front.

What Are the Disadvantages?

Software services are not without disadvantages such as:

1. You need broadband to make the most effective and efficient use of a software service. Most services don't work as well with a dial-up Internet connection.

2. The monthly fee is an irritant, particularly when it is more than nominal. Unfortunately, an expensive software service would also be expensive as a standalone program (i.e., one to be loaded on your computer), and you would have to pay the entire cost up front.

What's the Exception?

Even though you use the software service through your browser, sometimes it just makes better sense to have part of the software loaded on your computer and run on your computer. How is this different from normal computer programs? It isn't except for access.

Normal computer programs tend to be fat monsters that you install on your computer and that take a lot of space on your hard disk. Software service programs that you install and use on your computer tend to be lean programs that will download quickly. With your login and password, you can quickly download such software to any computer you use anywhere.

The truth is that many auction management services have a component that resides on your hard disk. It's usually the program that lists auctions. This is where you make the most data entries, and a desktop (your computer) component works more efficiently than a server (provider's computer) component. This is a hybrid approach, which seems to work well.

Andale

Andale is one of the leading third-party providers for eBay members and offers many different programming modules, some free and some by subscription. It's a good package to measure against the ideal auction management service outlined earlier in this chapter and against which to measure other auction management services. Below are some of the services it offers. Others are on the way.

Buying

Accounting systems for buyers didn't prove popular, but other buyer services are used by both buyers and sellers.

Search

The eBay search engine is pretty good. Andale claims theirs is smarter. It's a free service, so you might want to give it a try.

Research

eBay keeps several weeks of completed auctions in its archives for research. Andale claims to keep about six months of completed auctions (known to appraisers as comparables). It's about $3 per month for unlimited use. It provides detailed reports with statistics unavailable elsewhere.

Selling

The business people of eBay are primarily sellers, and Andale provides a broad range of seller's services.

Images

Like many other auction management services, Andale provides an image service to enable you to efficiently manage and store your auction photographs online.

Lister

This is an online service enabling you to create listings using templates (themes) that look professional. It costs a few cents per listing.

Gallery

The Gallery at about $6 per month is a great cross-marketing tool. The Gallery draws from all your auctions to present multiple photographs of items (in a gallery) in all your auction listings and even in email. It is, in effect, a mini catalog included to encourage additional product sales from an auction listing.

Email Manager

With a high volume of sales, it's easy to let the management of routine email communication with your customers get out of control. This new tool will help you.

Feedback

This $3-per-month service automates leaving feedback on your customers. This has the effect of increasing your feedback rating.

Checkout

This is a typical ecommerce checkout that you can provide as a convenience to buyers. It cost only a few cents per sale. You can use this anywhere. It's not just for your eBay customers.

Refunds

When the high bidder doesn't pay, you're entitled to a refund of your auction fees from eBay. This $3-per-month program enables you to take advantage of refunds in an organized manner.

Stores

This is a fixed-price storefront in the Andale mall. I'm somewhat skeptical that this or the PayPal mall can be very successful. They are competing with eBay and are probably not likely to garner a substantial market share. But who knows. Everything is up for grabs. We're still out on the Internet frontier. For about $6 per month you can try it, and it won't bankrupt you.

Information for Decision Making

Andale is also in the information business. Thus, some of its services are information services.

Counters

Andale supplies the free counters offered by eBay. You can put one in your auction ad. A counter indicates the number of visits made to your auction listing.

Sourcing

Need a source of inventory? This free service lists suppliers of merchandise and those looking for merchandise too.

Complete

Complete is a reporting service that gives you reports on your sales and compares you to others selling the same products. It's a great way to know where you stand so you can improve your sales.

Enterprise

Andale now goes beyond providing online services to individuals. It also provides tools and services for your organization.

Lister Pro

This is free offline software similar to eBay's Turbo Lister. You can use it for your whole organization. It has an Excel-like interface and will list and upload your auction listings.

Email Services

This service offers you a substitute for certain personnel you might otherwise have to hire. It is email customer service. It handles your customer service via email for as little as 50 cents per mail. That is, it handles incoming email and answers it.

New Services

Andale is committed, as are other auction management services, to providing a wide range of services for eBay members. Consequently, you can expect announcements of new services from time to time. It's an interesting time, because there is nothing static about what is emerging as the eBay industry.

eBay's Management Software

The eBay software service is the old Blackthorne software that has been around a long time. It competes directly with third-party software and services.

Seller's Assistant

This desktop software comes in two versions, basic and pro at $10 per month and $16 per month respectively. With Seller's Assistant you can make attractive listing ads, automate your email, track sales information, generate invoices, and file feedback. Additionally with Seller's

Assistant Pro you can manage inventory, print shipping labels, do bulk relistings, create sales reports, and build macros for frequent tasks. Go *Site Map*, *Sell*, *Seller's Manager* for more information.

Selling Manager

This is eBay's latest and greatest tool, an online service. You use it in combination with Turbo Lister to create listings, manage listings, store customer information, manage email, manage feedback, print shipping labels and invoices, and create reports. It's about $5 per month. It also comes in a *Pro* version at $16 per month, which does even more including inventory management and bulk processes management. Go *Site Map*, *Sell*, *Selling Manager* for more information.

Other Software

There is no shortage of other software and software services. I'm sure I haven't uncovered everything available, and by the end of 2003 there will be at least an additional 20 percent of new useful products. This is a dynamic market that takes an ongoing awareness just to keep up.

Auction Management Services

These are online services like Andale that work through your Web browser. They include:

Andale, *http://www.andale.com*

AuctionHawk, *http://www.auctionhawk.com*

AuctionHelper, *http://www.auctionhelper.com*

Auction Works, *http://auctionworks.com*

Auctiva, *http://auctiva.com*

ChannelAdvisor, *http://channeladvisor.com*

CollectorOnline, *http://www.collectoronline.com*

DEK Auction Manager, *http://dekauctionmanager.com*

HammerTap Manager, *http://www.hammertap.com*

ManageAuctions, *http://www.manageauctions.com*

Meridian, *http://www.noblespirit.com*

InkFrog, *http://www.inkfrog.com*

Vendio (previously Auction Watch), *http://www.vendio.com*

Zoovy, *http://zoovy.com*

Also consider PayPal covered in Chapter 16. PayPal is a payment service that also provide transaction tracking services for sellers.

Service or Program?

It is getting increasingly difficult to distinguish between programming delivered via the Web and programs that reside on your computer. Most auction management services provided via the Web also provide programs that reside on your desktop computer for part of their services, and some desktop auction management programs even perform certain functions with online assistance from a remote server. The important thing for you is to get the most for your money.

Auction Management Programs

If you prefer a more traditional software approach, you might consider one of these traditional auction management programs. Check out the following:

AuctionMessenger, *http://www.auctionmessenger.net*

AuctionTamer, *http://www.auctiontamer.com*

Auction Wizard 2000, *http://www.auctionwizard2000.com*

Blackmagik utilities (for Mac), *http://blackmagik.com*

Cricketsniper, *http://cricketsniper.com*

EZAd, *http://etusa.com*

EZLister, *http://www.ezlister.net*

Infopia, *http://www.infopia.com*

MyAuctionMate, *http://www.myauctionmate.com*

ShootingStar, *http://www.foodogsoftware.com*

Timber Creek Sold!, *http://www.timbercreeksoftware.com*

SpoonFeeder, *http://spoonfeeder.com*

Sundry programs, *http://www.hammertap.com*

SuperSeller, *http://www.databecker.com*

Veeo, *http://veeo.com*

Shovelware CDs

If you're going to buy eBay software, *buy eBay software.* That is, don't buy a CD with everything else in the world on it. CDs with everything in the world on them are known in the industry as *shovelware.* You can get a shovelware CD on eBay or at a local computer show for $4–$8. That's what shovelware is worth. If you want to buy an eBay program on a CD with shovelware, subtract $4–$8 and you'll know what the eBay program by itself is selling for.

Ironically, you can probably find the software and information contained in most shovelware CDs someplace on the Web for free if you use the search engines briefly.

Anything offered as part of a shovelware package is suspect. If the eBay software seems to get lost in the hyped benefits of the shovelware package, it's probably not worth much.

As you have probably discovered in your reading, I don't favor traditional programs for auction management. Auction management services offer far more. Unfortunately, not everyone has a broadband connection to the Internet. If you don't have a broadband connection, you have a solid reason for using a traditional program rather than an online service. Nonetheless, obtaining a broadband connection should be your goal due to the wider scope of services it will bring.

Auction Analysis Software

Some eBay-related software provides you with analysis capability. It can be quite enlightening to use, particularly if you are a high-volume seller.

AuctionIntelligence, *http://www.certes.net/auctionintelligence*

SeeBay, *http://www.seebay.co.uk*

Some of the auction management services also provide analysis software (e.g., Andale's Complete).

eBay's Standard Software

What is standard eBay software? It's software that's part of the eBay website and that provides extracurricular eBay services. In other words, it's built-in software created by eBay, not by independent software developers.

For instance, the eBay proxy bidding (see Chapter 9) is built into the system and provides a solid service to the current high bidder in an auction. In addition, eBay provides services that enable you to keep track of your activities on eBay. *My eBay* provides you with an automatic record of all your activities on eBay. A search on your name provides you with a record of your current auctions in *Seller Search* or your current bids in *Bidder Search*. Consequently, any independent eBay software you consider buying should offer more than these built-in eBay devices.

Advertising Services

The cross-marketing advertising services were mentioned earlier. Andale offers its Gallery and eBay offers its similar Merchandising Manager. In addition, eBay now offers *Keywords on eBay*, a new banner advertising program for eBay members. This enables you to actually sponsor banner advertising on eBay for products you auction related to keywords. Look for these new banner ads and for information on how they work.

Buyers

And what about buyers? When some of the auction management services were starting out, they offered buyer auction management services. Apparently there wasn't much demand, and it's rare to see such services offered today. Nonetheless, if you buy on a grand scale, you need to be well organized. You will need to devise a system to keep track of your auctions and purchases.

Summary

Well, there's no shortage of help, and more is on the way. The auction management services make running auctions on eBay and the entire process of selling as easy as it can be.

V

Useful Aids to Selling on eBay

18

Using Web Authoring Software

An authoring software program is one that takes media and arranges them into a presentation. You can think of a word processor as a text authoring program. For the purpose of this book, we are interested in Web authoring programs. Because the Web is a multimedia medium, Web authoring programs are multimedia-authoring programs, which means they handle a variety of media.

Multimedia and the Web

The media generally used on the Web are text, color graphics (images), animation, streaming sound, streaming video, MIDI music, and embedded programs (e.g., Java applets). Of the greatest interest for running auctions on eBay are text and color graphics (digital photographs). Anything more may interfere with the efficient functioning and appeal of your auction ads.

Implied in digital multimedia is interactivity. The primary interactive device is the link. The link enables you to have choices. The simplest is stay where I am or click a link and go somewhere else. Links can be important for eBay auctions. With these simple ideas in mind, you can learn to author your own eBay auction ads, and even webpages, using a Web authoring program.

Netscape offers Composer as its Web authoring program, and it comes free with the Netscape browser, also free. Microsoft used to offer FrontPage Express when it competed with Netscape. Now that it monopolizes the Web browser market, it no longer offers FrontPage Express.

FrontPage

FrontPage is Microsoft's website building program that comes with a price. Don't confuse it with FrontPage Express, which was more like a word processor and was free.

Netscape Composer is easy to use and is quite similar to both FrontPage Express and even FrontPage. In fact, they were all designed as Web word processors, albeit word processors for Web text. But remember, the Web is a multimedia medium. These Web authoring programs handle other media competently too.

You will find using these programs about the easiest way you can do Web work without knowing HTML.

I do not encourage you to use more than one of these programs on the same webpages. You're just asking for trouble. Choose one and stick with it. Because they are so much alike, this chapter covers only one, Composer (free). If you can understand Composer, you won't have any trouble using FrontPage Express or FrontPage.

You will also find that using these authoring programs is incompatible with hand coding and editing. If you can code HTML, you can work more efficiently using an HTML editor or authoring program, such as Macromedia's HomeSite, that does not change your HTML. Composer, FrontPage Express, and FrontPage, however, do their own thing, and that makes subsequent HTML editing both tedious and inefficient. Do not use these if you want to do your own HTML coding. You will be disappointed.

Composer

Open Composer and start typing. It doesn't get any easier. It's just like using a word processor (see Figure 18.1). Read my book *WebPages the Smart Way* (AMACOM, 2001) for more extensive coverage of webpage authoring. I hope to get it on the Web in HTML form as a tutorial in 2004. Check at *http://bookcenter.com*.

Want to add some headings? Do it. It's just as easy as using a word processor and virtually identical (see Figure 18.2).

Unless you know something about HTML, however, you may not fully understand how to format your headings and other typographical devices. For instance, <h1> is the largest heading, <h2> the second largest, <h3> the third largest, and <h4> the fourth largest. Few Web developers use <h5> or <h6> because you never quite know what you will get. Just understanding this HTML heading scheme will enable you to use Composer better, even if you never do any HTML coding. When you use Composer with templates too, it helps to know a little HTML.

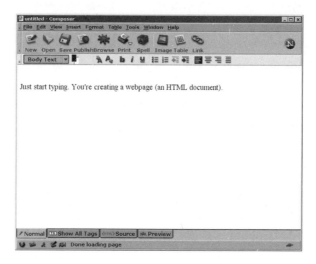

Figure 18.1   Open Composer and start typing.

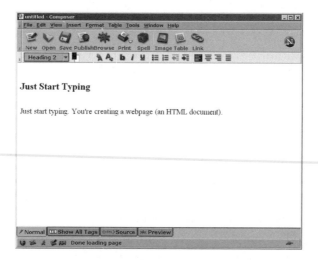

Figure 18.2   Add a heading.

Text

Don't do funny things with text. Keep it simple, readable, and well organized. Unless you have something unique (e.g., a work of art), potential bidders just want to read quickly and move on. If you have what they want at a reasonable price, they will be likely to bid. If you don't, they won't. No amount of jazzing up your eBay auction ad is going to change that. Help potential bidders to quickly get the facts and information that they need from your auction ad.

Typesetting

Typesetting is pretty straightforward for an eBay auction ad. Browsers have Times New Roman or Times (serif fonts) for their standard font; they have Arial or Helvetica for their sanserif font; and they have Courier for their monospaced font. Beyond those, you're kidding yourself; not everyone will see anything else you use because not everyone has the requisite fonts installed on their computers.

Graphics

You can easily place digital photographs in your eBay auction ad. Just place the cursor where you want the photograph to go in the webpage and click on the graphics button (see Figure 18.3).

The image markup is *<img src="[URL]">*. You will need to enter the URL of the photograph as you learned to do in Chapter 11, and it will magically appear. (The photograph must be stored on the Web somewhere.)

Unfortunately, it may not appear on your computer screen unless you are online. Test your eBay ad while online. You can see your webpage text at any time in your browser on your own computer, but the photographs and other media will not show unless you are online (assuming you use absolute URLs).

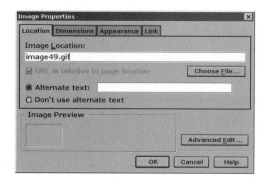

Figure 18.3   Inserting a photograph.

Links

You place a link (correctly called a hyperlink) just as you do a photo-graph. Click on the link button (see Figure 18.4).

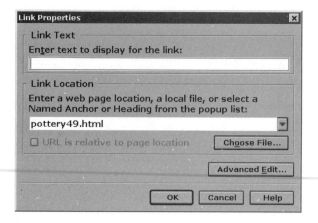

Figure 18.4   Inserting a link.

In this case, however, the link has a beginning markup <*a href="[URL]"*> and an ending markup </*a*>. Whatever is between these markups is the hot spot of the link. When someone clicks on the hot spot, he or she goes to the URL specified in the link markup.

You need to enter the URL for the link. Notice in your Web browser that the text that is in the hot spot of the link is a different color. That's how people find links.

Background Color

Changing the background color can prove attractive, but only if you are careful. Review Chapter 12, which covers browser-safe colors. Any colors you use that are not browser-safe may become slightly different colors in someone else's browser. Colors are not consistent unless they're browser-safe.

Keep in mind that you do not want to set the background color with the *<body>* markup for the entire webpage for your eBay auction ad. It will interfere with eBay's color scheme. That's practically suicidal. Use a table, and set the color background for the table. The Chapter 12 template shows how to limit your color changes to your portion of the entire webpage (i.e. inside the table that defines your auction ad).

You can have tables within tables. With different background colors, tables can provide a polished appearance to a webpage (see Figure 18.5).

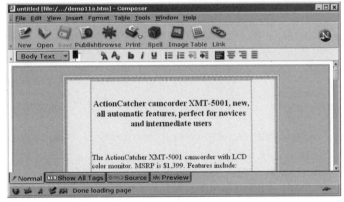

Figure 18.5   Two tables—one inside the other—with different background colors in the template. A third innermost table contains the text.

Creating tables is beyond the scope of this book, but a book on Web authoring or HTML will teach you tables and more.

Browser

You can check your work at any time with your Web browser. Just open the auction ad HTML file in the browser. Before checking your work, *first*, save the HTML file in Composer, and *second*, reload the webpage in your browser. You will see your latest up-to-the-minute work.

Chop It Off

Composer makes webpages. You need only a portion of a webpage. Therefore, you need to chop off the head and foot retaining everything between the body markups <body></body> of the webpage before you can submit it to eBay as the body of your auction ad.

This is your last act of webpage developing. Don't do this before you're ready to submit your work to eBay. Save your webpage file and close Composer. Open Windows Notebook or any other plain text editor. Load your webpage. Highlight the *<body>* markup and everything above it. Then delete it. Next go to the bottom of the webpage and highlight the *</body>* markup and everything below it, and delete it. Now you've got something you can copy and paste into the eBay auction input (*Sell Your Item, Description*) in the Sell section of the eBay website.

Summary

This chapter gives you a small start on webpage development. Webpage authoring programs are easy to use. Use one to make a webpage. Chop off the top and bottom and enter it via copy and paste as you would any description of a product to be auctioned. The result can be a nicely formatted presentation that can be better and *easier to read* than the presentation resulting from the normal entry of text in the *Description* input in the *Sell Your Item* form.webpage

19

Using Image Software

Why have an image software tutorial in an eBay book? Hey! It's fun to
touch up your digital photographs for your eBay auction ads. And you
will find a few other techniques useful too. Image editors range from
Adobe PhotoShop at about $700 to freeware or shareware programs
you can download from the Web. Some are quite easy to use. Some are
incomprehensible. But we will attempt only a few simple things and
leave the more incomprehensible programs to professional photographers and those who want to learn a lot more.

In fact, many image programs make easy-to-use darkrooms. Before you use a image program, however, you first have to digitize your photographs.

Digitizing Photographs

Chapter 12 covered digitizing photographs. If you have questions, review Chapter 12. This chapter will assume that you have the photographs on your hard disk or on a Kodak Picture CD. However, know something about those darn photographs? They're never quite as they should be.

Film Cameras

All we really need are a few simple photographs to use for our eBay auction ads, and we only have the time and money to take a few shots. It's not easy to always do our best photographic work with such time and money restrictions. That's where the image editing program comes in; it's a digital darkroom.

Digital Cameras

Digital cameras are just easier to use than film cameras. You will shoot many more photographs without a care because the photos cost nothing except battery power. You will get better photographs too. And the photographs are already in digital form. You simply transfer them to your computer's hard disk, usually with a USB cable. Then you're ready for the digital darkroom.

The Digital Darkroom

You can do amazing things with image editors. Using color graphics is highly complex technology that's impossible to understand without a lot of study. The top programs have extensive and robust capabilities. Using Adobe PhotoShop proficiently, for instance, entails applying it to specific graphics activities. You can spend months, or even years, learning how to use it with photographs. Then, if you want to use it to create digital watercolor paintings instead of photographs, the learning begins all over again.

In contrast, this chapter will simply cover four things you can do quickly and easily to improve your digital photographs. The program to use is the freeware IrfanView (*http://www.irfanview.com*).

IrfanView

This program was picked because it is a freeware program that you can download from the website mentioned. It's a capable program, but there are commercial programs that offer additional functionality and convenience. If you do a lot of image preparation work, you might consider buying a program like the popular Paint-Shop Pro (*http://www.jasc.com/products/paintshoppro*) for about $100 or for about the same price a copy of Photoshop Elements (http://www.adobe.com), a slightly less robust version of Photoshop, the leading image editor.

Today a computer or a video card (powers your monitor) usually comes bundled with an image editor. If you know you have one, try it on some digital photographs. If you don't know whether you have one, look around your hard disk for an unfamiliar program. You just may find an image editor. Image editors usually have the word *photo*, *picture*, or *paint* somewhere in their name.

And, of course, if you buy a digital camera, it invariably comes bundled with an easy-to-use image editor.

Contrast

When shades of black and gray are similar and when colors are similar, a photograph tends to have a flat, dull look. When you digitally increase the clash of the blacks, grays, and whites, particularly around the edges of objects, and when you digitally increase the clash of the colors, a photograph comes to life. This is contrast. You have to be careful, however, that you don't introduce too much contrast, or the photograph will look unnatural. But increasing the contrast just the right amount in a photograph will often make it look better. For Irfan-View, go *Image, Enhance Colors*.

How do you know what the right amount is? You can see it. As you apply the contrast, you will see the photograph change before your eyes (see Figure 19.1). Not all image programs will do this, but you want to use one that does.

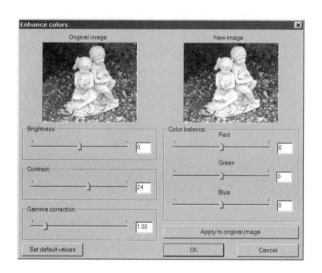

Figure 19.1   Applying contrast in IrfanView.

You can move the Contrast control panel (Figure 19.1) off the program window in actual use, enabling you to see the full photograph. It's hard to find a photograph that doesn't seem to improve with added contrast. You will probably find yourself adding contrast to all your eBay product photographs.

Brightness

Increasing brightness is less straightforward than adding contrast. Sometimes it works, and sometimes it doesn't. If you have a particularly dark photograph, you may want to increase the brightness. However, as you increase the brightness, the colors start to look increasingly bleached out. It's more likely that you will want to decrease the brightness just a little. The colors will often become richer and more saturated. You will notice that the brightness control is on the same panel as the contrast control in Figure 19.1 above.

You must use both of these controls to improve the look of photographs. More times than not, I reduce the brightness a little and boost the contrast to get a substantially improved photograph. Indeed, it's amazing how much you can improve the look of a dull photograph by changing only contrast and brightness.

Gamma

Gamma is the light intensity of the monitor. It is another way to adjust the brightness and works a little differently than the brightness control. It wouldn't be mentioned here except that IrfanView puts it on the panel with brightness and contrast. You can ignore it or play with it to see its effect.

How Do You Do It?

Again, as you adjust the brightness and contrast, the photograph will change before your eyes. Play with the controls (systematically). Have some fun. When you get a look that you like, it's time to save the photograph. (Click on *OK*.) The photograph is now the image that you adjusted it to be.

What if you want to go back to the original? That's OK. You haven't altered the original photograph until you save your work. That brings up an important point. You might want to keep all your original photographs somewhere special on your hard disk. When you decide to adjust one, make a copy first. Adjust the copy and save it. That way you'll always have the original.

Sharpen

Some image editors have a control called *sharpen*. This works a little differently than contrast. Use this instead of using contrast and brightness. It's quicker and easier, and it works well. But if it doesn't work the way you want, fall back on brightness and contrast instead. For IrfanView go *Image*, *Sharpen* and it instantly sharpens your photograph without any effort on your part. Slick!

Cropping

If you have the software to edit digital photographs, you don't have to frame your subject as carefully in your viewfinder when you take photographs. In fact, most inexpensive digital cameras take an image much too large for an eBay ad. Remember, anything larger that 400 × 300 will take too long to download, might be too large for your HTML work, and is much more than you need. That means you can crop a lot and still have a large image left.

Virtually every graphics editor has a cropper. You crop to get the right look for your photograph, not to reduce the size. After you do your cropping, you resize the image to the size you desire.

For IrfanView simply put the cursor on the photograph and hold down the left mouse button to create the cropping rectangle. Then go *Edit*, *Crop Selection*.

Resizing

IrfanView has a resizer wherein you enter the numbers (the dimensions) you want and IrfanView resizes to those dimensions. For Irfan-View, go *Image*, *Resize/Resample* (see Figure 19.2). Remember to preserve the aspect ratio (ratio of the width to the height).

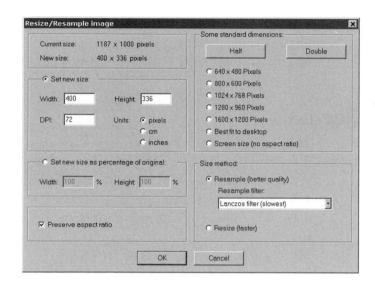

Figure 19.2   Resizing by the numbers.

Suppose your photograph is 1600 x 1200 pixels. You crop it to an image 1320 x 956. You want to get it down to a width of 400 pixels. So, you resize it to 400 x 290.

Normally, you resize your photograph as the last step in your image processing. Do your cropping first. Then resize to the dimensions you desire.

Orientation

When you shoot, you sometimes use the camera in the portrait position. When the image is in digital form, you can rotate it 90 degrees to the proper viewing position. For IrfanView go *Image*, *Rotate Right*.

Out of Focus

The one thing that's almost impossible for image processing to do is correct a photograph that's significantly out of focus. Sharpening can't work miracles. Thus, make sure that you focus properly when you shoot, and you will save yourself some wasted time. Cameras with automatic focusing don't always work perfectly, but overall they do a pretty good job. Use one to increase your efficiency in getting your photography work done.

File Formats

There are many graphics file formats. Whatever you start with, you must eventually convert your photograph to a GIF (.gif) or JPEG (.jpg) format. You can also use PNG (.png) format, but it doesn't work in early Web browsers. Most image editors will convert photographs from one file format to another. Simply save in the file format you want.

GIF

GIF files are compressed as much as 2:1 without loss of quality. However, they are only 8-bit files, that is, 256 colors. You need at least 256 colors to make a photograph look real, so GIFs work OK.

JPEG

JPEG files can be compressed a little or a lot. JPEG compression is "lossy," which means that quality diminishes during the compression process. The greater the compression, the smaller the file and the greater the loss of quality. But JPEGs are 24-bit files, that is, potentially 16 million colors. Consequently, JPEG files can look good, particularly when they're not compressed much. JPEGs work better than GIFs for photographs because they have more colors.

PNG

PNG is a new graphics file format just starting to come into use on the Web. It's an advanced file format that can carry with it extra information regarding the photograph. However, using its advanced capabilities is well beyond the scope of this book.

There's More

Image editors offer a lot more than this chapter covers. Some offer much more than others. You can spend as much time and energy as you want processing photographs. You have two steep learning curves to climb. The first is technical. Color is highly technical as is the digital technology that makes color possible on a computer. The second is artistic. To make good graphics, whether photographs or anything else, you have to have some artistic skills.

Using this technology is great fun. At the same time, our objective is a simple one: just post some good photographs with our eBay auction ads. It's not much fun to get bogged down in digital color technology just to accomplish something seemingly simple. Therefore, a good strategy is to stick with the simple approach of this book.

Summary

The procedure this book recommends for processing your photographs is simple:

1. Take a photograph.

2. Digitize it. (If already in digital form, transfer it to your hard drive.)

3. Adjust it (i.e., brightness, contrast, and perhaps gamma). Or, better yet, sharpen it instead. Step 3 is optional.

4. Crop it.

5. Resize it.

6. Admire it—or redo it. See Figure 19.3.

7. Upload it to your storage place on the Web that you use for your eBay photographs.

8. Put an image markup in your eBay auction ad to pull it in.

This is a simple strategy and an easy one that will accomplish your goal of posting good photographs to get more bids and, therefore, higher final bids on your eBay auction items.

Figure 19.3   The product photograph after sharpening and cropping.

VI

Advanced eBay for Sellers

20

Using eBay for Marketing

And you thought eBay was just for buying and selling. On the contrary, eBay may be your best marketing tool. What better way for you to promote your business than to get your name out in front of people who are motivated to buy what you have to offer.

Compared to What?

If you run an ad in a newspaper, your target market (potential customers) may be 1/10 of 1 percent of the readers. You pay the same advertising rate as another business that has a target market of 5 percent of the readers. What if you could inexpensively appeal to a market where 100 percent of the "readers" were potential customers? That would give you a significant business advantage.

Suppose you sell authentic Japanese prints (reproductions) for an average price of $85 each. If you advertise in the newspaper in your community of 200,000, the ad will be expensive (and small too) and the potential customers few. You will have to entice them with an appealing ad. You'll be looking for those few out of 200,000 who are ready to buy Japanese prints today. Those people will then have to travel to your place of business to purchase the prints.

In contrast, on eBay the people come to you (come to your auction) because they are interested in buying Japanese prints and have found you through eBay's directory system or search engine. It is only a very small percentage of the people using eBay, but a small percentage of millions of people is still larger than a small percentage of 200,000 people. And the cost of the ad is much lower.

The Plan

Now, let's say you have 120 prints in stock. If you put 50 or 100 in separate auctions at eBay, that's a *retail* sales plan that will be relatively expensive in regard to eBay fees (still inexpensive compared to newspaper advertising). If you put only one print up for auction, that can be a *marketing* plan.

How do you turn one auction into a marketing plan? Let's consider the retail plan first. If you put 100 prints on auction, that seems like a huge collection. In fact, art sells according to taste, and 100 choices are not very many, particularly if the prints are high-quality copies from several historical periods or artists (as is true with Japanese prints). Chances are most of the potential customers will choose to pass on the current collection. But they will be likely to return to see what you have to offer next time, and most will buy prints from you sooner or later. Nonetheless, this time most will pass. Therefore, sales may be disappointing.

If you auction one print, you'll probably attract the same people; but the time, trouble, and cost will be less. It's your job to leverage the visits to your one auction into multiple sales. You can do this with ingenuity if you realize that you're conducting a marketing plan instead of a retail sales plan. I'm not going to tell you how to conduct your marketing plan because there are many potential strategies. Invent some. Nonetheless, there are a few obvious ones that are worth mentioning.

Four Steps

First, you want people to see your entire collection, all 120 prints. You need to have an online gallery, a Web storefront. Your task then becomes enticing the potential bidders at your eBay auction to visit your website gallery. Second, you have to make it very easy for your potential bidders to leave eBay and go to your website. Third, you have to make it very easy for potential bidders to navigate your website and to buy something. Fourth, you have to make it easy for potential bidders to get back to the eBay auctions. Let's take these one at a time.

Entire Collection

People must be able to see your entire collection. That's the way to sell art. You need to have a website gallery. Setting up and operating a website is easier and less expensive than operating a real art gallery. It's also perhaps easier than running 120 auctions four times a month on eBay. If you already have a website, I don't have to sell you on this idea. Unfortunately, eBay no longer permits a link from your auction ad to your ecommerce website.

One alternative is to have a link to *About Me* where you can have a link to your ecommerce website. But that extra step is a killer that defeats an effective marketing program. Another alternative is to have an eBay Store instead of an independant website. You can link from your auction ad to your eBay Store directly.

How are you going to entice people to leave your auction and go to your eBay Store? I'll leave that up to you. One simple method is to ask them to.

Quick Link

Once you have talked bidders into going to your eBay Store, you have to make it easy for them. A link in your auction ad in the appropriate place accomplishes this nicely. For an ecommerce website, this is necessary (i.e., link to *About Me* and then to your website). For an eBay Store, you can argue that the link already exists. There's a red tag after your name in the auction listing if you have an eBay store. But that's not enough. Put a link to your eBay Store right in the copy for your auction ad.

Website

Your website needs to be attractive, up to date, and well operated with easy navigation. Chapter 21 covers what a basic ecommerce website looks like. You need to offer all means of payment and make it easy for people to complete a transaction.

With an eBay Store you don't have as much flexibility, but you can still upgrade the look and feel as much as possible. eBay is committed to making eBay Stores better and more attractive in the future as well as to giving sellers more digital control over their stores. So, look for eBay Stores to turn into an attractive shopping Web shopping portal as it grows larger.

Return Link

There should be multiple return links in your eBay Store or website to make it convenient for potential bidders to return to your auction on eBay. You will have to revise these links for each new auction (i.e., each week—each new auction has a different URL). That's extra weekly work. If you do this, you have effectively made eBay auctions part of your eBay Store or your website. If you don't provide return links to eBay, you'll have fewer repeat visitors to your eBay Store or your website in the future. People don't like to be left stranded.

In the Long Term

This is a long-term marketing plan. You want to make the appearance of your auction consistent so that people recognize it. You want to make the link to your *About Me* webpage consistent so that people will learn to feel comfortable leaving eBay to visit your *About Me* webpage and then your website. In the alternative, you want to make the link to your eBay Store consistent so that people come to recognize it. And you want to make the return trip consistent too.

Repeat Auction

You need to run the auction constantly; as soon as one auction is over, another should be in place. Naturally, you should change the Japanese print being auctioned each time to maintain interest in your auctions.

As a practical matter, if you're marketing on eBay, you may find it cost-effective to run multiple auctions in different categories as part of your marketing campaign. Usually, one auction at a time doesn't achieve the market penetration you can achieve by a more ambitious approach.

Serious Auction

Is this a serious auction you're running? From one point of view it's just a token auction to keep your business before the print-buying public as part of a marketing plan. Nevertheless, you have to take the auction itself seriously. A sale at each auction will definitely help your marketing plan. If potential bidders get the idea that it's a phony effort, they will resent it, and your marketing plan will not be as effective. If you do not make a sale at most of your auctions, you may be conveying the impression that you're making a bogus effort. In fact, your price may be too high. Sales are crucial to your marketing plan. Take your auctions seriously.

Other Businesses

Keep in mind that the Japanese print business is just one business. Each business has its own peculiarities. For instance, suppose you sell nine models of electric guitars ranging in price from $200 to $4,500. Rather than offer a different electric guitar at each auction (like the different Japanese print at each auction), you might offer the low-end guitar at each auction at an attractive price as a strategy to attract entry-level customers to your retail sales operation at your eBay Store or your website. Each business will have a different strategy, and even businesses selling the same things will have different strategies. A variety of strategies will work, and some won't. Experiment.

Marketing, Not Retail

The thing to remember is that a marketing effort on eBay is different from a retail sales effort. The objective of a marketing effort is to use eBay auctions as a promotional or advertising vehicle. The sales are not necessarily made in eBay auctions, and in some cases, sales will be made off eBay at an independent website. The objective of a retail sales effort (not a marketing effort) is to sell merchandise on eBay. If you keep these two efforts separate in your mind and pay attention to details, you will be more effective in whichever strategy you choose to pursue. Confused planning regarding marketing and retail sales may yield disappointing results.

Retail and Marketing

Retail sales and a marketing effort on eBay can also be one and the same in some circumstances for some businesses. As long as you understand the difference between a retail sales effort and a marketing effort and decide to combine the two in a creative way, a combined effort might prove very successful for you. For instance, rather than sell 1 Japanese print, you might sell 15 each week on eBay but do it in such a way that it promotes marketing as well as retail sales volume. But a retail sales effort is not automatically a marketing effort, and a marketing effort can be something very different.

eBay User Agreement

When using eBay for marketing, be careful that you don't violate the eBay User Agreement. It requires that you do not sell an item on a website linked to your *About Me* webpage for the same price or a lower price than the reserve price (or minimum bid) for the same item being auctioned on eBay.

eBay seems to like the two-way-street approach. It allows links to your website (subject to the eBay User Agreement) from your *About Me* webpage, but it likes to see links from your website to eBay in return. It seems to me that this is a sound marketing approach for both you and eBay.

Professional Services

Services are perhaps more difficult to sell on eBay than merchandise. Professional services are often intangible or loosely defined, and costs are often difficult for customers to estimate. But even if there is not a substantial opportunity for actually selling professional services on eBay, there is a solid marketing opportunity.

The Package

An attorney could offer divorce services at $120 per hour, real estate services at $145 per hour, estate planning services at $160 per hour, etc. That does not seem particularly appealing.

How about a marketing plan instead? Each week offer one package of well-defined legal services at a specific price. Do it simply as a promotion. Specificity attracts better than ambiguity. The package will attract potential bidders to your auction and then to your website (through *About Me*) if you cleverly enticed them. What are the chances of selling the package? That depends. When it comes to legal services, they are usually performed on a custom basis to accommodate specific problems that clients have. However, the package gives people something specific to consider, and it may eventually attract them to your website where you can provide them with as much information about your legal services and qualifications as they can digest.

But wait. Why not use *About Me* as your promotional website? If you're not trying to sell anything on your website that requires a catalog and if you're just providing information on yourself and your legal skills to entice people to come to you for custom legal services, then *About Me* might work. eBay puts no limit on the amount of information you can present in *About Me*, and you can make a robust website out of one long webpage. Something to think about.

A few people will want the package as presented in your eBay ad. You need to be ready to perform the services specified for the price stated. Indeed, steady sales of the packages will help your marketing program, so an attractive package is important. However, many people who buy the package will eventually find that they really need custom legal services instead. So, the package will draw in new clients who will eventually buy more services. Indeed, even those who do not bid on the package may be drawn to your website (or *About Me*) to see what similar or other legal services you offer. Thus, the package will draw in potential clients.

Institutional Advertising

Normal advertising sells specific products. Institutional advertising sells companies. Because the scope and cost of *services* are often difficult to pin down in advance, specific advertising or promotion is difficult to devise. That's why institutional advertising is common for services. If you can sell someone on the idea of doing business with you or your law firm, you can negotiate the specific legal services and fees after a consultation session. What brings the client to you in the first place is institutional advertising, that is, the firm's name.

Unfortunately, institutional advertising doesn't seem to fit in on eBay where specific goods and services are auctioned. That's where the package of legal services fits in. It seems to be specific; but even after someone buys it, it may turn into something else due to most people's need for custom services. It's a hybrid idea. It's a package that interests people in doing business with you, but it's a package that most likely will turn into something else when the services are actually performed. It seems to me that selling packages of services on eBay is similar to the institutional advertising you need.

Information Products

Many professionals provide information (e.g., advice) as a considerable portion of their normal services. Therein lies an eBay opportunity. Create information products and auction them on eBay. This makes a great marketing program and may even generate some significant extra income. Information products might be books, reports, surveys, audio takes (or CDs), or newsletters. Naturally, they will be specialized, reflecting the specialized expertise of the professionals creating them. People who are likely to be potential clients may buy such information products. And such information products help create knowledgeable clients who are more able to use your valuable advice. If you don't like the packaged services idea, try information products.

This is not a new idea, of course. Consultants (including attorneys) have been doing this for a long time. But it's an idea that might work well for you in the huge new eBay marketplace.

The Professions

Of course, professionals are a funny lot. Some professional organizations have rules about advertising and marketing that inhibit their members from doing the normal things to get business that other businesspeople do all the time. Consequently, if you are a professional, check your code of ethics carefully to determine what kind of a marketing plan you can ethically operate on eBay.

General Services

The general services category is much broader than professional services. Some services are, in fact, more like merchandise than services. For instance, an oil change and lubrication for your car are more like buying a bag of groceries than buying legal services, even though the actual oil and lubrication make up a modest portion of the purchase price. Yet the same service station that sells you the $25 oil and lube service acts like a lawyer when you bring your car in with a funny clunking noise. Sure, you get an estimate, but who knows what the scope of services and the final price will be. The point here is that general services can be anything from a merchandise-like package to a custom service. This makes general services quite appropriate to auction on eBay in packages. You may even be able to auction general services in a retail program. You can certainly auction services as part of a marketing plan.

Services Included

It always seemed to me that manufacturers should give you the copy machine and charge you to service it. As it is, they charge you a modest price for the copy machine and a substantial monthly payment for the service. That's almost the same thing.

Selling copy machines on eBay doesn't look very promising. Too large, too heavy, and who's going to service the copy machine when it goes from the seller in one city to a buyer in another city. But in a local market, a copy machine is easy to deliver and to service. And as eBay grows, the auctions for each local market grow too. Selling copy machines might work on eBay, particularly as your local eBay marketplace grows.

This is an example of a service that's attached to a product. If you want to sell your service, auction the product on eBay. There are probably better examples than the copy machine, but the idea is a powerful one. Because most services are performed locally, as local eBay markets grow, they will provide fabulous new opportunities online for those who provide services attached to a tangible product. And if your service isn't attached to a tangible product, find one to attach it to. Then sell the product on eBay.

Speculative

Perhaps I should have warned you at the beginning of this chapter that all these ideas are speculative. They are unproven on eBay. Yes, some people and companies sell professional services or other services, but the practice is not yet widespread. If you want to sell services, it is a time to experiment. In the meanwhile, take a look at Elance in Chapter 28, which is special auction for certain types of services. Elance has grown, albeit not nearly as fast as eBay itself. So, selling services on eBay is not a pipe dream.

This is the third edition in which I've speculated about selling services on eBay. But I'm not the Long Ranger. Recently I found out that eBay has been trying to figure out how members can sell services effectively on eBay. By the time you read this, there may be some special eBay programming that supports this idea.

You might note that the eBay/Elance relationship goes back a long way. Elance all these years has had a link to its website right from the eBay home page. Had Elance been spectacularly successful, eBay would have bought it. If it had been unsuccessful, eBay would have dumped it. Apparently it has had only modest success, so eBay is left to do research & development (R&D) on selling services via eBay. Someday down the road, you will see the results of that research.

Summary

Theoretically, you can use eBay to support a marketing or advertising plan. So long as you keep the ideas of an eBay retail effort and an eBay marketing effort separate, you can do either successfully. You can even combine them creatively.

eBay provides you with a substantial marketing opportunity. Don't abuse the opportunity. Abide by the eBay policies that put certain restrictions on what you can do to link to your ecommerce website. And those restrictions seem to change often. Integrate your ecommerce website with your eBay auctions using links that run in both directions and through *About Me*.

Better yet, use *About Me* as a robust webpage for advertising. Use an auction to bring attention to your *About Me*.

Marketing is one idea that can make eBay useful for professional and other services. Auction a package of services, an information product, or any product in order to promote your services via eBay. Find out that eBay is an inexpensive marketing medium with a great deal of potential.

21

Building a Website

An ecommerce website can be a profitable operation in conjunction with running multiple auctions on eBay. What is an ecommerce website? Typically, it's a website that sells products. It has a catalog; a shopping basket for customers to accumulate products; a checkout procedure including automated shipping and sales tax calculations, credit card processing, and warehouse shipping notification; and order accounting. Not too long ago, a system as just described was a major Web construction project and was expensive to create and operate. Today such capabilities are offered by dozens of Web commerce software packages for websites, and operating expenses can be quite low. Indeed, almost every host ISP offers free Web ecommerce software to its customers.

eCommerce

So, ecommerce websites are no longer difficult to create or expensive. What does this mean to eBay retailers who run auctions on eBay? It means that auctions on eBay and an ecommerce website can work together to increase business. For instance, Dutch auctions are a good way to sell inventory in quantity on eBay. It's almost like selling inventory out of a catalog. Likewise, the *Buy It Now* feature of eBay enables you to turn eBay into an online fixed-price catalog, in effect. Turbo Lister enables you to upload auctions in bulk quickly and efficiently. And, of course, eBay Stores are ecommerce websites themselves.

If you do conduct a retail operation on eBay, you might ask yourself, How can I get customers from my auction ads to my ecommerce website without violating eBay rules? As you will recall from Chapters 4 and 20, eBay does permit a link to your *About Me* webpage from your auction ad and a link from your *About Me* webpage to your ecommerce website. However, eBay policies state that you cannot sell the same products you are auctioning on eBay at your ecommerce website at a lower price. Otherwise no link is permitted.

It's clear to me that an ecommerce website and eBay are potentially two powerful online retailing tools. Why choose one over the other? Can you use both together to generate the highest possible volume of Web retail sales?

Cool on eCommerce Websites

In the prior two editions of this book, I was hot on ecommerce websites. Today I am not for three reasons.

Link

eBay has taken away the direct link from an auction ad to one's ecommerce website. Indeed, it appears from a current reading of the eBay rules that even publishing your ecommerce website URL in your auction ad (not as a link) is a violation of the rules. Although you can still link to your *About Me* webpage from your auction ad and from there to your ecommerce website, it's not the same. It's too indirect and much less effective.

Marketing

Operating an ecommerce website is the easy part of Web retailing. Getting significant traffic to your website, however, will take at least half your time and resources. Yes, half. With the weakening of the website-eBay link, as discussed above, the idea of an ecommerce website doesn't seem quite as compelling and is likely to be much less profitable.

The great feature of eBay is that the marketing is built in. You can have an eBay retail business without doing much marketing. When you could link your eBay auctions directly to your ecommerce website, you could take advantage of eBay's tremendous marketing power and forego expending time and energy on marketing your ecommerce website. You can't count on that any longer.

eBay Stores

Today you can have a storefront on eBay. Although eBay Stores have an anemic and feeble design, they are functional. However, by the time this book went to press, eBay had announced an intent to enable more flexibility in creating attractive storefront designs. Such flexibilkity may be available by the time you read this. Unlike your independent ecommerce website, eBay Stores have the marketing built in. You don't have to do much marketing to make an eBay Store work. You might have to do a lot of other things to be successful, but eBay does your marketing for you. Since marketing is such a large component of what you have to do to make an ecommerce website profitable, eBay Stores look like a much better place to spend your time and resources to become profitable than an independent website.

Conclusion

If you already have an ecommerce website and it's successful, by all means keep it going. If you operate an ecommerce website and it's not profitable, you need to give consideration to switching to an eBay Store. If you're just starting out to expand your eBay selling, my advice is to forego creating an ecommerce website and go with an eBay Store.

Nonetheless, the remainder of this chapter will treat the ecommerce website as if it were a good idea. Indeed for some, it will be a profitable enterprise. But I'm afraid for many eBay businesses it may prove a waste of time and money.

Links to eBay

You can link from your website to eBay three ways:

1. eBay home page

2. Your list of current auctions

3. A specific current auction

Linking to the eBay home page is a service to your website visitors and helps promote eBay. You have a vested interest in promoting eBay if you are running auctions there regularly. Someplace on your website—most likely your home page—you need to put this general link.

Linking to a list of your current auctions on eBay is not only a service to your website visitors but an arrangement that directly promotes your retail effort on eBay. You may want to use this link together with every item in your catalog that you auction on eBay.

Linking to a specific auction is tough. The longest auction is ten days. That means that if you are linking to current auctions, you need to change your website every few days to keep up. This is a great way to operate, but it's only for the ambitious and diligent. If you have links on your website that don't work (stale links), it reflects negatively on your credibility.

Sure Beats the Alternative

If you do link to your current specific auctions from your ecommerce website, it's almost the same as running auctions on your website. The eBay auctions will be much more effective; you won't have to buy and operate any special expensive website auctioning software; you won't have to run a marketing campaign to get traffic to your auctions; and you won't have any of the headaches of running your own auction marketplace. Indeed, keeping your eBay auctions current on your website (via links) sure beats the alternative of running your own auctions.

URLs

To determine the URLs of the links you want to use, simply find the various webpages on eBay. Then look in the Web address (URL) window of your Web browser (middle near top - see Figure 21.1).

Figure 21.1   URL window in a Netscape Web browser.

Highlight and copy (to the clipboard) the URL in the URL window (use right mouse button). Paste the URL into the appropriate hyperlink markup in the appropriate webpage on your website (use right mouse button).

eBay Buttons

If you want to use official eBay buttons for links instead of using text, eBay provides a way to do so. You can use eBay buttons with your eBay links, if you agree to the eBay Link License Agreement. You will find it on eBay under *Site Map*, *Buying and Selling*, *Promote your listings with link buttons* (see Figure 21.2).

One button is for a general link. The other button is for a link to specific items currently being auctioned. Your general link to the eBay home page will be as follows:

```
<a href="http://www.ebay.com">eBay Home
Page</a>
```

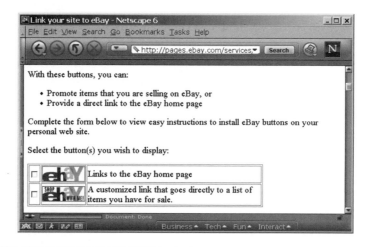

Figure 21.2   Link buttons provided by eBay.

Your link to a specific item being auctioned will be similar to the following:

```
<a href="http://cgi.ebay.com/aw-cgi/
eBayISAPI.dll?ViewItem&item=13682875">Blue
Ridge Cup and Saucer Crabapple Design</a>
```

Again, to get the address, go to the auction and look at the Web address window in your browser. Highlight the URL in the window, and copy and paste.

Institutional Advertising

At your website, you should have a webpage dedicated to your business. For instance, put in a photograph of your retail store, warehouse, or office if you have a physical location. Provide the history of your firm; if you've been in business for 20 years, toot your horn. Show photographs of your employees and yourself. You can do as much as you want to do. This is not an ad in the newspaper that costs $400 per inch.

Incidentally, you can do this in your *About Me* page too. If you're a serious seller on eBay or run a part-time or full-time business on eBay, this is a wonderful opportunity.

Information

Information can promote your business. The Web is an information medium. The amount of information you can put on a website is practically unlimited. Pull these three ideas together and you have a real opportunity to promote your selling effort. For instance, it's not unusual for professionals to give free seminars to attract potential customers. You can easily create a text tutorial on any topic on a website. Thus, a tutorial on dog grooming will tend to bring potential customers to a website that sells canine products.

Once, while I looked for a camcorder to purchase, I ran across an ecommerce website (video retailer) that had a complete tutorial on shooting video with a consumer camcorder. It was quite valuable (and free), and I gave that particular website a more thorough visit than other video retail websites I visited. But, most interesting, I found that particular video retailer by searching (using a search engine) to see what information was available on the Web about shooting video. (Note that I eventually bought the camcorder at an eBay auction.)

A tutorial is a good example of a website attractor. And you are in a unique position to provide attractors for your products. For instance, if you sell watches on your website, a tutorial on how to plant and raise tomatoes is not relevant nor do you have the apparent credibility to create it. However, a tutorial on how to tell a real Rolex from a fake is relevant to what you sell, and people will assume you have the knowledge to create it.

The About Me Home Page

The interesting thing about the Web is that you can have a website made from webpages on different servers; that is, different places on the Web. It's all in the links. Consequently, you can use *About Me* as a home page for your website. From there, various links could take your customers to various webpages. So long as you don't violate eBay restrictions on linking to competing product sales, you apparently have license to do anything you want to do. You could build a website featuring tutorials to promote your business using *About Me* as the home page, in effect.

Information Website

If you create an institutional advertising website and if you feature tutorials on such a website but do not sell products, you can link to such a website from an eBay auction listing under the eBay rules. Why? Because you're not selling anything there that competes with the items you sell on eBay. This might prove a very good reason to create a website to boost your sales. But this is not an ecommerce website.

Catalog

It's not unusual for even small retailers to have hundreds or thousands of different items in inventory. It's probably not realistic to put all of your products up for auction each week, but you can put all of them in a Web commerce catalog like the one that Miva Merchant (*http://www.miva.com*) provides. I know one individual who has 7,000 items in the catalog for his one-person Web retail business using Merchant.

Catalogs can include thumbnail photographs, full photographs, short descriptions, long descriptions, logos, prices, and shopping carts. You can choose to use any or all. I know one retailer who just names the products, gives the prices, and provides no photographs or other information. His reasoning is that his customers know the products (commodity-like products) well and don't need photographs or descriptions. They buy strictly on price, and he sells at attractive prices. Other types of retailers might be ill-advised to do the same. They need to feature photographs and voluminous specifications. Every retail business is different.

A catalog is an important component of ecommerce software and is included in most ecommerce software packages.

Transaction Services

One of the most important elements of good Web ecommerce software is the transaction services it provides. A customer goes to the checkout where the shopping basket shows up with the products that have been ordered. The prices of the products are totaled, sales tax (if applicable) is calculated and added to the total, shipping is calculated and added to the total, and a choice of payment methods is provided. Then the information for a particular payment method is received. All this information passes back and forth in a secure digital environment. This is all done by the Web ecommerce software. It provides an easy-to-use and convenient way for a website visitor to make purchases.

If it works for website visitors, why not for eBay bidders? If you have an ecommerce website, you can direct the high bidders at your eBay auctions to your website to make payments. It's convenient for the bidders, and it's convenient for you.

Auction management services also provide checkout mechanisms similar, if not identical, to those included in ecommerce software; you can use some of these services, such as Andale, both for eBay auctions and for an independent website. What a deal!

Online Processing

Once ecommerce software has accumulated all the information about the order and the requisite information for the particular payment method chosen by the buyer, what do you do with that information? There are two answers to this question. The first answer is that you do with the information what you would normally do if the information were collected at a retail store. For instance, if you have collected credit card information, you can call up via telephone and get approval (e.g., from Visa) for the transaction in the normal way. You also fill out a credit card charge slip and handle it as you normally would that way. The charge slip will not have the customer's signature, but you have electronic documentation (proof) that the customer charged the purchase.

The second answer is that you can also subscribe to an online service that will handle the credit card processing automatically for you online. Your ecommerce software will interact with a number of online credit card processing services should you choose to use one. This is a convenience to you, for which you pay, and has nothing to do with your customers. But you don't need this service to accept credit card payments from customers via Web commerce software; you can do it the normal way instead.

Merchant Account

You can't take credit cards unless you have a merchant account. So, without such an account, you will be unable to accept credit card payments through your Web ecommerce software and will therefore have no use for online credit card processing.

You get a merchant account through your bank. They are difficult to obtain without prior retail history and good credit. However, there are businesses online that will extend you merchant account privileges with certain restrictions. There are many different programs. Read and understand the details of the programs and find one that fits your situation before you sign on the line. Some of the programs are quite costly.

A bank's reluctance to grant a merchant account to someone without assessing their credit is based on the fact that a merchant account holder can run up phony charges to amass a large bank balance.

Alternative

Mentioned many times before as an alternative to a merchant account is PayPal, now owned by eBay. You can use PayPal off eBay; it's not just for eBay transactions.

Accounting

Many Web ecommerce programs provide a record of all the orders. If you do not have a separate accounting system to handle orders, this can be very handy. Even if you have a separate accounting system to handle orders, you can use the accounting capabilities of your Web ecommerce software for interim accounting. Some ecommerce programs will plug nicely into popular accounting software, and you will be able to handle orders seamlessly. For instance, modStop (*http://modstop.com*) sells a module for Miva Merchant that enables it to pass order information to QuickBooks (*http://www.quicken.com*).

Cost

The cost of ecommerce software varies widely. Miva Merchant software costs $500 the first year and $200 for upgrades thereafter. You must use it at an ISP that has a Miva server; there are over 100 of them. The nice thing about Merchant is that you can often use it for no additional fee over and above your normal ISP Web host service (e.g., $30 per month). Some ISPs simply provide it free. Other ecommerce software packages charge differently. Typical is a cost of $500–$15,000 for the ecommerce software and $40–$400 per month for the ISP service to run it on. Virtually all Web ecommerce software requires a special server in addition to a Web server to operate. Some ecommerce software is even provided for at no additional cost by some ISPs, but you need to investigate what such free software offers. The features of Miva Merchant provide a good standard against which to measure competing software products because Merchant is quite robust.

Merchant Modules

ModStop sells many Merchant modules that extend the features of Merchant, including many that enrich customer service. Other modules are available elsewhare for sale or free. Also, check out other ecommerce software for special features, including customer service features.

Who?

Who is going to take care of your ecommerce website? The nice thing about Merchant and some of the other ecommerce software is that you don't have to be a programmer to use them. For instance, once you get Merchant up and running properly at your website, you can keep it going with minimal technical maintenance (e.g., perhaps a few hours a month). The maintenance of your Merchant catalog via a database, which routinely takes time, is actually a time-saver over other methods of accomplishing the same things and can be done at the desktop.

A webmaster or Web developer can handle Merchant. A webmaster doesn't have to be a database expert to design and use a simple database, but he or she does have to learn how to use a database program. This may be a task that your bookkeeper or another skilled employee can learn to handle. Database managers such as Paradox, FileMaker, and Access are easy to use.

eBay and Merchant

eBay, with all its database expertise, decided not to reinvent the wheel. eBay used Miva Merchant for its eBay Store (now eBay-o-rama) catalog for several years.

eCommerce Website Database

In order to stock your ecommerce website catalog efficiently, keep your inventory in a desktop database such as Access. Make your daily inventory adjustments; change your prices; delete sold inventory; and do it all offline with an interface that's easy, quick, and convenient to use. (Online interfaces for Web ecommerce software are notoriously slow to use.) Then in one quick gesture, upload the data you need to your website commerce catalog. The result is an entire new catalog with up-to-date information, that is, up-to-date inventory and prices. Some corporate ecommerce websites have catalogs connected directly to database servers, but you have to have tens of thousands of unique items in your inventory before you need such a system or can justify the cost of it.

Database Overview

If this database stuff seems complicated to you, let's review it. Here are the steps:

1. Use a desktop database manager such as Paradox, FileMaker, or Access.

2. Put all the data you need for everything in the ecommerce catalog into one database table by creating as many columns as you need.

3. Maintain the data at the desktop in the database manager where you can do it quickly and efficiently.

4. Export the data to your ecommerce software catalog database.

5. The data will add to or revise the catalog entries in your ecommerce webpage catalog.

It's pretty straightforward. If you use your own overall database system for managing your auctions, the scheme outlined above can fit nicely into your overall system.

Auction Management Services

If you use an auction management service for your eBay auctions, you may be able to use the checkout mechanism on your ecommerce website too. For instance, Andale enables this. Your auction management service may even provide a catalog you can use on your website. Check out the features of your auction management service, if you use one, to see what's available that you can use on your website as well as for auctions.

ecommerce software from an auction management service might be easier to install on your website but perhaps not as flexible as the ecommerce software provided by your ISP. One compelling reason to use the catalog and checkout from your auction management service on your website is that you don't have to learn more than one ecommerce program.

Finally, let's mention that it's a two-way street. There is a plug-in for Miva Merchant that handles eBay auctions. Eureka! If you use Merchant, you can use your ecommerce software to manage your eBay auctions too. Check out Veeo (*http://veeo.com*).

A Less Serious Website

Do you need to have a full-fledged ecommercial website? It seems to me that if you go to the trouble to create your own website, making it a commercial website does not entail much extra operating effort, although the initial setup work is much greater. However, you can create a webpage or a series of webpages at some webpage hosting services without going to the extra effort of creating an entire website. There are even free webpage hosting services:

- Angelfire, *http://www.angelfire.com*

- FortuneCity, *http://www.fortunecity.com*

- Geocities, *http://geocities.yahoo.com*

- Tripod, *http://www.tripod.com*

Certainly, you can do many things at a webpage hosting service, short of creating a ecommerce website, that can help your retail efforts on eBay. Some webpage hosting services may even offer ecommerce software.

If you want to take this idea a little further, you can opt for a hosting service that specializes in providing storefront websites. Some of those are free too. Try:

- DiscountBuy, *http://www.discountbuy.com*

- Veeo, *http://veeo.com* (caters to auction sellers)

- webPeddle, *http://webpeddle.com*

Marketing

Your ecommerce website will not sell anything without an aggressive Web marketing campaign. People have to know about you, be motivated to visit you, and find you. Marketing is just as difficult and expensive on the Web as it is in real life. The difference is that offline, virtually everything costs money. *Time* magazine is not going to do a tradeout with you (e.g., a half-page ad for sweeping out the Chicago bureau for three months). On the Web, however, you can substitute time for money. You can carry out an aggressive Web marketing campaign if you want to spend the time to learn to do it and then the time to do it. It's clear that without a serious marketing effort no one will come to your ecommerce website.

eBay can be part of that serious marketing effort. But the eBay link (eBay auction link to your website) is not what it once was, so to speak. If you're starting out to expand your selling, check out eBay Stores before you rush to make your own website.

A Teaser

A challenge to eBay is arising, and you might hedge your bets if you're thinking about running an online retail business. Although beyond the scope of this book, I urge you to check out Froogle. That's right, it's Google's shopping search engine. You might want to develop a strategy that enables you to sell on eBay and sell on Froogle too. Get more information at Froogle Information for Merchants (*http://froogle.google.com/froogle/merchants.html*).

Summary

Can you have a retail business that exists only on eBay? Yes. Nonetheless, there are a lot of benefits to establishing an ecommerce website too. One is that you can offer better customer service generally, and you can specifically offer better service to your eBay customers too.

Unfortunately, an ecommerce website is a considerable project to get off the ground. It requires routine maintenance to keep it going, and you can't make an ecommerce website successful without extensive marketing. That's where the idea falls down. You are probably better off with an eBay Store.

In short, if you're successful selling at retail on eBay, establishing a ecommerce website takes you to the next level. But establishing an eBay Store will take you to the next level, too, without the necessity to spend your time and resources on marketing. Does that mean that I absolutely advise against establishing an independent website? Not necessarily. The *About Me* website and Information website ideas covered earlier in this chapter might be a good idea for many eBay sellers, but they were proposed as information websites, not as ecommerce websites.

22

Sources of Inventory

Some readers will want to expand their efforts from selling occasionally to selling routinely. What's the secret behind an eBay selling business? It's inventory! Where are you going to get some inventory to sell, inventory at a low price that you can sell at a higher price? This chapter surveys a few ideas. But it only makes a ripple in the surface of the endless sea of available inventory.

Acquiring Inventory

First, you need to consider and keep in mind some retailing basics. Then you move on to consider some ideas on where to find inventory to sell.

Sales Tax License

You are not a retailer until you have a sales tax license. Once you have one, a lot of doors will open for you. It's your ticket to the wholesale world. It's also a lot of ongoing paperwork (e.g., reports to the state).

Drop Shipping

Unless you have the money to purchase inventory and the warehouse space to store it, your best bet is to think *drop shipping*. Drop shipping doesn't come cheap, but when you're starting out, it makes a lot of sense. You inventory nothing. When you make a sale, the wholesaler (drop shipper) ships directly to your customer. You never have possession of the merchandise. Slick.

Inventory Ideas

An assortment of inventory acquisition ideas follow. It's my hope that these ideas will get you thinking. But the best ideas for you will be your own, not mine.

Traditional Ideas

Straightforward ideas for acquiring inventory have sustained many eBay sellers desiring to make money on eBay.

Wholesale

Talk a wholesaler into selling you inventory, perhaps even extending you a little credit. Sell the merchandise on eBay for a profit. This is a proven method of retailing that hardly needs much explanation. Some wholesalers will sell to anyone who knocks on the door. Others are superselective. There are a hundred positions in between.

As simple as this seems, it's not a no-brainer. Some wholesalers sell at prices as high as, or even higher than, discount stores. You have to know your market very well and make sure you have a healthy spread between your wholesale prices and your eBay auction prices. Needless to say, eBay bidders are not looking to pay full retail prices.

Special Mail-Order Wholesale

There are special wholesalers that sell merchandise to amateur retailers operating in special markets such as mail order. Are such retail sales profitable? Probably for some people. Probably not for most people. Don't enter a contract with one of these wholesalers with your eyes closed. Evaluate the opportunity carefully, and do a little test marketing (test auctioning) before you commit yourself fully to this scheme. One advantage that these wholesalers usually offer is drop shipping.

One variation on this is the wholesaler that buys a huge closeout and breaks it up into smaller quantities to sell to retailers. Try Luxury Brands (*http://luxurybrandsllc.com*).

Government Surplus

Army-Navy-Air Force surplus. Now there's an interesting business. But I don't think it's one I'd like to be in. Still, military surpluses are not the only surpluses that the government has. The governments (federal, state, county, and municipal) all have surpluses, and they all sell off used and even new merchandise and supplies from time to time. They do it at special sales and auctions, seldom without public notice. Watch the public notices. Be there, and buy some inventory cheap. Make sure it's something you can resell easily for a profit on eBay. Try Liquidity Services (*http://www.govliquidation.com*).

Closeouts

Closeouts are excess inventory that someone wants to unload quickly for whatever reason. The seller might be a manufacturer, a wholesaler, a retailer, or even a high-volume user (e.g., the government). The price is often well under wholesale. Ten to twenty cents on the dollar is not uncommon. You must usually buy in large quantities to participate.

There is an entire closeout industry with closeout shows and periodicals. Get plugged in, raise some money for inventory, buy for ten cents on the dollar, auction for 35 cents on the dollar on eBay, and make your fellow eBay denizens happy. A profitable deal all around. One closeout retailer that uses eBay extensively is eValueville (*http://evalueville.com*). Visit its website to see what's happening.

The following are some potential sources of useful information about closeouts or closeout inventory:

- CloseOutNow (*http://www.closeoutnow.com*)
- Discount Warehouse (*http://www.closeouts.digiscape.net*)
- Lee Howard's Business Inventory Closeout Sources Directory (*http://www.chambec.com/closeout.html*)
- Liquidity Services (*http://www.liquidation.com*)
- Maverick Enterprises (*http://amaverickent.com*)
- MUSA (*http://www.merchandiseusa.com*)
- redtagbiz (*http://www.redtagbiz.com*)
- RetailExchange (*http://retailexchange.com*)
- RO-EL On-Line (*http://www.ro-el.com*)
- Sav-On-Closeouts (*http://www.sav-on-closeouts.com*)
- TDW Closeouts (*http://www.tdwcloseouts.com*)
- Tradeout (*http://www.tradeout.com*)
- UBid (*http://www.ubid.com*)

Not That Easy

Closeouts sound like an easy business. However, dealing in close-outs is competitive, like any other business, which means you have to work hard to find closeouts on which you can make a reasonable profit. Remember, too, that closeouts usually include merchandise that a manufacturer or retailer could not sell in the normal course of business.

Auctions

Local auctions are known for their bargain prices. Ironically, as most of us know from experience, this isn't necessarily true. Sometimes things sell for more at auctions than they do elsewhere. Nonetheless, local auctions do remain a potential source of bargains. If you can buy low at an auction and sell higher on eBay, you have yourself a business. This works well with individual items such as antiques. But it also works for bulk inventory. Frequent your local auctions, and buy stuff you know you can resell on eBay for a profit.

Fewer and Further

Unfortunately, more and more local auctioneers are using eBay to guide their pricing (e.g., opening bids). Consequently, the bargains are fewer and further between. Nonetheless, give this a try as a potential source of inventory.

Special Products

There are some special products around that have a lot of appeal but aren't generally available. You know. You see them advertised for $19.95 on obscure TV channels, like the superpotion that shines your car and makes your coffee taste better too. Find out how you can buy them at wholesale. Auction them on eBay.

Find an inventor who has manufactured some clever product, has 500 in his garage, but doesn't know what to do with them. These guys are all over the place. I knew a guy who invented a clever rack that holds a supermarket plastic bag open for the purposes of garbage disposal. The rack goes on the back of the door under the kitchen sink. It's quite handy and eliminates the need for plastic garbage bags that you have to buy. He never was able to market it effectively and probably still has 300 in his garage nicely packaged. Perhaps you can auction a product like that on eBay at wholesale prices to dealers in lots of four dozen. Or perhaps you can auction such products individually at retail prices.

Manufacturers

You don't always have to go through a wholesaler. Many manufacturers will deal with you directly and sell you inventory at wholesale prices. It makes sense to ask.

Special Manufacturing

Have something made for you to sell. Gee, you could invent something. But you don't have to go quite that far. How about lining up a beer mug manufacturer to reserve some time for your production run two weeks before the Super Bowl. You license the logos from the National Football League (NFL) prior to your production run. As soon as you know which teams will play each other, you plug the team logos into your Super Bowl beer mug design and start your production run.

You immediately start your Dutch auctions on eBay. In fact, you can do preliminary Dutch auctions at early-bird prices even before you or the bidders know which teams are going to play. Some people will buy the mugs even if their favorite team doesn't make it.

By the time the first auctions are finished, you should have inventory to ship. Better yet, have the mug manufacturer drop ship. You'll do most of your business in two weeks, but there will be some late sales, too, perhaps even a second run for mugs proclaiming the winner.

Special manufacturing doesn't have to be for a special event. It can be any mass-produced product that is customized for your retail sales.

Remanufacturing

Defective items plague manufacturers. They are returned (under warranty) new, or almost new, with some small thing out of whack that can be easily fixed or replaced at the factory. Once fixed and tested, the unit goes back on the market as refurbished merchandise. For all practical purposes, it's as good as new.

Laws in some states may prohibit such practices, and returned items must be disassembled for parts. The parts then go to a special assembly line where they are reassembled into refurbished merchandise. Quality is high.

Normal dealers often do not want to carry refurbished merchandise because it competes with the sales of their new merchandise. This creates an opportunity for special retailers who will market the refurbished items at prices below market for new goods. There are a lot of people successfully selling refurbished merchandise on eBay.

Small-Time Manufacturing

Small local manufacturers often have trouble marketing their products for lack of high-horsepower marketing departments. And some small manufacturers make some pretty unusual things that will draw a lot of attention in a large marketplace like eBay. Look around your locale. You may find a manufacturer with some attractive products, not widely available, that you can sell on eBay.

Art and Handicrafts

Artists and craftsmen are small local manufacturers. Some have unique products that have significant market potential. Others have bread-and-butter products that always sell. Many do not have any marketing skills, or even if they do, they still do not like to market their products. This common situation creates opportunities for you to buy low and auction appropriate products on eBay for a profit. With intelligent choices, you can realize a higher profit with these sales because many of the products have no standard prices and will not be compared to discounted goods.

Estate Sales

People buy so much stuff. Some of it they wear out, and it isn't worth much. Some of it they hardly ever use and perhaps never even take out of the box. Then they croak. The relatives just want to get rid of the junk. Voila, the estate sale. If you're a buyer at an estate sale or auction, you can buy low and sell higher on eBay. If you're the auctioneer for the estate, perhaps you can auction for higher prices on eBay than you can at a local auction and make more money for less work.

Make the Rounds

One way to pick up general inventory is to make the rounds of the places in your community where you can routinely purchase goods well below their market value. These include:

- Garage sales
- Thrift stores
- Flea markets
- Swaps, exchanges, and trade shows

In addition, you can occasionally pick up wholesale inventory locally from:

- Going-out-of-business sales
- Retailers' excess inventory

For instance, a retailer that has to put 200 towels on sale for 60 percent off list price might be willing to sell them to you for 70 percent off list price, if you take them all and pay cash.

Good Cause Goods

How many times have you been involved in selling Girl Scout cookies or other goods to raise money for a cause or charity? Some of those goods (not Girl Scout cookies) are also available for normal commercial sales. One can't buy them in the stores, and many are high-quality goods in high demand. Find the wholesale source, buy low, and sell high on eBay.

Discount Stores

Costco, Sam's Club, and similar discount stores often offer terrific deals on specific products. You can buy merchandise at wholesale or even closeout prices in quantity and sell on eBay for a significant profit. If you're like me, you shop there anyway. Keep you eyes open for the super deals.

Special Ideas

A few special ideas are for the more energetic eBay members who wish to devote themselves to selling on eBay.

Packages

Sometimes putting products together into packages adds value and brings higher prices. For instance, digital cameras are easy to buy. Digital camera accessories are hard to find. There is a lens mount, a close-up lens, a telephoto lens, several filters, and a professional flash attachment—all difficult to find for purchase—for one of the medium-priced point and shoot digital cameras. If you put together the camera and the accessories into a package, the package might sell for more than the sum of the parts.

For the bargain hunter, a package doesn't appeal. The bargain hunter has fun taking the time to assemble the package himself. But for the busy person who has more pressing matters to attend, the package is a convenience and worth more than the sum of the parts. This is particularly true when everything sells below list price, and the person buying the package can still rationalize that he is getting a good deal. Hint: some accessories sell at a much higher markup than primary products.

The Web Department

You have the product knowledge, know some HTML, and know eBay, but you don't have the money for inventory. A local retailer has the inventory but doesn't understand the Web or eBay and doesn't have time to start or operate a multiple auction effort on eBay. Make the following proposal:

You will:

1. Set up to operate with an auction management service.

2. Auction the inventory on eBay.

3. Manage the eBay fulfillment operation.

The retailer will:

1. Supply the wholesale inventory.

2. Provide merchant credit card services.

3. Split the profits with you.

You become, in effect, the retailer's "Web Department" but on a partnership basis. This arrangement has a lot of flexibility. It can start out informal. Then, if successful, it can evolve into a department of the retailer's operation or into a separate business by itself.

The point here is to work for a share of the profits, not for a salary. Insist on a share of the ownership. That makes you an entrepreneur, not an employee. It may be lean pickings for a while, but if the business is successful, you will make more money over the long haul.

Consignment

Consignment selling is almost a tradition on eBay now. Many people have been doing it for years. This is simply selling other peoples' merchandise on eBay for a fee. eBay now has a Trading Assistant program where eBay will list you as a consignment seller, in effect. Go *http:// pages.ebay.com/tradingassistants.html*.

Interestingly, this seems to be a growth business. Auctiondrop (*http:// auctiondrop.com*) in San Carlos, California, is a physical location where people can leave something to be auctioned on consignment. Look for an Auctiondrop franchising program to appear in the future. Likewise, Drop It Off (*http://dropitoff.com*) in Delray Beach, Florida, is a place where people can drop off something to be auctioned on eBay or other auctions. It will likely be offering a franchise program by the time you read this.

A Future Idea

The inventory idea for the future? It's importing. There's a whole world of products out there (abroad) suitable for importing and selling at a profit. eBay's auctions in other countries make it easier for you to find products and to make contacts without expensive and extensive traveling.

Summary

The ideas covered by this chapter are covered more thoroughly in my book *eBay Business the Smart Way*. There are plenty of places to get inventory. When you start looking, you will find many more than I have covered in this chapter. eBay is a new international 24-hour-per-day marketplace with millions of consumers who scream for more inventory. If you can find the right inventory at the right price, you can sell it on eBay.

VII

Specialty Auctions

23

Local Auctions

If a nationwide auction makes sense, what about local auctions? After all, many items don't trade well at long distances but do trade well inside metro areas. eBay answered this question by creating "regional" auctions, which are essentially the leading metro areas.

Unfortunately, the local auctions have all but disappeared from the scene. They have been relegated from the eBay home page to the Browse section of eBay and don't stand out as well as they once did.

Regional Auctions

Local (regional) eBay auctions provide a convenience for bidders and extra exposure for sellers. They are designed to handle large or heavy inexpensive items or other items not appropriate for long-distance shipping due to size or cost. For instance, a desk worth $100 that costs $150 to ship almost anywhere will be difficult to sell nationally on eBay. But in a local auction, a buyer will drive across town in a borrowed pickup or van to take delivery.

Office equipment, industrial equipment, hardware, garden supplies, livestock, and the like are all good candidates for local eBay auctions. If it's large or heavy and inexpensive and if eBay has an auction in your area, sell it at a local eBay auction.

For Bidders

You will find local eBay auctions in about 65 regional areas in the US named for their metro area. You can access these local auctions on eBay's navigation bar. Go *Browse*, *Regions* (Figure 23.1).

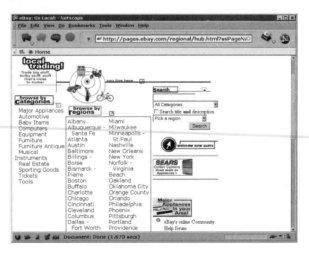

Figure 23.1   Selecting a local auction.

Each local auction used to have its own attractive home page. No longer. The local auctions are somewhat lackluster. They always were just a subset of the general eBay auctions. But now they look like a subset.

In other words, eBay creates the local auctions by filter. Everything is filtered out except auctions originating from within the local area. Consequently, this is a convenience for potential bidders rather than a truly separate auction.

You will see in Figure 23.2 that the local auctions do not have directories as robust as the full eBay auctions.

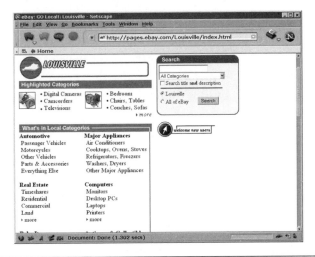

Figure 23.2   Local auction home page for Louisville.

eBay designed the local auctions this way to avoid blank lists for thinly traded items. Nonetheless, you can use the eBay search for specific local items productively if you decide the catagory directories are unproductive.

eBay local auctions have great potential, although eBay has apparently relegated them to the back burner for a while. In a few years, as eBay expands its general membership, it will generate a critical mass for

some of its local auctions.Perhaps then eBay will learn the magic formula for making local auctions work well.

For Sellers

The local auctions give a boost in marketing power for your items,
particularly the items that do not make sense to sell nationally. When
you auction an item, you do not have to elect a local area, but you lose
nothing by doing so. You gain having your item appear in a regional
auction as well as the national auction. There is no additional cost for
local auctions.

The question comes up, What if potential buyers want to see the item?
You need to handle this just like you would if you put an ad in the
local newspaper; that is, if you don't want someone to come to your
home, you may have to arrange to have the item inspected somewhere
else. Keep in mind, too, that you can normally get more information
on an eBay bidder than you can on someone who answers your newspaper ad by phone.

Street Address

eBay has stated that it will not give out your street address to anyone. Presumably no other eBay member can get it except from
you.

Use common sense and be clear in your auction ad what your policy is
regarding inspection and shipping. For items appropriate for local
auctions but inappropriate for shipping, you might want to indicate
"For pickup only."

Real Estate

Most states regulate real estate auctions, and you have to have a real
estate license to hold such auctions. Generally speaking, eBay is sup-
posedly licensed in real estate in every state. Nonetheless, eBay runs

mostly non-binding real estate auctions. It has experimented with binding real estate auctions. The complexity of real estate transactions does not seem to conveniently fit into the normal eBay procedures. Real estate auctions have a different eBay fee structure. In effect, running a non-binding real estate auction on eBay is essentially a form of advertising.

Real estate is a growing category for eBay, and more and more sellers are finding their way to eBay to advertise by running auctions. In particular, Realtors are making good use of eBay to advertise their listings. Naturally, local auctions give real estate sales a boost.

Strictly Local

Some other goods and services are strictly local. That is, it doesn't make as much sense to auction them on national eBay as it does on a local. Chapter 20 uses an attorney for an example of marketing services on eBay. Yet, most attorneys provide services only locally. Such a marketing plan will get a boost from a local eBay auction.

A restaurant provides another prime example. It doesn't make much sense to auction off a dinner for two nationally, unless the restaurant happens to be in one of the top-ten tourist destinations in the country. But a local eBay auction might prove enough of a boost to make such an auction effective.

As this book goes to press, there are over 27,000 categories of goods and services being auctioned on eBay. There are probably 1,000 ways to effectively sell these goods and services on eBay. (Many of them haven't been invented yet.) The local eBay auctions will eventually add even more ways to effectively auction goods and services.

If you think you've missed getting in on the ground floor of eBay, you haven't. The local eBay auctions will someday be the next ground floors. The local eBay auctions will develop different dynamics and new opportunities.

I must say it's brave of me to say this. I may have more faith in the future success of local eBay auctions than does eBay. I believe that eBay just hasn't figured out yet how to operate local auctions. When it does—and it will—the local eBay auctions will indeed provide opportunities for greater sales and new ways to sell.

24

eBay Stores

Don't go to sleep at this crucial point. This whole chapter is one big hot tip for you if you operate an eBay business. Your easy-to-use, low-cost Web storefront is now available. It's a way of selling and marketing you need to consider carefully, because it beats the alternative. It's the old golden opportunity knocking at your door

In the prior editions of this book I advocated creating an ecommerce website and using it in conjunction with your eBay auctions. I no longer recommend such a strategy. Three factors have changed the

411

eBay business environment to make this prior recommendation a less desirable alternative.

First, eBay no longer permits a link from your auction ad to your ecommerce website. Second, eBay now provides you with a storefront (eBay Store) and does your marketing for you. Three, auction management sevices now provide you with a checkout device for your eBay customers, and the eBay checkout is much improved.

Online Realities

eBay is still being invented. New twists in the invention process can quickly render useful techniques obsolete. In this case, eBay has evolved in a direction that is both restrictive and at the same time expansive.

The Magic Link

It used to be that eBay allowed a link from your auction description to your ecommerce website. This enabled you to promote (advertise) your website on eBay. In the spring of 2002 eBay disallowed this useful link, severely restricting your capability of promoting your ecommerce website on eBay. Today eBay still allows a link to your ecommerce website from your *About Me* webpage. But it's not the same. It's too indirect.

Apparently, if I read the rule correctly, eBay doesn't even allow the URL for your ecommerce website to be published in your auction description. eBay characterizes it as a "static link," whatever that is? You will do well to review the rules about this if you have questions about it. Go *Services, eBay Policies, Rules for Sellers, Listing Policies for Sellers, Link Policy.*

The Website

Why have an ecommerce website in the first place? It gives you a chance to put up an online catalog with fixed prices. It gives you another means of selling your merchandise. But it doesn't come free. A website costs time, effort, and money to create. It requires even more time, money, and effort to maintain. This is true if you can do it yourself. If not, you have to hire someone, and it costs even more.

If you already have a profitable website, great! Don't give it up as long as it's worthwhile for you to operate it. But many eBay businesses discover that having an ecommerce website is more trouble than it's worth. Before jumping into creating your own website, you need to give careful consideration to the alternative: eBay Stores.

The Checkout

A reason to have had your own website in the past was to provide a checkout procedure for your eBay customers. There was a time when the eBay checkout procedure was weak. Ineffective really. Nonetheless, most ecommerce websites had capable checkout procedures. If you could steer your eBay auction winners to your ecommerce website checkout, you could handle them more efficiently, and they would see your website too.

Today eBay offers a much improved checkout procedure, although it's only capable if the seller sets it up properly. The auction management service checkouts work well, and you can even use some of them on your ecommerce website in place of traditional ecommerce software. Consequently, today it's not important to have a website just to provide a capable checkout procedure.

Marketing Realities

The reality of operating your own ecommerce website is facing the great marketing problem. Marketing your website will take at least half the time, effort, and money you put into your business. Without being able to piggyback on eBay, you have the same marketing problem as any ecommerce website on the Web. The piggyback was the direct link from your eBay auction ads that eBay no longer allows.

Without the link, the marketing effort required to make your website successful is enormous. It's not any easier or less expensive on the Web than it is off the Web.

For instance, the search engines are probably the best marketing device on the Web. The reality is that you will have to hire an expert or a special service to analyze and restructure your webpages to be "found" by the search engines and put at the top of the lists. This will cost you $3,000 to $10,000 or more and will also require a lot of work on your part or require a lot of work by your website designer, an additional expense. There are other effective Web marketing techniques, too, but I don't know of any that don't require money or huge amounts of time.

The great thing about eBay is that it relieves you of the burden of doing anything but token marketing. That saves you considerable time, energy, and money.

Use the Stores

Now an eBay storefront can be yours for a reasonable fee. Granted, the eBay Stores aren't very pretty, but we can assume that's just a temporary situation. Granted, the eBay Stores aren't generating a huge amount of business yet, but we can assume that they will eventually command an impressive retail market share. Granted, you can't do much with your eBay Store other than list items for sale in a catalog, but we can assume eBay will enable many refinements in the future.

What the eBay Stores do today is present to you a grand opportunity to run an ecommerce website, in effect, without all the headaches, hard work, and expense. For most eBay businesses, an eBay Store will bring them more business immediately than an ecommerce website. And the best is yet to come.

Judge Separately

eBay auctions have grown so fast in the last eight years that we tend to expect everything eBay does to perform as well—or it's a failure. The fact is that eBay has had plenty of failures, and most of them aren't with us any longer. Nonetheless, it has plenty of submarkets that grow at a much slower rate than eBay auctions. That doesn't mean they're failures. It just means we need to judge them separately from the eBay auctions. Some eBay features, such as eBay Stores, will take a longer time to reach full fruition. But when they do, you'll want to be a part of the success.

Stores is well on its way with over 100,000 participating businesses! Now that's a pretty good start.

Storefront

When you become an eBay Store, you get a storefront and a catalog. You decorate the storefront, if you want to, and you fill the catalog with *Buy It Now* (fixed-price) listings.

Incidentally, Elance is a good place to find a low-cost but skilled webworker who will design a nice Store for you as well as a nice *About Me* webpage. Until eBay upgrades the appearence of Stores—and it will eventually—this is a worthwhile step to take.

Special Features

Look for special Store features. For instance, eBay already enables you to have your own custom search categories for searching through your Store items (once customers reach your Store). This becomes an increasingly more powerful benefit the larger your Store gets.

Reports

eBay also gives you sophisticated monthly sales reports for your Store. These can be a powerful tool in analyzing your business and identifying opportunities for greater sales.

eBay Is No Slouch

Note that the auction management services offer you many features, some free and some for a fee. But eBay is no slouch. Although eBay may not be as inventive as the third-party service vendors, it eventually attempts to match their successful services feature for feature. The monthly reporting for Stores is a good example. (And, of course, eBay has invented a few things itself.)

The thing to watch with the auction management services, and with eBay too, is that they will experiment with a new service and offer it free. If it's successful, it often turns into a service for a fee. Nothing wrong with that. I encourage you to join the experiments. But you do have to watch the nickels and dimes. Your overhead can skyrocket quickly if you don't.

Items

A Store is a normal store idea. Its shelves, in effect, are stocked with goods selling at a fixed price. The listing for an item looks much the same as an auction listing, and you create and treat the listings much the same as you do an auction listing. One thing to keep in mind is that the Stores have their own general search mechanism and category classifications separate from the ones for auction listings.

The catalog of Store items looks much the same as an eBay member's list of pending auctions. Not very fancy but functional. It's only a matter of time before eBay will provide enhancements that will improve the appearance of the catalogs. The current benefit to you is that you can process your auction listings and your Store listings the same for all practical purposes, and the available software and services enable you to do so.

Merchandising Manager

Don't overlook the eBay Merchandising Manager. Go *Site Map*, *Cross Sell your Store Inventory*. This is much like Andale's Gallery, which puts a mini catalog of other items on each Store item ad. It's a terrific cross marketing tool inside your Store.

Fees

The Stores operate on a different fee schedule than auctions, and that seems to be changing. The posting of items is longer (even unlimited) and the fees generally lower. You can find the latest fee information at *Site Map*, *Learn about eBay Stores*, *Fees*.

Cross Marketing

Pay attention to cross marketing opportunities between your auctions and your Store. For instance, suppose you sell digital cameras in your eBay auctioning business. You can use your Store to sell accessories. Refer your bidders to your Store (including a link) specifically to purchase the accessories they need for successful digital photography.

Links

The key to making your Store successful is to use auctions to bring bidders to your Store. To do so you need to link to your Store from within your auction ad and even suggest to bidders that they visit your Store. Don't rely on the red tag link at the top of the auction listing.

If you have something specific to cross market, like the example in the previous section, that's fine. But beyond cross marketing, you will want to skillfully use your eBay auctions to promote your eBay Stores. Someday perhaps this won't be necessary for success, but today it is. The primary way to promote is to always include a link from your auction ad to your eBay Store and always tell bidders to visit your Store. And I will say again, don't rely on the red tag link at the top of the auction listing webpage.

Read Chapter 20 on using eBay for marketing to gain some insight on how you might use your eBay auctions to carry through a marketing program that promotes your eBay Store.

Unique URL

Your eBay Store is your new website. You even get your own permanent unique URL! You can treat it just like your own website. You can even promote it outside eBay. It's your permanent Web address.

Dynamic Duo

Don't forget, your *About Me* webpage is also a unique URL. This is where you can do institutional advertising. This is more than it seems, even though it's just one page. It can be a gateway to something bigger as mentioned earlier in the book. The combination of your *About Me* webpage and your eBay Store gives you a powerful place on the Web. Make sure you have a lot of links going back and forth.

Summary

The eBay opportunities are expanding. The powerful threesome of your eBay auctions, eBay Store, and *About Me* provides you an exciting opportunity to sell to a huge market, an idea never comtemplated in anyone's dreams just a short time ago. eBay's philosophy is to create a level playing field for all, large and small; that is, a democratic playing field. eBay Stores are another step (another opportunity) to take toward realizing success if you are a serious eBay seller.

25

eBay Motors

Does it make sense to buy a used car in Boston when you live in Phoenix? It might. It depends on what you're looking for. The local market even in large cities tends to be thin when you're looking for something specific. There are so many brands and models.

Now if you're selling a popular car, you probably won't have any trouble quickly selling it locally. Unfortunately, most cars are not in high demand, and they can be difficult to sell locally. But expose them to a larger market, and you have more chance of finding a buyer who wants what you've got (see Figure 25.1).

With the above in mind, eBay makes a perfectly logical place to buy or sell cars. If you buy a car and live within 1,000 miles of the seller, you can hop on an airplane for less than $200 and drive the car home in a weekend. If you live 3,000 miles away, you can have the car shipped for under $900. If your prospective purchase is a good deal even after factoring in the cost of delivery from a distant city, why not buy it?

Indeed, eBay Motors sold 300,000 vehicles in 2002 worth $3 billion, and 75 percent of those transactions took place across state lines. That was 23 percent of eBay members' total sales for the year.

Figure 25.1   eBay Motors home page.

Dream Vehicle

In 1998 I saw a ten-year-old Chevy Suburban for auction on eBay with reasonable mileage about 3,000 miles away—in Florida. The seller had an excellent reputation on eBay after several hundred transactions. He represented that the vehicle was in excellent condition and that he could provide all the service records. His eBay auction ad provided a wealth of information about the vehicle. Because I backpack, climb mountains, and explore canyons in Utah and Colorado and leave vehicles at remote trailheads for ten days at a time, this vehicle had special appeal for me. Chances of finding a similar vehicle in similar condition nearby in the *San Francisco Chronicle* classified ads were not great.

The question was, Would I fly to Florida to buy this vehicle? It was a moot point because I already had a similar vehicle that got me where I needed to go. But if I had not had such a vehicle, I would have seriously considered flying to Florida to buy that Suburban. It appeared to be a well-maintained vehicle in great condition with plenty of miles left. The flight would have cost several hundred dollars, and the drive back several hundred more, but the extra money may have been worth it for a vehicle in good condition that's not so easy to find.

As a seller, you can potentially generate more interest in a vehicle in the national market. eBay provides a cost-effective means of reaching that market.

Think Local Too

Even if you don't like the idea of a national market being a good place to buy or sell a used vehicle, don't forget eBay reaches local markets as well.

Buying a Car Nationally

Being a national marketplace, eBay often offers more choices, particularly when you want something specific or unusual. Researching the value of the vehicle provides you with the basic information you need to negotiate well. A possible drawback to an eBay purchase is your inability to inspect the vehicle before traveling to the seller's faraway city. But that might not be such a disadvantage with the proper safe-guards agreed by buyer and seller before the auction is over.

Determining Value

Determining value is essential to intelligent negotiation. Vehicle values fall within certain ranges. If you know what those ranges are, you can do your best to purchase wisely. Otherwise, you're operating in the dark.

The Blue Books

The best way to determine the value of any car is to consult a publication containing the value data on a wide range of brands and models (see Figure 25.2 – Edmunds website).

Figure 25.2   Edmunds website.

These are generically referred to as "blue books" and are published by several publishers:

Edmunds (*http://edmunds.com*)

Kelly, the original "Bluebook" (*http://www.kbb.com*)

NADA (*http://www.nada.com*)

They offer a wholesale (trade-in) value and a retail value for used cars. Somewhere between these two values is likely to be the purchase price of your next used car.

The Spread

What does the spread between wholesale and retail value mean? It's simply the markup a dealer seeks. A dealer acquires a vehicle at its trade-in value when a buyer buys a new vehicle and trades in the old one. Dealers also acquire used vehicles in auctions at wholesale (trade-in) prices. The dealer sells the vehicle traded in (or purchased at auction) for a markup to cover expenses and make a profit. A dealer's expenses include the following:

- Preparation of the vehicle for sale

- Financing to carry inventory

- Dealership overhead

- Advertising

- Salesperson's commission

A private sale is not exactly the same. Typically, the seller in a private sale has lower expenses than a dealer. That's a primary reason that private sales tend to have a purchase price between wholesale value and retail value, usually closer to wholesale.

The Lender

A lender will usually loan the wholesale value of a vehicle or higher. In fact, some blue books list a loan value. That means that if you can purchase at wholesale instead of retail, you can get a 100 percent loan, assuming your banker has confidence in you.

How to Protect Yourself

How do you protect yourself against purchasing a defective vehicle? Well, how you do it for a local purchase shows how you might do it on eBay.

Local Purchase

The standard buying procedure is to visually inspect a vehicle. You can judge the exterior and interior condition reasonably accurately. But it's the engine that requires some expertise. I always take the vehicle to a mechanic who does inspections for car purchases. These inspections cost $50–$100.

Between your visual inspection and a mechanic's inspection, you will get a pretty good idea of the true condition of the vehicle. This procedure is not foolproof, but it's much better than sticking your head in the sand.

eBay Purchase

Alas, when you buy a vehicle on eBay in a faraway city, what can you do? First, you need to deal only with eBay sellers who have good reputations (solid positive feedback). Second, you need to get full information on the vehicle. Third, you need to see plenty of photographs, one from every angle, to do a preliminary visual inspection. Fourth, if these are not included in the seller's auction ad, you need to request them. If the seller won't provide them, forget the vehicle and move on to another. Fifth, there is a free one-month, 1,000-mile warranty on most vehicles less than ten years old with less than 125,000 miles. Sixth, there is free fraud insurance up to $20,000.

With honest information and a reputable seller, you can make a reasonably safe decision. It's not a risk-free decision, but it's workable. Remember, if the vehicle turns out to be as represented, you're stuck buying it. Better test drive one exactly like it at home before you commit yourself to some heavy bidding. If it's not as represented, the eBay Seller Guarantee program if offered by the seller may protect you.

Seller-Arranged Inspections

eBay has set up a system of seller-arranged vehicle inspections for only $25 (through Pep Boys, a national chain of auto mechanics). The idea is that the seller takes the vehicle to a third-party mechanic for inspection (at seller's expense) and then uses the results of the inspection to help sell the car by providing the buyer with useful and presumably accurate information. If this program will come to be used by all sellers nationally, it will help alleviate a serious concern of buyers.

If you arrive in the faraway city to find the vehicle is not as represented, you have reasonable grounds to back out of the deal, and you should do so. For that reason, you should, if possible, travel to the faraway city to inspect the vehicle immediately after the auction before the seller requires you to put down a deposit. Otherwise, in a dispute, you may lose your deposit.

Test Drive and Engine Inspection

It's up to the seller whether to allow you a test drive or an engine inspection before completing the transaction. These inspections are your best protection against getting a lemon, and it seems silly to travel all the way to the seller's city to pick up the vehicle if the seller won't let you (an out-of-towner) do what most sellers will allow buyers in their locale to do. The honest seller takes little risk in allowing these inspections. After all, it's the buyer who travels at his or her own expense to make these inspections. It takes a serious buyer to do so. Consequently, if these inspections aren't allowed, take a pass and go on to another vehicle.

Of course, if a seller pays for a Pep Boys inspection before auctioning the vehicle on eBay, she will probably not be inclined to accommodate your desire to have another inspection.

Before the Auction

Some sellers allow an inspection and test drive before the end of the auction but not after. This is obviously not workable for out-of-town buyers.

Victor Owens of Brooks Automotive, the chief mechanic who has taken good care of my family's cars for many years, recommends the following:

- Ask for a pre-purchase check similar to one normally done during an oil change and lubrication, except more thorough. Check to see that everything on the vehicle both inside and outside works.

- Ask for a smog check (required upon transfer in some states). A successful smog check generally indicates that a vehicle operates properly, but it is not conclusive.

- If a vehicle has over 80,000 miles, have each engine cylinder's compression checked manually. A compression check done on a scope saves time and sometimes costs a little less but is not as accurate as a manual check.

- Always have a vehicle checked in daylight, not at night.

- Have the mechanic do a test drive. In a test drive, a mechanic can uncover problems that others would miss.

A pre-purchase check costs $50–$100. A compression check is often extra and costs $50–$100. An emissions check is also extra, and the price is set by the state and varies from state to state.

Where does the Pep Boys $25 check-up fit in? It's adequate for vehicles with under 80,000 miles. For mileage above that, you will definitely want to have a manual compression check, which will undoubtedly cost more.

Any Purchase

For any purchase, whether local or on eBay, you can collect paperwork to protect yourself. Don't miss this opportunity to make your prospective transaction as safe as possible. Get a Carfax Vehicle History Report (*http://www.carfax.com*), formerly known as the Lemon Check, to determine the history of the vehicle (see Figure 25.3).

Figure 25.3   Carfax website.

Carfax reports the following in its Vehicle History Report: salvage history, odometer fraud, multiple owners, flood damage, major accident damage, and fire damage.

eBay also offers a similar service arranged through AutoCheck for only $6. Click on the VIN in the auction listing.

Warranty

Buying a warranty for the vehicle you purchase is always a good idea. You can purchase your own warranty, at the time you purchase the vehicle, from a firm such as 1Source (*http://1sourceautowarranty.com*). Warranties cost from $300 to $1,800 depending on the vehicle, what you want covered, and for how many miles or years you want coverage. eBay has arranged to provide 1Source warranties as part of its website services.

eBay sponsors a Seller Guarantee program. Ask the seller to take part in the program. It provides additional assurances to buyers.

Consummating the Transaction

To complete the transaction, go with the seller to the Department of Motor Vehicles (DMV) or whatever it's called in that state to complete the transfer of ownership and collect all the paperwork. Make sure all the seller's liens are removed from the title and that the title is free and clear. You pay sales tax and vehicle registration fees in your home state. If you are buying out of state, you will pay only nominal transaction fees, nominal temporary registration fees, and no sales tax. Going through the transfer process at the DMV with the seller is your only assurance that everything is done correctly.

Don't forget to have your car insurance in place prior to the transfer of ownership. You are liable for your newly purchased vehicle. You can actually get auto insurance through eBay too. The eBay resources are INSWEB and Progressive.

And what else? eBay will get you together with Dependable Auto Shippers if you need to ship your newly purchased car home. eBay will also find financing for you if you don't already have it arrangesd. And finally, PayPal comes into the picture with a special Secure Pay service for car buyers. It is essentially an escrow service provided through Escrow.com. Not a bad group of services, all at the eBay Motors website. Where can you get this kind of service anywhere else?

Escrow

You may need to set up the transaction in escrow if:

> You cannot be present in the faraway city when the transfer of ownership takes place;

> There is a lender lien on the title (the seller owes on the vehicle);

> You are borrowing from a lender to make the purchase; or

> You just want to protect yourself.

This is extra paperwork that is sometimes tedious to arrange, but it may be necessary. Before the purchase funds are released to the seller, you must be satisfied with the vehicle.

Escrow.com

For a graduated 3 to 1 percent fee, Escrow.com (*http:// www.escrow.com*) will provide an escrow transaction. It will verify payment for the seller, and it will withhold payment from the seller until the buyer has inspected the vehicle and is satisfied. Although the fee seems reasonable, as the book went to press, this service was inadequate for many situations. It did not handle loan payoffs.

Through eBay you can get the Secure Pay arrangement (for vehicles) for $75, also provided by Escrow.com.

Bank Escrow

An escrow agreement is particularly valuable when the seller still owes funds to a lender on the vehicle, and he or she will use your purchase money to pay off the loan. The escrow is your only assurance that the seller's loan gets paid off.

Perhaps the best place to arrange the escrow in the case of a loan pay-off is the seller's lender. The seller's bank can adroitly handle the transaction because it can pay off the seller's loan instantly with the buyer's purchase payment.

Informal Escrow

Many lenders will do informal escrow arrangements. When two lenders (seller's and buyer's) are involved, you can expect them to work out the details of completing the transaction, sometimes without a formal escrow agreement.

Let the escrow agent worry about the transfer details. But don't over-look the problem of taking responsibility for the vehicle immediately after the transaction is complete. The escrow agent isn't going to put your vehicle in his or her garage until you get to town if you happen to be buying from afar.

TitleTransfer.com

Try this dot com company to handle the transfer documents. It might make your transaction easier and more smooth, particularly when there is not a lender involved on either the buyer or seller side. How-ever, understand that this is not necessarily an escrow arrangement and does not provide all the protections of an escrow arrangement.

Escrow Fee

An escrow arrangement is so germane to an eBay vehicle transaction, which involves a seller's loan payoff, that the escrow fee should be split. Indeed, this is true for most eBay vehicle transactions except where the seller can provide clear title and the buyer and seller can go to the DMV together to complete the transaction. eBay is not going to dictate the terms of agreement for a transaction, but as a practical mat-ter and as a matter of fairness, the buyer and seller should split the escrow fee. Ask the seller to do so prior to the conclusion of the auction.

Dealer

Dealers do vehicle transactions every day as part of their business role. If the seller is a dealer, leave the details of the transaction to the dealer-seller and don't worry about an escrow arrangement. Dealers are regulated by the state and can lose their licenses not handling transactions properly.

Verification

To bid more than $15,000 on eBay, you have to either put your credit card on file or go through the ID Verify process (see Chapter 4). This is something to note because many vehicles will cost more than $15,000. This assures eBay and the seller that the bidder is a known person, not someone fraudulently hiding behind an alias and playing bidding games.

Agency

In some cases you will find that the seller doesn't really own the vehicle. He or she is selling it for someone else. Before you take a plane ride from Phoenix to Boston as the winning bidder to pick up the vehicle, you need to make sure that the auction is binding on the seller. The only way to do so is to get a copy of the agency agreement between the true owner of the vehicle and the person or company that auctioned it on eBay.

Mediation

Insist that the seller agree to mediation in regard to disputes that may arise from an auction transaction. SquareTrade, the eBay recommended service (see Chapter 8), is a great way to do this inexpensively and effectively. Vehicles require financially large transactions. It's well worth it to have the most complete protection possible; mediation through an organization like SquareTrade can provide you with assurance that you will get treated fairly. In fact, SquareTrade thinks of itself as a type of insurance.

eBay Local Purchase?

Can you do a local purchase on eBay? Certainly. If a seller in your city sells your dream vehicle on eBay, it makes things simple for you. Treat such a purchase like any local purchase. You can insist on the proper protections covered in this chapter, and you're present to act in a timely manner to complete the transaction. Indeed, some eBay vehicle transactions are local transactions.

Seller "Maltactics"

Some sellers state that they reserve the right to cancel their auction at any time. That means they will sell the vehicle on eBay unless they get a reasonable offer locally in the meantime. This is unfair. Pass on such sellers (which are usually used car dealers).

eBay rules, however, state that sellers cannot cancel auctions unless they cancel all the bids first. To explain themselves, sellers need to give a credible reason for the cancellation, which potentially subjects them to angry bidders.

Impulse Buying

Americans love cars and trucks. It's easy to get carried away when buying one. And impulse buying for cars and trucks, unlike for other merchandise, tends to linger for days instead of hours or minutes. Don't let impulse buying affect your rational approach to buying a vehicle on eBay. Don't take shortcuts. They usually lead to unnecessary risks. Do what you have to do to protect yourself.

If you need a vehicle immediately and you insist on getting what you want, you will probably spend several thousand more dollars for the same vehicle than you will if you can shop for a vehicle casually.

Selling a Car Nationally

Selling a vehicle nationally potentially brings in more buyers than a local effort. More buyers mean a higher price, a quicker sale, or both. This is particularly true for unusual cars, antique cars, or classic cars, but it's also true for ordinary vehicles.

The best place to start finding out how to sell a vehicle on eBay is to read the section for buyers earlier in this chapter. That will give you some ideas about the plight of the faraway buyer. If you can accommodate buyers, faraway buyers, you're more likely to sell your vehicle for the highest price possible on eBay.

Three-quarters

As mentioned at the begining of the chapter, three-quarters of the 300,000 vehicles sold in 2002 on eBay were in transactions that crossed state lines. In other words, only 25 percent of sales were in the same state, of which a smaller percentage were in the seller's locale.

Determining a Car's Value

Read the earlier section in this chapter on determining value. If you realistically want to sell your vehicle on eBay, you will need to sell it at a price that appeals to eBay buyers. It's not likely that you will sell it at full retail value for the following three reasons:

1. In the local market you will have a difficult time selling a vehicle at full retail. A typical private sale (not a dealer sale) in my experience is closer to wholesale than to retail value.

2. A normal eBay buyer has to spend $200–$900 to pick up the vehicle or have it delivered. That has to come out of the price, or what's the point of buying on eBay?

3. A buyer runs the risk of traveling to pick up the vehicle in a dis-

tant city, being dissatisfied with the misrepresented condition of the vehicle, and returning home empty-handed. That could cost as much as $500 or more, a substantial risk. It's not smart to take that risk and pay full retail too.

As a seller you might ask, What's the point of trying to sell a vehicle on eBay if sales prices are likely to be lower than full retail? There are several answers to that question:

1. A local sale is likely to be lower than full retail too.

2. A $200–$900 downward price adjustment looks less significant as the price of the vehicle increases.

3. Some vehicles will take a long time to sell in the local market, perhaps many months. It may be quicker to find a buyer on eBay.

4. For many vehicles, there are more potential buyers on eBay than locally. That means more possibilities and a greater likelihood of a successful transaction.

5. If you sell only via eBay, you are not likely to have a lot of people coming to your home to take a look at the vehicle.

6. Selling on eBay is easier than selling locally in many cases.

7. There are always potential eBay buyers who live in your city. Thus, an eBay auction has local possibilities.

Perhaps a more relevant question is, What can you do to maximize the purchase price that an eBay buyer is willing to pay?

Winning Bid

To inspire the maximum winning bid, you need to lower the buyer's risk and make it easy for a buyer to purchase the vehicle from you. That's why reading the early part of the chapter is so important. If you see things from the buyer's point of view, you can make a purchase more appealing at little or no cost to yourself.

Do the following to entice potential buyers:

- Provide complete information on the vehicle.

- Permit a test drive and engine inspection after the auction and prior to making the sale final (for out-of-town buyers only).

The less risk the buyer has, the more the buyer will be willing to bid.

Verification

I believe ID Verify is essential to both buyers and sellers in vehicle transactions. The ID Verify costs you about $5 (one time only) and verifies to eBay and the world that you are who you say you are. eBay requires verification of sellers, or at least a credit card number and bank account number in lieu of verification. If as a seller PayPal (or eBay) has not required you to become verified, you should become verified anyway. It will build confidence with buyers.

eBay requires that a buyer who bids over $15,000 have ID Verify. This requirement is not good enough for vehicle transactions. You should require that any winning bidder, regardless of the purchase price, have ID Verify.

Title

Don't assume that because the buyer has paid for the vehicle he or she will carry through on the paperwork, such as getting a new title. Buyers have many reasons why they don't get around to registering the transaction and officially taking title. One of the primary reasons is that they must pay sales tax when they officially take title to the vehicle.

Suppose a buyer sits on the paperwork and does nothing. As the seller, you still have your name on the title. If anything happens with that vehicle (e.g., an accident), you may be liable.

Therefore, walk buyers through the closing transaction at the DMV and make sure they have title to the vehicle before you bow out of the picture. Otherwise you might find yourself faced with a legal claim based on the fact that you're still the owner of record for the vehicle.

Mail-In Forms

Some states, such as California, have a mail-in transfer report that the seller can send to the Department of Motor Vehicles (DMV) after the transfer to report the transfer. As the seller, make sure you mail this to the DMV after the transfer, if you didn't do the transfer at the DMV.

Information Sells

This book continually stresses that information, not hype, sells merchandise on eBay. This is particularly important for big-ticket items such as vehicles. Provide prospective buyers with complete information on the vehicle that you auction. Take a look at some auction ads from auction listings on eBay Motors to get an idea of what *complete* information means. If you provide anything less, you will lose potential bidders for each item you don't include. The ultimate result will be a lower winning bid. Always include good photographs and a description (and photograph) of every defect.

I believe it's practically impossible to sell a normal vehicle on eBay without providing at least one good photograph. The more, the better. Look at dealer auctions on eBay. They always include at least a few good photographs, and they're the expert sellers.

Seeing photographs is the primary way a potential buyer has of making a purchase decision. If you ignore this fact, you eliminate most potential buyers and make yourself look like an eBay rookie.

Check out Dealer Assist, available to everyone, a new photography and presentation service offered by Auction 123 (*http://*

www.auction123.com). They will come and take photographs of your vehicle for a modest fee and provide a professional Web presentation of the photographs.

Success

In the second edition of this book (written in 2001) I predicted, "I'm bullish on eBay Motors. It will evolve into a more secure and more dynamic vehicle marketplace over the next few years and gain a significant market share at the expense of local newspapers (classified advertising)." And so it has. eBay Motors is one of eBay's great success stories.

Summary

It works! Yes, it makes sense to buy and sell vehicles in the national vehicle marketplace that eBay enables. It's not perfect. Like any other means of buying or selling, it has its problems and its expenses, but it can work for you. This chapter explains how it can work for you, whether you're a buyer or seller, safely and with minimum financial risk.

If you don't believe in the national market for vehicles, eBay reaches the local vehicle market too. With over 69 million eBay members, there are plenty of members in your state or your locale to consititute a significant market. About 25 percent of eBay Motors transactions take place inside the seller's state, and a good percentage of those are undoubtedly local.

eBay Motors will continue to evolve until it becomes a more convenient vehicle emporium for both buyers and sellers. But it works well already. Try it (see Figure 25.4).

Figure 25.4   Sell your car the smart way.

26

Business Marketplace

Businesses can auction new and used goods and equipment on eBay's specialty auction, the Business Marketplace. These types of transactions are known as B2B (business to business). They take place between businesses rather than between consumers or between businesses and consumers. Although eBay overwhelmingly dominates consumer (personal) auctions, it has focused its B2B efforts on small businesses. The big corporations have numerous B2B transaction hubs for particular industries in which they can participate. Small businesses are left out of many of those corporate B2B hubs, and eBay gives them a home at its Business Marketplace (see Figure 26.1).

Figure 26.1   eBay Business Marketplace.

The Business Marketplace used to be the Business Exchange. You might find it at *http://ebaybusiness.com*, or you might find a link to it from the eBay home page or from the Browse page. In other words, eBay continues to experiment with it. It is growing albeit not as fast as eBay overall, and eBay does seem to have a commitment to it. Nonetheless, you may have to root around to find it.

In addition, the Business and Industry category (plus the Wholesale category) in the category list on the eBay home page is much the same as the Business Marketplace. It's somewhat confusing that there are two collections of business auctions. Alas, eBay isn't perfect yet. Both the Business Marketplace and the Business and Industrial category are part of the vast eBay auction listings. Neither is a separate auction.

Basic Considerations

The eBay Business Marketplace auctions work the same as normal eBay auctions. eBay provides no special considerations or special mechanisms for conducting these B2B auctions. Thus, you need to examine the normal eBay auction buying-selling procedures to see how your business can make best use of the Business Marketplace.

Review

Review the Risk and the Transaction Overhead sections of Chapters 2 and 3 to get a better feeling for how costs (buyer's or seller's overhead) may affect a transaction.

Opportunities for Buyers

Businesses, as buyers, need single items (e.g., equipment), and the Business Marketplace is a good place to buy goods and equipment on which a business can realize a meaningful savings. Additionally, a business can buy the bulk merchandise it needs to fuel its everyday operations. That requires that the availability of such goods at the Business Marketplace be dependable and that shipping not be a prohibitive expense.

Time Factor for Businesses

The time commitment for businesses to buy something is not favorable. An eBay transaction is a long process from a buyer's point of view. Whether it makes sense for a business to have an employee go through the procedure will depend on the size of the transaction and the potential for savings compared to other means of purchasing similar items. However, with the widespread use of fixed prices (*Buy It Now*), eBay has become more efficient from a business buyer's prospective. Of course, a steady diet of proxy bidding takes much of the time commitment out of buying on eBay too.

Supply for Businesses

The supply for buying at auction has yet to materialize for businesses, although there are certainly plenty of goods and equipment available at the Business Marketplace and elsewhere on eBay. As eBay figures out how to make its local auctions and its Business Marketplace more useful, it will develop more potential to create a healthy and steady supply of the type of goods and equipment that businesses buy.

Individual Buyers

See Chapter 2 for similar considerations for individuals. But what works for individuals does not necessarily work for businesses.

Opportunities for Sellers

Businesses need to sell goods and equipment. Suppose you manage a small radio station that has four Sony TCM5000EV portable audio-cassette recorders (expensive field recorders for news reporters) in good condition. You are installing an all-digital studio system, and you can no longer use analog recorders even for field use. Where do you sell four TCM5000EVs? To another radio station perhaps, but beyond that, it might be tough. eBay provides a ready, willing, and capable market in which you can sell such equipment.

Businesses always have something to sell, such as old office machines, old office furniture, and excess office supplies. eBay provides an appropriate place to sell such goods and equipment. Everyone needs office things. The primary drawback here is the shipping cost.

If you sell a heavy-duty copy machine for $2,000, the $150 for shipping isn't going to kill the deal. But if you sell a run-of-the-mill office desk for $100, the $120 for shipping will kill the deal.

This points out one of the weaknesses of the eBay market: Large or heavy items that aren't worth much don't make good items to sell on eBay. The shipping costs will kill the deal. However, this also points out a hidden strength of eBay: A portion of the eBay market will always be local to a seller. It's not a stretch to think that you can find a local buyer via eBay who will buy your heavy office furniture and come across town in a pickup truck to take delivery.

The Time Factor for Businesses

The tough consideration for businesses is: How much time does it take to sell something on eBay? An employee will have to do it. Will it ultimately be less expensive to haul the merchandise to the city dump than to attempt to sell it on eBay?

Auctions don't require much time. You need to create the advertising copy and create the eBay auction. Because the auction is a silent auction, no further action is required except to answer buyers' questions, if any. When the auction is over, you have to communicate with the buyer to arrange payment and shipping. The process seems manageable without a great deal of employee time. If buyers renege or other problems appear, the time expenditures by employees will increase. If multiple (identical) items are sold one at a time to different buyers, the time commitment also increases.

The Market for Businesses

The market for businesses will always be substantial. There are always new business start-ups looking for usable assets at reasonable prices. Many businesses need more office equipment or specialized industrial equipment each year. Even individuals need equipment for home offices and businesses.

When businesses need to get rid of something, it's often not just one item. It might be 10 cartons of 8½ × 11 inch paper (100 reams) or 40 cases of 10W40 motor oil (480 quarts). The Business Marketplace is a good place to auction such surplus supplies to other businesses.

New Goods and Equipment

Just as in the normal eBay auctions, there are businesses selling new as well as used goods and equipment on the Business Marketplace. This can make a good business for the entrepreneur who has enough capital to deal in high quantities, high-priced goods, or surplus goods.

Individual Sellers

See Chapter 3 for comparable considerations for individuals. What works for individuals, however, does not necessarily work for businesses.

Specialty Auctions

Below are a sampling of the Business Marketplace categories:

Agriculture

Construction

Electronic Components

Healthcare

Industrial Supply

Laboratory

Metalworking

Restaurant

Retail Fixtures

Printing Equipment

Test & Measurement

Networking & Telcom

Office Products

PDAs

Printers & Accessories

Software

Wireless Telephones

Wholesale Lots

Businesses for Sale

Commercial Real Estate

Commercial Trucks

Pro Audio Equipment

Pro Photography

Professional Services (Elance)

Pro Video Equipment

This list gives you an idea of what's included, but take a look at the Business Marketplace to get a better idea of what it has to offer. Some of the categories are also listed by region.

My Review

I reviewed the Business Marketplace in the first edition of this book soon after it started while it was still a little green. I was moved to treat it humorously because the offerings were a little thin. Today, however, B2B on eBay is alive and well, indeed robust. eBay needs to put more effort into promoting it. At least putting a link to it on the home page would seem appropriate.

The subsections below give you a flavor of this non-consumer market-place. This is a down-to-earth business marketplace. Someday it will be much larger with a greater selection of goods. Nonetheless, it has already grown into a place quite useful to businesses.

Agriculture

Under *Agriculture, Tractors* you will find tractors, about 2,703 items in the summer of 2003. See Figure 26.2 for a John Deere, which could be yours for about $18,000.

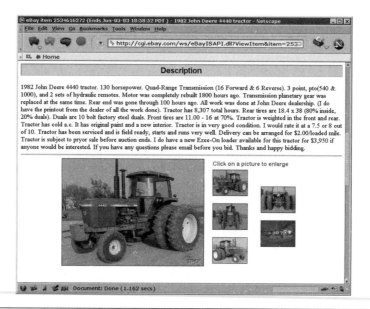

Figure 26.2   1982 John Deere 4440 tractor.

Metalworking Equipment

Under *Machine Tools, Fab Machines*, you will find stuff that you will probably not buy for home use. Who needs a $25,000, 4-ton, vertical mill in the basement? See Figure 26.3.

Figure 26.3   A mill for all seasons.

Healthcare

In the first edition of this book I said, "It's not clear that eBay can get a good start in this category. The only two subcategories are X-ray Equipment and Stethoscopes, an odd selection." Boy, was I wrong. Today (four years later, summer 2003) there are almost 8,000 items for auction in many different subsections. This is not exactly setting the world on fire, but it's well on its way.

Restaurant

In my first edition, I said, "Restaurateurs are entrepreneurial. This could turn into a really robust B2B auction." Hey, I was right about something. The Restaurant section is going crazy and has blossomed into a smorgasbord of equipment, so to speak. See a nice range stove with oven in Figure 26.4.

Figure 26.4   Imperial 2000 Series Model #IR-6.

A restaurant supply company in Atlanta decided to start selling used equipment on eBay. They couldn't make their efforts profitable. But they learned how to use eBay. Then they tried selling new restaurant equipment via eBay. Bingo! They developed a vigorous business selling expensive equipment to consumers with a large number of their orders coming from California. Finally they started experimenting again selling used equipment, this time with some success. While this change in their business was going on, they shut their doors—no more walk-in traffic—and stayed nearby their computers. They were doing most of their business on eBay or over the phone.

Construction

I was talking with the owner of a metal fabrication company in Huntsville, Alabama, who told me he bought his metalworking machines on eBay. He was in the process of building a 3,000 square foot metal building to expand his business. Naturally he looked to eBay to find construction materials. He purchased his drywall via eBay in a city a few hundred miles away because it was cheaper than buying the drywall in Huntsville, even after the shipping cost. He indicated that all together he saved about $30,000 by buying construction materials on eBay.

Warmed-Over eBay

Although included in the Business Marketplace, *Office Products* which includes computers and other office equipment, is not specifically Business Marketplace stuff. This is simply a subset of the normal eBay auctions and not unique to the Business Marketplace.

Future B2B Auctions

What does the future hold for the eBay Business Marketplace? It's hard to tell. Clearly, eBay has captured the consumer-to-consumer market and the small business-to-consumer market. Its hold on these markets will be tough to break.

The B2B market, however, is fragmented and specialized with plenty of competition. It may never be dominated by one Web auction the way eBay dominates the consumer markets. Nonetheless, eBay's B2B effort has enjoyed reasonable success and has tremendous potential for growing and for providing a useful outlet for used goods and equipment, for excess inventory, and even for new goods and equipment.

eBay is smart to focus on small business. Big business will continue to develop its own B2B transaction hubs and processes. Small business will look to eBay and eBay's competitors to establish smoothly functioning auctions to accommodate small business B2B needs.

Summary

eBay has established a solid foundation for its Business Marketplace. It's business will increase, although in smaller numbers than consumer activities. If eBay had strong local auctions, the B2B market would be better served (low-cost delivery for large or heavy items). But eBay hasn't quite figured out local auctions yet, and the B2B marketplace doesn't have the dramatic high volume enjoyed by the consumer auctions.

27

Half.com and Live Auctions

Wow! I discovered Half.com while writing the second edition of this book. It's a powerful and easy-to-use website that enables you to purchase goods at a fixed price—millions of items. The idea is that the goods are used and sell for less than half price. But the goods can be new, too, and sell for more or less than half price.

This chapter also briefly covers eBay Live Auctions. These auctions are limited to certain kinds of merchandise, and must be considered experimental.

Half.com

eBay originally bought Half.com. to supplement the eBay consumer-to-consumer auction transactions with fixed-price transactions. Alas, say goodbye to Half.com. eBay intends to merge it into eBay. The problem is that since eBay instituted its fixed-price system (*Buy It Now*), Half.com is redundant. After the merger, will the resulting system be similar to Half.com or just more eBay auctions? That remains to be seen. In the meanwhile, the best I can do is write a brief chapter section on Half.com assuming that some, if not all, of its characteristics will survive the merger (see Figure 27.1).

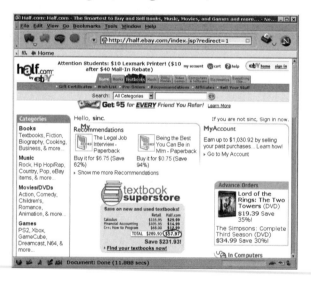

Figure 27.1   Half.com website.

Buyers' Benefits

Now, we're not talking about selling everything as eBay does. Half.com limits its offerings to books (printed), music (CDs), movies (VHS, DVDs), and games (electronic). These are called intellectual property, although Half.com also sells computers, software, and other electronic equipment. The nice thing about some intellectual property is that once you've used it, you usually don't want to use it again (e.g., once you've read the book or seen the movie, you don't want to do it a second time). Yet the benefits are the same for the next person who uses it (e.g., the next person who reads the book or sees the movie). For digital intellectual property (e.g., CDs and games), the experience is just as high quality for the second user as the first. Half.com provides a mechanism that enables anyone to sell such goods at low fixed prices in an efficient and smoothly operating national and international market.

Books

Think of Half.com as a used bookstore online, one that offers hundreds of thousands of titles.

Buying Books

Here's what I bought on my first try (see Table 27.1). I've been meaning to buy and read these books for a while.

The savings provided me with an incentive to buy. My savings were $42.82, that is, 64 percent off list. A shipping and handling charge of $6.85 was added to my order. Keep in mind, these are not impulse purchases that I happened to see on a table as I walked to the checkout counter of a bookstore and will never read. I actually read the first and the third books and will read the second just as soon as I can break my indentured servitude to my publisher.

Table 27.1   Books and Savings

Title	Purchase Price	List Price
Passage to Juneau: A Sea and Its Meaning (Raban)	$6.37	$26.50
Passionate Sage: The Character and Legacy of John Adams (Ellis)	$6.47	$15.95
The Power Broker: Robert Moses and the Fall of New York (Caro)	$10.79	$24.00

Alas, I could not find the eighth and final volume of Page Smith's *People's History of the United States*. But Half.com has over 8 million items for sale, and it turned up later.

Since my initial purchase, I have purchased an additional few dozen books. Now, before I buy books I don't need immediately, I always check with Half.com first.

And If It's Not in Stock

If you need a book immediately and it's out of stock, Half.com will display several online bookstores, where you can purchase the book new, and show the prices. This enables you to go to the online bookstore with the lowest price and purchase the book new for immediate delivery.

Out of Stock

For Half.com, "out of stock" means that no seller has submitted the book for sale. The catalog database for Half.com is huge, but Half.com cannot possibly have all titles in the catalog. Half.com depends on its sellers to provide the inventory. As soon as a seller provides a book, it is in stock and available for purchase. Half.com has millions of books in stock.

Music

Right from the beginning Half.com offered plenty of popular music. Today it offers all. Even J.S. Bach, who was invisible when I first tried Half.com, has 13 webpages of titles today. This is a great source of music CDs.

Movies

I found the Kenneth Branagh version of *Hamlet*, a favorite of mine, listed (along with nine other versions) as well as *Chariots of Fire,* about the 1924 Olympics, a wonderful movie. This is undoubtedly the largest selection of movies in the universe. I don't know that for a fact, but if it isn't, it's certainly close.

Games

Because I don't play computer games, I don't have much to report here. Keep in mind, however, that the digital game industry is larger than Hollywood in dollar sales. We're talking big money. Any website that can save a kid a few bucks, or parents a few hundred, is a welcome relief to purchasing full retail.

Searches

The search engine at Half.com at one time didn't work very well. You could only do a definitive search with an ISBN number. However, it is now much improved. But when all else fails, go to Amazon.com and search. Come back to Half.com with the ISBN or UPC numbers.

Numbers

The ISBN (International Standard Book Number) and the UPC (Universal Product Code) are standard industry inventory numbers, often expressed as bar codes, found on products in the Half.com catalog.

The Half.com database is independent of inventory. Therefore, you will find books that are "out of stock." This makes a very complete database possible, enabling you to order books that are not in stock. As soon as someone offers such books for sale, your purchase will automatically take place, and you will get the book. Or, rather than purchase automatically, you can elect to be notified when a book you want comes into Half.com's inventory. (Searches work similarly for other items.)

Reputation

The feedback system works a little differently on Half.com. Only sellers get feedback. After all, the buyer buys for a fixed price immediately with a credit card. Therefore, why rate buyers? Consult the Half.com rating guide to learn how to rate sellers.

The feedback is based on how quickly the seller confirms the order, how quickly the seller ships, how well the seller classifies the condition of merchandise, and how well the item is packaged for shipping.

Selling on the Half

As a seller, you have to be on your toes to remain successful. Just as in eBay auctions, good customer service is a must.

When you are just a casual seller, you may not worry too much about your reputation. Nonetheless, the system requires that you give good customer service. In the spirit of eBay and Half.com, you need to make an effort to take care of details and ship promptly. Most merchandise is shipped by the US Postal Service media rate, which is slow. Any delays you add to the inherently slow shipping will be agonizing to many customers.

Selling Procedures

It's easy to offer an item for sale. You just enter the ISBN number (for books) or the UPC number (for other items), the price, the condition, and comments. You can also offer shipping by Priority Mail (faster than Media Rate). Your item goes into the vast Half.com catalog; that is, the item appears in stock.

It's your responsibility to ship the item adequately packaged. When someone buys your item, you are notified via email by Half.com and must confirm within 48 hours that you have the item and will ship it. You must then ship within 24 hours after confirmation. If you do not follow this procedure, the order may be canceled, subjecting you to a low feedback rating. If you're slow, you may not get a top rating.

Generally, you need to set your prices realistically. I recommend the following price structure (percentage of list retail price new - based on my observations, not a scientific study) for used books:

Like new 60%

Very good 45%

Good 35%

Acceptable 25%

Remainders, which are new books that did not sell in the bookstores, might be sold for more than 60 percent. In practice, however, remainders sell for lower percentages. Many books sell for below the suggested percentages. For each item, Half.com does list a selection of retail prices at certain online retailers (e.g., Buy.com) that are generated automatically.

Shipping

Unless you offer Priority Mail and the buyer elects it, you can ship the item any way you want. The media rate for books is the least expensive and is what will be expected by buyers. Half.com will reimburse you for shipping according to Table 27.2. The reimbursement is the same regardless of what the actual shipping costs are.

Table 27.2   Reimbursement for Shipping

	Special Rate	Priority
Hardcover		
First item	$2.33	$4.70
Subsequent items	$0.90	$2.75
All Other Items		
First item	$1.89-1.94	$4.70
Subsequent items	$0.65-69	$1.50

You need to send the bottom half of your order confirmation with the merchandise. You can also send a receipt. You are not permitted to send anything else (e.g., promotional materials) with the merchandise without Half.com's permission.

Fee

Half.com takes a 15 percent fee on sales. The fee is graduated with more expensive items over $50 being a lower percentage. Half.com provides the Web catalog, completes the sales transaction, and collects the purchase price on all sales (via credit card). Sellers merely list the merchandise and ship it. Seems like a reasonable arrangement. Half.com takes no listing fee; listing is free.

Business?

Can you make a business out of selling on Half.com? Sure. In the publishing industry, books that don't sell in the bookstores are said to be *remainders*. Since books are sold on consignment (a practice started during the Great Depression), the bookstores return unsold books to distributors, which in turn return them to publishers. You may be able to get remainders from bookstores, distributors, or publishers at very low prices. Sell them on Half.com. Likewise, you can find sources of excess inventory for textbooks, music CDs, movie VHS tapes and DVDs, video games, computers, software, and electronics.

Live Auctions

eBay bought the old San Francisco auction house of Butterfields to acquire the expertise to auction valuable fine art and artifacts online. eBay Premier for offline auction houses and art dealers was the result. That didn't seem to work. Then eBay made a deal with Sotheby's. That didn't last either. Today eBay continues the experimentation with its Live Auctions. These auctions are primarily for high class art objects that require lots of paperwork such as authentication documents. And they are held live online. Included in these auctions are collectors' books, antiques, fine arts, manuscripts, art, and the like.

It was bound to happen sooner or later on eBay, a live auction via the Web. And eBay Live Auctions makes a great place to experiment with live auctions. Fine art auctions handle the expensive items that make it worthwhile to go to the expense of broadcasting such auctions live on the Web. You can hear the auction via RealMedia (audio) and participate in the bidding via a form in the webpage. Although live auctions are not necessarily meant to be experimental, you should certainly view them that way. Jump in and experiment. Live auctions via the Web will have their place apparently.

Consult the Live Auctions section of eBay for specific instructions on participating and bidding. You must sign up ahead of time to bid in live auctions, and of course you must be an eBay registered and verified user. This provides you with an opportunity to participate in something a little different on eBay, even if you don't bid.

Summary

Half.com is not an auction, but it complements eBay nicely with fixed-price inventory for a few types of standard merchandise (and more). Soon it will be incorporated completely into eBay. It's a special type of sales because it uses catalog databases for books, textbooks, music, movies, and video games. If you buy such merchandise, give it a try. Or, if you want to sell what you've got, give it a try.

Live Auctions have their place, but it's not a huge place. The items are limited to art, art objects, and similar things. It's more like going to Sotheby's to bid than it is like going to eBay to bid. eBay continues to pursue this venue, and perhaps someday it will accommodate a broader range of items.

28

Elance

Talk about marketing your services on eBay, well here we are. Elance!
The service has been affiliated with eBay for so long that I reported in
the second edition that eBay had purchased it. Don't know where I
read that, but it's not true. The name stood for electronic freelancing.
Today it is a successful, but not wildly successful, marketplace that
offers certain professional services via eBay. That is, the sellers sell professional services, and the buyers buy and use such services. But
Elance has a twist to it. The sellers do the bidding, so to speak.

How does this work? The buyer posts a project requiring services, and sellers bid to do the work. Theoretically, the low bidder gets the project. It's pretty straightforward, but it has a few wrinkles that make it work well.

Professional Services

Although eBay features the name Elance for this marketplace, it uses the words "professional services" in the home page link leading to Elance.

Professional Services

First, this marketplace does not accommodate all professional services. Your service needs to be on the list before you can make this work for you. Second, this is really advertising and marketing for your skilled services, and as such it doesn't come free or even at a nominal cost. It will cost you real money to participate. Third, Elance doesn't guarantee your success. The low bidder isn't necessarily the winner.

Who Can Play This Game?

Occasionally eBay adds or subtracts a category, but at the time this book went to press your skilled services had to fall into one of the following categories to enable you to participate:

1. Accounting and Finance

2. Administrative Support

3. Business Strategy

4. Graphic Design & Multimedia

5. Legal

6. Personal

7. Software and technology

8. Training & Development

9. Web Design and Development

10. Writing & Translation

In Four Months

In the four months since I last reviewed the Elance offering of services in 2003, the category of Engineering and Design disappeared and the Personal category appeared.

To give you an idea of the depth of the categories, Administrative Support provides the following services:

- Data entry
- Event planning
- Presentations
- Printing
- Transcription
- Travel planning
- Word processing

You don't have to sift through these categories. You can use the Elance search to find Elance services too.

Appendage

eBay has appended to Elance a small listing of services categories (auctions) available on eBay itself. And one can use the regular eBay search to find services auctions on eBay. There are no category restrictions on such auctions. See Chapter 20 for more discussion about marketing services on eBay.

As you can see, Elance continues to attempt to identify categories that will work. But the categories are anything but open ended. Of all the services and consulting available, the Elance categories represent but a small percentage.

You might also wonder what the term "professional services" means. To eBay it means whatever they can fit into Elance. A more descriptive term might be "white collar" services. Clearly, Elance does not include "blue collar" services.

Seller's Cost

You are skilled and want to provide services working from home or in an office with a small staff. You understand that to keep busy you have to spend half your time marketing your services. Is there any other way?

I doubt that Elance will solve your marketing dilemma. There just isn't enough work available on Elance to keep most freelancers busy. But if you can pick up some work with a minimum amount of marketing activity, you're further ahead. Elance can help you get that additional work.

Elance Fees

Elance fees aren't cheap. To be listed as a professional services provider, the listing costs about $75-$250 per month or $360-$1,200 per year. In addition, there is a transaction fee of 8.75 percent of the project amount.

On the other hand, if a listing on Elance is repeatedly successful, the Elance fees start to look like smart inexpensive marketing.

Overhead

The Elance fees are not the only cost. For Elance, you must be ready to bid on projects quickly, accurately, and efficiently. This means you

must be well organized, and you must be organized digitally. It takes
time and energy to pursue a strategy of constant bidding on Elance.

How It Works

The buyer defines the work project. The sellers bid to do the work on
it in a reverse auction (low bid presumably wins).

What Buyers Do

The buyer has a work project. He puts it in writing. To use Elance he
can take two approaches. He can review the resumes of appropriate
service providers and choose a few to send his project to for bidding.
Or, he can post it on Elance to open it to all for bidding.

What Sellers Do

Sellers put their best face forward and bid a price for a project. There
is no obligation, however, to bid on anything.

A Buyer's Opportunity

Elance claimed $75 million in posted projects and 300,000 free-lancers
ready to go to work, as the book went to press. That averages about
$250 worth of services per freelancer. This clearly shows that this is a
buyer's market.

Sellers

As a seller, if you want to make something out of Elance, you'll have to
hustle. There are far more people ready to work than there is work to
go around. It's unlikely that you can rely upon Elance as your primary
source of business. The real question is, Is it a worthwhile source of
business?

To get business, you'll not only have to pay Elance but you'll have to
get organized to efficiently work the Elance system. Only experimentation and hard work will reveal whether Elance will work for you.

Buyers

As a buyer, Elance provides you with an great opportunity to get high quality work done on the cheap. Let's take a look on how that works.

Working at Home

First, the market is unbalanced. There are more sellers than buyers. Second, one reason for the imbalance is the slow economy. Nonetheless, even in a strong economy, the imbalance will remain for most categories. Third, many freelancers work out of their home with minimal overhead and can do the work less expensively for you than people working in an office. Fourth, most freelancers don't charge enough. They establish fees based on what they need to make to get by and seldom cover the benefits they would get on a normal job. Such benefits typically add 10 to 40 percent to an employee's salary.

The bottom line is that you can purchase needed services at bargain rates. The question then becomes, How can I use these services?

Keep in mind that a considerable percentage of white collar workers work at home today. The Census Bureau shows Colorado with 4.9 percent home workers while some communities have as high as 6.4 percent home workers according to the *Rocky Mountain News*, June 5, 2002. These are freelancers. These figures, however, don't take into account employees who work at home for employers, so called "telecommuters."

The Maryland Department of Transportation did a survey that indicated 12 percent of the employees in the Washington metro area telecommuted in 1998 (for at least part of their work week).

What do these figures mean? Simply that a significant percentage of the national work force works at home. With inexpensive telephone service, fax, cheap computers, and the Internet, one can work at home, do productive work for a business, and fit right in at the office from afar. In fact, my wife telecommutes one day a week for her employer (a major corporation) and gets several days' work done in one day with no meetings and few telephone calls to distract her.

If you have a business and haven't tried using a freelance teleworker, Elance may provide a money-saving opportunity for you to experiment with out-of-the-office workers; that is, you can "outsource" the work. If you have an eBay business, you will need some kind of white collar work occasionally, if not regularly, and Elance may provide just what you need.

Hiring

Your first reaction might be that it's hard to hire people in distant places. You can't meet them. You won't have any local references for them. And they can't come into the office to do part of their work. That's all true and perhaps will prevent you from hiring some freelancers for some tasks. Nonetheless, for many tasks or projects, such considerations will not be a barrier.

First, although you can't meet them, you can have an extensive telephone conservation with them, perhaps more conveniently than meeting them. Second, you can review a freelancer's track record on Elance. It's perhaps easier to do via Elance than it is to do for a local freelancer. Third, email and the capability to attach a file to an email message greatly improves business communication. It means that you can expect to pass back and forth with a freelancer almost any type of information required for productive work. In addition, there are dozens of ways for workers to collaborate via the Internet. In fact, working with people you've never met and never see face to face has become commonplace.

Habit Breaking

What do you do when you want to make 10,000 entries in your database from electronic documents and your staff is too thin to handle it? Do you ask around to find out if anyone knows someone? Do you run a classified ad? Do you call a temporary employment service? Do you post a Help Wanted ad at the local supermarket? It seems like using Elance might be the easiest way to get this task done.

It's not easy, however, to break old habits. You have to try something new and be successful. Elance provides you with a chance to try something new conveniently, get the job done, save money, and perhaps get even higher quality services than you might otherwise.

On the front end, your eBay business is a virtual business. It exists primarily on a computer connected to a network (i.e., the Internet). Elance gives you the opportunity to make your back office operations virtual too. And the intensive use of computers and communications in business means greater efficiency and lower labor costs.

Give Elance a good look soon. You may find something there that you can use in your business, even for small tasks and projects.

eBay Services

eBay has indicated that it is trying to develop effective ways to sell services on eBay itself. In the future, look for eBay to try some new schemes in its normal auctions to enhance the sale of services.

Conclusion

The jury is still out on whether Elance will be successful. If it isn't, all is not lost. Normal eBay auctions have potential for marketing professional services. And if you're a buyer of services, both Elance and the normal eBay auctions offer you real opportunities to get your project done at a reasonable cost.

29

eBay International

eBay provides a smorgasbord of international buying opportunities. eBay operates auctions in over 27 foreign countries:

Australia

Austria

Belgium

Brazil

Canada

China

France

Germany

Ireland

Italy

Korea

Mexico

Netherlands

New Zealand

Singapore

Spain

South America

Sweden

Switzerland

Taiwan

United Kingdom

You can find the links to these auctions on eBay's home page.

This represents the results of an amazing expansion, which continues. Don't overlook the fact that PayPal continues to expand internationally too. Consequently, you can go shopping in many faraway places.

As a seller, a quick way to expand your market for your merchandise is to sell internationally (i.e., to foreign bidders) via eBay in the US.

Buying Far Away

With all those foreign auctions available, you can find something you want if you can navigate the auctions. Or, you can find something to import for sale in your retail business.

You might be able to find some interesting, even exotic, merchandise on eBay's foreign auctions. They present a unique opportunity to shop abroad without ever leaving your home. You have five serious considerations, however, that might make foreign shopping difficult.

Language

First, you must be able to search and find items. Then you must be able to pick out items in which you are interested. Finally, you must be able to read the auction ad. If you can't speak German, this is going to be almost impossible to do on eBay's auction in Germany.

Communication

Once you want to bid, or are a winning bidder, you will have to communicate with the seller. Unlike most foreign buyers who buy on eBay US, you cannot count on the foreign sellers speaking English. You will most often have to speak the local language.

Currency

The eBay auctions in other countries use the local currency. You will have to make arrangements to pay for the items you purchase in the currency of the auction. Some sellers may agree to take payment in US dollars, but it's not something you can count on. Some sellers may accept US credit cards. Some may accept PayPal, which has a built-in currency exchanger you can use. But it's up to you to find a practical means of paying that is acceptable to the seller.

Shipping

Shipping becomes a problem for purchasing in many foreign countries because distances are so long. You have to make a financial judgment as to whether the shipping costs preclude purchasing the specific item you want to purchase abroad.

Taxes

You need to learn about taxation in the country in which you want to make a purchase. US citizens are used to considering the sales tax (paid to states). Similar taxation in foreign countries may seem abusive and financially unacceptable. Indeed, the local taxation may be complex or have multiple layers compared to the simple sales tax collected in the US. Probably, you will be exempt from such taxation, but that is something you need to determine.

Then there is the import tax (tariff). When you import something to the US, you may have to pay an import duty. There are certain exemptions, but the law is not simple, and you might get surprised. Some things are even banned for import.

What to Do?

If you are serious about buying in foreign countries on eBay, it will require some research on your part to be successful. Nonetheless, eBay will permit you to bid on its auctions abroad without obtaining special memberships, and foreign buying on eBay opens opportunities to you not easily available by other means.

If you're a seller on eBay, the capability to buy on foreign eBays presents a wonderful new opportunity. There is a huge amount of merchandise sold abroad that is not available in the US but that will sell well in the US. In buying such merchandise abroad for resale in the US, eBay gives you a cost-effective import opportunity unimagined before the Web. Although you probably can't buy enough merchandise at an eBay foreign auction to sell in volume, you can make contacts with foreign people who will help you import in larger quantities.

Selling Internationally

This is a no-brainer. If you're willing to collect payment and ship abroad, you can expand your sales significantly.

For Aggressive Sellers

One reason sellers on eBay have been able to sell so well to people in other countries is that certain US merchandise is popular but unavailable or much more expensive.

Selling Via eBay US

Your job is to find out what merchandise sells well abroad. It is only a percentage of all US merchandise. What it happens to be in any particular country depends on local tastes, taxation, commercial customs, competing goods, and a variety of other considerations. It's your job to find out and meet the market by auctioning specific goods on eBay US.

Books about Computers and Software

Computer books sell in Europe for about three times the cost in the US. Why? That's a tough question to answer, but they do. That presents an opportunity for someone like me to sell computer books in Europe at a profit but also at a price considerably below the local market. Many high-tech personnel in Europe can read English, making the computer book market in Europe an attractive opportunity for US authors and publishers even for books in English.

But you don't necessarily have to find out anything to make foreign sales on a haphazard basis. Foreign buyers will come to you when you sell something they need or want. Indeed, such buyers are a constant presence in many categories of auctions, particularly auctions for consumer items.

Selling Via Foreign Auctions

It's one thing to sell to people abroad via an eBay US auction. It's another to actually offer merchandise for sale on eBay auctions in foreign countries. If you do so, you will have many of the same problems as buyers, so read the earlier section *Buying Far Away.* You will have to consider language, communication, currency, shipping, and taxes in addition to discovering merchandise that will sell well. Keep in mind that foreign countries have cultural differences far greater than the differences between the states in the US. Generally, what sells well in Nebraska can be expected to sell well in North Carolina. What sells well in France may not sell at all in Germany.

Specific Opportunities

For occasional selling on eBay's foreign auctions, the effort is more trouble than it's worth. The real opportunity is becoming a specialist in one country and making it a business.

With a little determination, you can learn to speak, read, and write a foreign language. That's perhaps the toughest part. Learning the commercial byways and the taxation aspects is almost certainly easier. Finding products that make sense to export is a matter of endless experimentation.

Certain US merchandise is popular abroad. If you can sell it on a foreign eBay auction profitably but at a lower cost than it is available locally, you have a cost-effective business opportunity not imagined before the Web. Go for it!

Get a Partner

Want to short-circuit the learning curve? Instead of learning the foreign language and byways, find a US resident (immigrant from the target country) who knows them already. Form a partnership and start an import/export business using eBay.

An alternative and perhaps a long shot is to find someone in the target country to be your partner, that is, find him or her via the Internet (e.g., via eBay). It's difficult enough to form workable partnerships with direct personal contact. It's clearly a long shot to arrange a partnership with someone you don't know via the Internet. But it's been done successfully.

The important thing to remember here is that most people will not do what is suggested here. The effort is simply too much. The entry to the import/export business is said to have a high *threshold* that will keep most people out. After all, how many people will learn French in order to sell American merchandise in France? If you're willing to cross that threshold, you may find it profitable.

The Threshold Is Lower

The threshold to enter the import/export business remains high because of language barriers. But due to the Web, the capital requirements have dropped. Formerly, to enter the import-export business took significant capital for travel and communication as well as the personal effort to master the language learning curve. Today, due to the Web (specifically eBay) and Internet communications, the capital required to start an import/export business is potentially much lower even though the learning curve remains as high.

Who's the Competition?

If capital requirements are lower today, where is your competition? An immigrant to the US who speaks English and already knows the language and byways of the target country, is not only a potential partner but a potential competitor. By learning English and living in the US, immigrants potentially understand the two cultures well enough to make the import/export business work on eBay.

You need to be cautious about what you export. There are certain highly competitive export businesses that almost certainly will not be good opportunities for you. But these are usually major industries that do not represent the niche opportunities in which you are more likely to be involved. There are also some products banned from export. You don't want to get into trouble with the feds by exporting the wrong things.

Professional Export

If you want to be more than an aggressive seller, you can use eBay both at home and abroad to get yourself into the export business and still use eBay as your marketplace. To do so, however, means taking the business more seriously. And that means learning the export regulations, getting export licenses, using customs brokers both in the US and abroad, and doing a dozen other things to make your exporting successful.

Resources

A good source of import/export information that wants to cater to eBay members is TamTam (*http://www.tamtam.com*). Visit their website to see what they have to offer. A solid source of information, publications, and Web services is World Trade Press (*http://www.worldtrade-press.com*). They provide everything from books to up-to-date specialized trade services via the Web that will keep you informed. If you need a customs broker, A&A Contract Customs Brokers, Ltd. (*http://www.aacb.com*), is looking for eBay business. For information on import/export with Canada try Canada Post BorderFree (*http://borderfree.com*).

Don't Forget PayPal

In the first six months after eBay bought PayPal, it expand it to 38 foreign countries and now exchanges money in five currencies. When you learn more about the import/export business, you will realize what a fabulous service this is. Suffice to say, it makes taking payment much safer, something that many experienced eBay members can appreciate. PayPal is a big story on the international scene. Think of PayPal as an international bank that facilitates both sides of the transaction easily, quickly, and inexpensively. If you do so, you suddenly wake up to the fact that PayPal is going to take over the world, literally. It makes small business import/export so easy that it's a nobrainer for anyone doing business on eBay. You can substantially expand your markets for your goods with a minimum of bureaucratic hassle.

Summary

The genius of eBay is that it creates a huge national market for goods and even services. But some goods sell well in the international markets as well. As the eBay foreign auctions grow and as foreign people bid in the US auctions, eBay will come to encompass a greater variety of goods and services and provide new markets. This evolution provides new opportunities for eBay members.

eBay's foreign auctions deliver the eBay magic to new markets. Such auctions also open opportunities for all eBay members as eBay takes on more of an international character. Although part of the eBay market has always been international, the new foreign eBay auctions, and PayPal as well, will rapidly expand between nations the type of people-to-people and retail-to-consumer trade that eBay auctions support.

Appendix I Top 10 Tips

The top 10 tips for success on eBay for both buyers and sellers follow, not necessarily in order of priority:

1. Play by the Rules. The eBay rules were set to make sure that people deal with each other fairly. If you don't play by the rules, you may be unfair to others and undermine eBay. You may even break laws or incur legal liability.

2. Take eBay Seriously. eBay is not a game. It's a new international marketplace where valuable business is transacted.

3. Protect Yourself. Don't be paranoid, but don't be foolish either. Follow standard protective practices that make sense, just as you do offline.

4. Give Feedback. The core of eBay is trust. Feedback determines an eBay member's reputation. You want to make sure that the eBay members with whom you deal get the reputations they deserve so that eBay patrons will know who to trust.

5. Pay Attention to Detail. This means know eBay rules and procedures and follow them carefully. Provide plenty of detail on the items that you auction and on your sale requirements. For items on which you bid, review carefully the seller's auction and sales requirements. Whether seller or winning bidder, follow through diligently after the auction.

6. Research Market Value. Whether you're a buyer or seller, your best technique is to know the value of the item auctioned. With an accurate value, you can make smart decisions.

7. Keep a Cheerful Attitude. Buying and selling can be fun. No one likes to do business with a sourpuss, whether it's at a retail store or on eBay. Being pleasant can go a long way toward solving a lot of difficult problems.

8. Treat eBay as a Lifelong Asset. It's already eight years old, and it will be around for a long time. You will be able to use it profitably for longer than you think. Some pundits have said it's only a passing fad. Don't believe them.

9. Contribute to the eBay Community. A dynamic and successful marketplace is always a community. Sooner or later you will have opportunities to make a contribution to eBay or to other eBay members. Answer those opportunities.

10. Develop Your Own Approach. Only experience will lead you to auction practices with which you will be comfortable and successful. A book can be helpful, but what works for an author may not work for you. Invent a new eBay technique.

———

This top 10 list is not loaded with specific details that will make you an eBay wizard immediately. Nonetheless, it points out some things for you to consider in developing successful eBay practices.

Although this list does not provide the *details* you need for success on eBay, this book does. Read it through once. When you have a question later, use the book as a reference. Most authors, including me, write books they would like to use as references. When I buy and sell on eBay, I use this book as a reference for details that I have forgotten.

Appendix II Top 9 Tips

The top 9 tips for successfully auctioning items on eBay follow, not necessarily in order of priority:

1. Research the Market Value. This is the first and most important step in listing something for sale. If you set your minimum bid or reserve too high, no one will bid. If you set it too low, you will short-change yourself.

2. Pile It On. Put as much information about the item as you can gather in your auction ad—information, not hype. The Web is an informational medium, and there is no practical space limitation.

Lack of adequate information is almost certain to bring lower winning bids and in many cases no bids at all.

3. Always Include a Photograph. Pictures sell. Good pictures sell even better. There are a very small percentage of items that don't need a photograph. The rest do. Provide multiple photographs for expensive items (e.g., at least five or six sharp photographs for a vehicle).

Sellers Beware

I know of a woman in Sonoma County, California, who has an interesting eBay strategy. She buys items on eBay from auction listings that include poor photographs. She then takes good photographs of the items, relists them on eBay, and sells them for a profit. Great moneymaker.

4. State Your Requirements. Clearly state your requirements for sales to inform bidders of what to expect. Be sure to include everything that will cost winning bidders money.

Tell Them Before

If you intend not to sell to bidders with undesirable feedback, state that in your sales requirements. Then check the feedback on the leading bidders. If one is undesirable, email him or her before the auction ends to state that you will not accept the bid and ask him or her to retract it.

5. Remember the Search. Craft your auction *title* to include keywords for buyer searches and to be readable.

6. Answer Inquiries Immediately. Always answer bidder email inquiries immediately. If you wait, you may lose a bidder. A robust auction ad will help reduce bidder inquiries.

7. Follow Through. Most winning bidders will expect you to take the initiative to complete the transaction after the auction ends. Contact winning bidders by email within a half-day (a half-hour is better) after the auction ends and restate the details of your sales requirements. Keep a record of all documents, including the auction ad and all emails, for reference. Provide the buyer with a receipt. After the transaction is complete, don't forget to submit feedback on the winning bidder.

eBay Retailers

If you sell regularly on eBay, you will need to develop a system for handling auctions that will keep you well organized and responsive to buyers. It doesn't take more than two or three auctions at the same time to completely confuse you if you aren't organized to handle the action.

8. Use an Auction Management Service. If you sell routinely, use an online auction management service to manage your eBay business. The benefits far outweigh the cost.

9. Provide Good Customer Service. You are the seller, and the winning bidder is your customer. The customer is always right. Put customer service first. Keep a cheerful attitude. It's your responsibility to set a cheerful tone for the follow-through process. On eBay, customer service is the name of the game.

———

This top 9 list will help you focus on what's important for success in auctioning your items on eBay. Always keep in mind that excellent customer service has come to be expected online, and eBay is no exception.

Appendix III Top 8 Tips

The top 8 tips for successful bidding on eBay follow, not necessarily in order of priority:

1. Research the Market Value. There will always be alternative places to acquire at market value any item on which you bid. By researching market value, you know when you are getting a bargain and can move aggressively. You also know when there is no bargain to be had, and you can look elsewhere to obtain the item. Knowing the market value of the item is the single most important technique for successful bidding on eBay.

2. Save Your Insanity for Unique Items. Don't get carried away bidding on a Sony camcorder. There will be dozens more exactly like it available on eBay soon. However, when you bid on a unique item (e.g., an antique eight-color painted steel sign advertising the Monongahela Bakery), the market value of the item may be of less concern to you than the amount you are willing to spend to get the item.

3. Check the Seller's Feedback. Once you check the seller's feedback, you will either develop confidence in dealing with the seller, or you'll avoid the auction.

4. Consider the Details. Review carefully the auction offering and the seller's requirements. Also consider the bidder overhead expenses (e.g., shipping costs). Factor these into your bid.

5. Look for Unsavvy Sellers. Look for auctions where the seller has not followed good eBay practices. The bids will be fewer, and the winning bids will be lower. You might find a bargain. Serious seller listing mistakes include a misspelling in the auction title, no photograph, too little information, and the like.

6. Contact the Seller. Email the seller to get any additional necessary details you don't have to make a well-informed decision regarding whether to bid and what maximum amount to bid.

7. Develop a Repertoire of Bidding Techniques. No one bidding technique works best for all auctions. Learn and experiment with a variety of techniques and use them when appropriate.

8. Follow Through. Follow through in a timely manner after the auction. If the seller doesn't contact you within a reasonable time, take the initiative to contact him or her. Keep a record of all the auction documents; save the auction ad and all emails for reference. After the transaction is complete, don't forget to submit feedback on the seller.

———

This top 8 list does not guarantee success in every auction, but it will help you develop an intelligent and successful approach to bidding on eBay.

Put Defeat in Perspective

Being outbid almost always means that someone else was willing to bid more than you. It doesn't necessarily mean that your bidding skills are deficient. You will rebound to bid again another day.

Appendix IV HTML Tutorial

You can learn Hypertext Markup Language (HTML) easily. It's not programming, although many Web developers now call it *coding*. This tutorial does not attempt to give you a comprehensive grasp of HTML. It does give you a good start on using HTML basics in the auction ad portion of your auction listing.

Sometimes when using a Web authoring program, you just can't get things quite the way you want them. If you know HTML, you can tune up your webpages more precisely. Sometimes you see an auction ad page you really like on eBay. You can copy it to your hard disk. If you can read HTML, you can look at the markups to see how the auction ad is constructed. Although copying the content of someone else's auction ad may be a copyright infringement, copying layout and typesetting is not.

For a more thorough introduction to HTML, you might read *Teach Yourself to Create Webpages in 24 Hours*, Third Edition (SAMS, 2001) or any one of a number of similar books readily available in many bookstores. I hope to have my book *Web Pages the Smart Way* (AMACOM, 2001) available on the Web as a tutorial at *http://bookcenter.com* in 2004.

The angle bracket characters (< >) indicate markups (also called "tags"). The markups instruct the browser how to display the content (text, graphics, etc.). The markups also enable some interactive functions such as links. Markups are not case-sensitive; that is, you can use either upper- or lowercase characters inside the angle brackets. As you can see, I prefer lowercase markups; I can read them faster.

Some markups stand by themselves.

```
<br>
```

Most require a closing markup.

```
<b>content</b>
```

The forward slant indicates the closing markup.

Spaces

HTML doesn't like spaces unless you specify them. Therefore, it will change two or more consecutive character spaces into one space. It will change redundant line spaces into one line space. See the   markup later in this appendix for a way to increase spaces.

Refer to Chapter 12 for an example of an auction ad that goes into an auction listing. It uses only a few markups.

Markups Alphabetically

This section presents the most elementary HTML markups in alphabetical order.

<a href=" "></a>

You use a link to go to another webpage anywhere on the Web. For instance, suppose you want to go to the *Hike-Utah* website. You might use the following link.

```
<a href="http://www.hike-utah.com">canyon
trail maps</a>
```

This link will take you directly to the Hike-Utah website which features information on hiking and backpacking in Utah.

Notice that the opening and closing markups surround the words "canyon trail maps." In the webpage, these three words will be underlined with a different color to indicate that they are a link.

<b></b>

This is the markup which creates bold type. The browser will render the text inside the markups as bold. Consult Chapter 8 for the proper use of bold in typesetting.

*
*

Use this markup to create a line break. This differs from the <p> markup in that a blank line does not follow the line break.

```
Charlie Craft<br>
Wilderness experience: 21 years<br>
Canyon experience: 10 years<br>
779-341-8533 Ext. 409<br>
```

See Figure A4.1 to see how this looks in a browser.

Figure A4.1   Use *
* for line breaks not followed by a blank line.

<dl></dl>

This markup makes a list of terms and definitions like a dictionary with words and definitions. The <dl> markup creates the list. The <dt> markup marks the term. And the <dd> markup marks the definition of the term.

```
<dl>
<dt>term
<dd>definition
<dt>term
<dd>definition
</dl>
```

<dt>

This markup creates a term in a *<dl>* list. It is flush left. It must be used with the *<dl>* markup.

<dd>

This markup creates a definition in a *<dl>* list. It is indented. It must be used with the *<dl>* markup.

This makes a good markup to use for general layout purposes too. For instance, suppose you want to make an unnumbered and unbulleted list. You can use the <dl> and <dd> markups (see Figure A4.2).

```
<p>You will need the following 7.5 minute
topographical maps for the Slickhorn
trek.</p>

<dl>

<dd>Slickhorn Canyon East

<dd>Slickhorn Canyon West

<dd>Pollys Pasture

</dl>

<p>You can obtain these maps at your
nearest US Geological Survey office.</p>
```

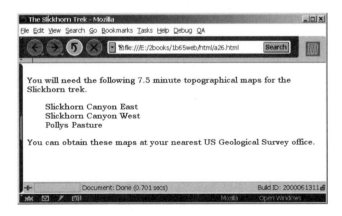

Figure A4.2   An unnumbered unbulleted list.

Note that the indent is on the left side only, not on the right side.

<div> </div>

This division markup by itself is not much use. Its attributes make it useful. Use this markup (with attributes) to lay out a section of text. The section can be a heading, a paragraph, or multiple headings and paragraphs. For instance, one attribute is *align*. You can use this to center a heading or other text (see Figure A4.3).

```
<div align="center">Slickhorn - East
Slickhorn Loop, Utah</div>
```

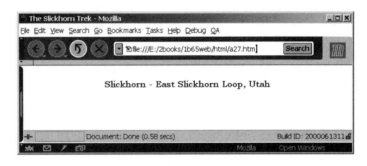

Figure A4.3   A heading centered with the *<div>* markup.

For other attributes of the *<div>* markup, consult an HTML book. Note that for the above example, you can also use the *<center>* markup. But the HTML standards committee wants to discontinue the *<center>* markup, so use the *<div>* markup instead with the *align* attribute.

<h1> </h1>

Use this markup for headings. It comes in six sizes: 1-6. For most uses, only sizes 1-3 prove useful (see Figure A4.4). Sizes 4-6 are too small for normal use.

```
<h1>Slickhorn - East Slickhorn Loop, Utah</
h1>
```

```
<h2>Slickhorn - East Slickhorn Loop, Utah</
```

```
h2>

<h3>Slickhorn - East Slickhorn Loop, Utah</
h3>

<h4>Slickhorn - East Slickhorn Loop, Utah</
h4>

<h5>Slickhorn - East Slickhorn Loop, Utah</
h5>

<h6>Slickhorn - East Slickhorn Loop, Utah</
h6>
```

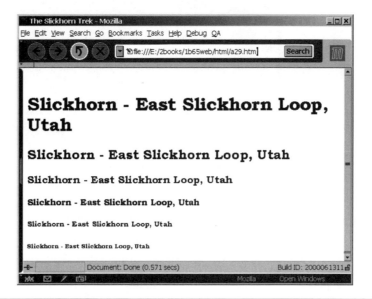

Figure A4.4   Six different headings.

The headings display in bold with a blank line before and a blank line after.

<hr>

Use this markup to make a line (a rule) across the page. The attributes control how the rule looks (see Figure A4.5).

```
<hr align="center" size="2" width="300">
```

We took one five-gallon container out of
the vehicle at each trailhead and stowed it
in the bushes. This is an arid area. If
your car is stolen at the trailhead, you
don't want to come out of the canyon to
find no water.

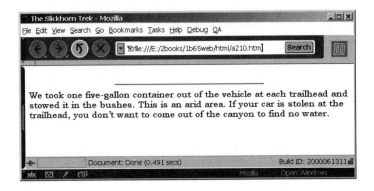

Figure A4.5   Use the *<hr>* markup to create a rule.

The rule shown in Figure A4.5 is 300 pixels wide and 2 pixels thick.

<i> </i>

This is the markup which creates italic type. The browser will render
the text inside the markups as italics. Consult Chapter 12 for the
proper use of italics in typesetting.

<img scr=" ">

To include an image in a webpage, use this markup. Place the URL of
the image file in the *scr* attribute. The URL can be local or somewhere
else on the Web. The image displays at the location of the markup.

```
<img scr="slickhorn23.jpg">
```

The *src* refers to an image file, which must be a GIF, JPEG, or PNG. Use the attributes of the *<img>* markup to control how the image displays in a browser (see Chapter 11). Note that the URL for the image file can be anywhere on the Web. It doesn't have to be at the same URL as the webpage.

<ol> </ol>

This markup makes a list of numbered items. You do not specify the numbers. The items are numbered in order. You must use the *<li>* markup to designate the list items.

```
<ol>
<li>item
<li>item
<li>item
</ol>
```

The list is indented. For example, the earlier unnumbered list displays with numbers when you use the *<ol>* markup (see Figure A4.6).

```
You will need the following three 7.5
minute topographical maps for the Slickhorn
trek.

<ol>
<li>Slickhorn Canyon East
<li>Slickhorn Canyon West
<li>Pollys Pasture
</ol>

You can obtain these maps at your nearest
US Geological Survey office.
```

<li>

This markup creates a list item in a numbered or bulleted list. It must be used with the *<ol>* or *<ul>* markups.

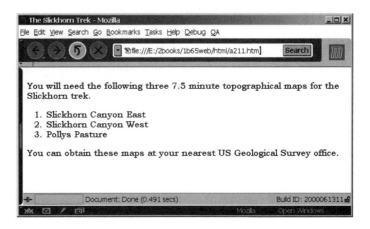

Figure A4.6   A numbered list.

<p> </p>

Use this markup for all your paragraphs. The difference between this and the <br> markup is that the <p> markup adds a blank line of space before and after (see Figure A4.7).

```
<p>To find the ruins, you have to
speculate. (It helps to know they are
there.) Look for a place where there might
be ruins (under an overhang). Then climb up
and look. In most cases, you will not be
able to spot the ruins from the canyon
floor.</p>

<p>We traveled about three and a half miles
for the day, not exactly a death-defying
pace. The wet potholes, although still
small, appeared more often. It's evident
```

that without recent rain, and particularly
in a drought year, there would be no water
in the canyon. Even with water present, we
topped off at almost every wet pothole not
knowing whether it would be our last.</p>

<p>We camped at another wide place in the
streambed with flat rock and small potholes
with fresh water. Ravens and lizards seemed
to be the only wildlife in the canyon.</p>

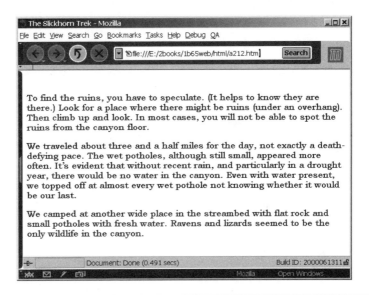

Figure A4.7   Use the *<p>* markup for all your paragraphs.

Note that today just the beginning markup *<p>* is enough, and you
don't need the end markup *</p>*. But soon the browsers may require
the end markup, too, and you don't want to have to go back and add
the end markups.

<table> </table>

Use the *<table>* markup to create a table. The *<tr>* markup (table row) indicates a row (record), and the *<td>* markup (table data) indicates a column (field). The following is a two-column table with three rows.

```
<table>
<tr>
<td>data</td>
<td>data</td>
</tr>
<tr>
<td>data</td>
<td>data</td>
</tr>
<tr>
<td>data</td>
<td>data</td>
</tr>
</table>
```

For example, the following table shows three products (topographical maps) and their current prices (see Figure A4.8).

```
<table cellpadding="10">
<tr>
<td>Slickhorn Canyon East</td>
<td>$4.00</td>
</tr>
<tr>
```

```
<td>Slickhorn Canyon West</td>

<td>$4.00</td>

</tr>

<tr>

<td>Pollys Pasture</td>

<td>$4.00</td>

</tr>

</table>
```

Note that to create some space between the data of this table, you need to use the attribute *cellpadding* to add 10 pixels of padding within each cell. The default use of *<table>* uses no border as Figure A4.8 shows. To add the border, add the *border* attribute set to *1* (see Figure A4.9).

```
<table cellpadding="10" border="1">
```

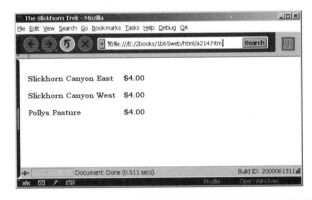

Figure A4.8   The <table> markup makes attractive tables.

As you can see, the <table> markup is handy for tables, but most of us don't use tables very often. However, tables provide another tool in creating attractive layouts.

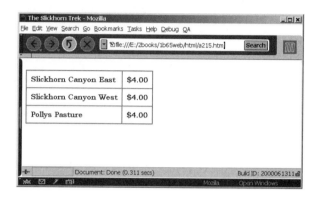

Figure A4.9   A table with borders.

As Chapter 4 explains, you can use tables to lay out a readable text column. The following one-cell table 480 pixels wide creates a convenient reading environment (see Figure A4.10).

```
<table width="480" align="center"><tr><td>

<p>To find the ruins, you have to
speculate. (It helps to know they are
there.) Look for a place where there might
be ruins (under an overhang). Then climb up
and look. In most cases, you will not be
able to spot the ruins from the canyon
floor.</p>

<p>We traveled about three and a half miles
for the day, not exactly a death-defying
pace. The wet potholes, although still
small, appeared more often. It's evident
that without recent rain, and particularly
in a drought year, there would be no water
in the canyon. Even with water present, we
topped off at almost every wet pothole not
knowing whether it would be our last.</p>
```

```
<p>We camped at another wide place in the
streambed with flat rock and small potholes
with fresh water. Ravens and lizards seemed
to be the only wildlife in the canyon.</p>

</td></tr></table>
```

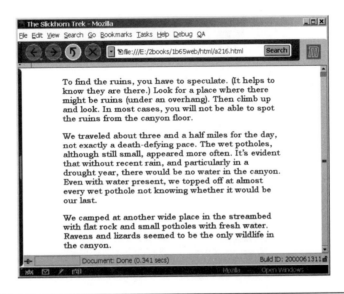

Figure A4.10 Use the *<table>* markup for special layouts such as a text column.

This is a good example of how with a little imagination you can use the *<table>* markup creatively to concoct a variety of layouts.

<tr> </tr>

This markup creates a row (record) in a table. It must be used with the *<table>* markup.

\<td\>\</td\>

This markup creates a column (field) within a table. It holds the data (content) for one table cell. Used with the *\<table\>* markup.

\<ul\>\</ul\>

This markup makes a list of bulleted items. You must use the *\<li\>* markup to designate the list items. Figure A4.11 shows how the browser displays this list.

```
You will need the following 7.5 minute
topographical maps for the Slickhorn trek.

<ul>

<li>Slickhorn Canyon East

<li>Slickhorn Canyon West

<li>Pollys Pasture

</ul>

You can obtain these maps at your nearest
US Geological Survey office.
```

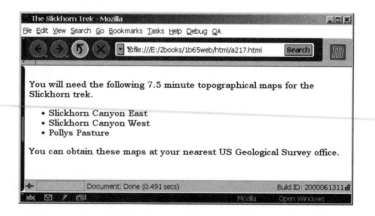

Figure A4.11   A bulleted list.

A browser eliminates redundant spaces between characters or between text blocks. In other words, a browser allows only one space between characters and only one blank line between text blocks. This particular markup establishes a space that will not be eliminated by a browser (see Figure A4.12).

```
Charlie Craft<br>
Occupation:    Wilderness Trekker
```

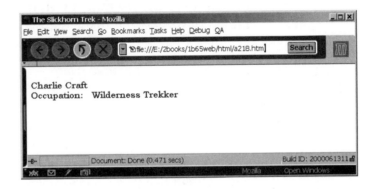

Figure A4.12 Use   to extend spaces.

<!-- -->

You can put this markup to good use. It marks text that does not display.

```
<!-- Change the color of this page to
offwhite when using it to display photos. -
->
```

You can leave instructions (reminders) to yourself or to others who will be working on the authoring of your webpages.

```
<!-- This article is not part of the series
of articles by the same author that appear
in the 4/97 archive. This article belongs
```

```
in the 2/99 archive. -->
```
You can use the comment markup for almost anything, but it's not a good idea to use any other markups inside this markup.

Viewing the Webpage Source

Want to see the HTML in a webpage? You can do so with any webpage. In your browser go View, Page Source. You will be able to see the HTML markups together with the page text.

Viewing the HTML in webpages that you find attractive is a great learning technique. The next step is to use these webpages to help create your own templates for your own webpages. (One can copyright content but generally not typesetting and layout.)

Summary

This basic tutorial is designed to whet your appetite for understanding and using HTML. It doesn't include much information on attributes for the markups covered, and it doesn't include all the HTML markups. But it will get you off to a good start for making an eBay auction ad in an auction listing.

Appendix V Two-System Marketplace

Everyone knows Google, the most popular search engine. eBay considers Google its hottest competition. Indeed, many people use Google to shop. Name a product you want, plug it into the keyword entry, and Google will give you plenty of places to buy it online at a good price. I've used it that way many times myself.

eBay is acknowledged to be the number one selling machine on the Web. But it may not be. Although it would be difficult to prove one way or the other since statistics are not available, more merchandise may sell on the Web via Google. Because it's the number one Web search engine by a substantial margin, a huge number of people find their way to merchandise via Google, and many more via Google than through the other search engines. Indeed, the number one Web marketing technique is to get your website "found" by Google. Many ecommerce business owners spend a lot of money to do so.

But you know something? The leads you get on Google for finding merchandise online are mixed in with everything else regarding the item for which you are looking. For instance, plug in *Marantz PMD-222*, a journalist's audio recorder for interviews, and you will get reviews, public information, foreign language websites, research results, and almost anything. If you just want to buy a PMD-222, everything else but vendors that Google lists are just folderol. That's where Froogle comes in.

As this book goes to press, Froogle is still in beta, and you can try it at *http://froogle.com*. It works amazingly well. What does it do? It simply filters out all the non-commercial websites of a Google search. With Froogle, you get only the vendors. It's a powerful purchasing mechanism, a new ecommerce phenomenon.

This is great news for buyers. You can find more, easier on Froogle. But what about sellers? What does this new phenomenon do for sellers? Surprisingly, quite a lot. You don't have to have your website found by Google. You can enter your catalog (items) directly into Google via the Froogle data feed, and your items will be found by Froogle. And it's free!

Alas, what can we make of all this? In my most recent eBay books, I advise people not to get a website (to go with their eBay operations) but to get an eBay Store instead. (Remember, eBay outlawed a link from an auction ad to a website soon after eBay Stores were introduced.) For most small businesses, an eBay Store enables more efficient marketing than a separate and independent website. eBay Stores sell fixed-price merchandise. Using the Froogle data feed, you can index your eBay Store items right into Froogle for a super powerful 1-2 marketing punch. This is quite easy to do with the right software setup.

Still, we have to return to database techniques to understand how this works. Your eBay Store is just a database of the items you sell. From your existing data for eBay you can extract a subset of data for the Froogle data feed. Go to *http://froogle.google.com/froogle/merchants.html* for detailed information. If you operate your own database system for your eBay business, you'll know what I'm talking about.

Otherwise, don't worry about it. Your auction management service (or software) will include a Froogle data feed feature soon, if it doesn't already. Even eBay's own auction management services may eventually include a Froogle data feed feature (pure speculation). Regardless, one way or another, you can use your eBay Store as a website and index it to Froogle with little extra effort or expense and thereby easily tap into a vast marketplace that may be larger than eBay itself. Opportunities like this don't come along often.

If you operate an independent website and use ecommerce software for a catalog, shopping cart, and checkout, your software vendor should include a feature in the future to make a Froogle data feed. For instance, FASTFEED is a Miva Merchant plug-in for Froogle.

Unfortunately, to give details on the specifics of exactly how to do this Froogle thing is premature. Froogle is still in beta. We don't know how eBay will ultimately react. We don't know what roadblocks might materialize, if any. And if roadblocks do appear, we're not sure what the work-arounds will be. That's why this information is in an addendum. But it seems clear now that one way or another, as an eBay seller you will be able to substantially increase (double?) your marketplace soon. By the time you read this book, some of these issues—unresolved at the time this book went to print—will have been resolved.

Lets take a look at the current Froogle requirements for being indexed:

- Must be a US vendor
- Products must fit into a Froogle category
- Must sell at fixed prices
- Must sell goods (not services)
- Must ship your products (i.e., affiliate websites not permitted)
- Must apply to Froogle to open an account

To open an account, you submit the following information:

- Contact information
- Vendor information
- Name
- URL
- Product information
- Number of products
- Product categories

If you are permitted to open an account, you can submit your data feed as often as once a day and must submit it at least once a month. The data feed columns are as follows:

1. **product_url**
2. **description**
3. **price**
4. **image_url**
5. **category**
6. **offer_id**

Column (field) 1 contains the URL of the product webpage where the product is for sale. Column 2 contains the description of the product (no HTML permitted). Column 3 contains the fixed price. Column 4 contains the URL of the image of the product. Column 5 contains the Froogle category in which the product belongs. Column 6 contains a unique ID for the product. There are also other columns you can use if you need to run a more complex selling operation.

The Froogle data feed is a normal tab delimited data (text) file with headers that you can export from any database. You simply upload the file to Froogle; that's the data feed.

For more information on this exciting new breakthrough in ecommerce, try some of the following resources:

CartKeeper, *http://www.cartkeeper.com/froogle.htm*

Froogle, *http://froogle.google.com/froogle/about.html*

MvCool, *http://www.mvcool.com/compiled.mv* (WCW-FAST-FEED)

Risk Ebiz, *http://www.usgaragesale.com/products_services/froogle.htm*

Search Engine Optimization Consultants, *http://www.seoconsultants.com/articles/1383/froogle-optimization.htm*

SiteAll, *http://siteall.com*

Subia, *http://www.subiainteractive.com*

Tatem Web Design, *http://www.tatem-web-site-design.com/froogle_datafeed.htm*

TerenceNet, *http://www.terencenet.com/capabilities/websiteservices-froogle.html*

Universal Description, Discovery, and Integration, *http://www.uddi.us.com/datafeed.html*

Vendio (previously Auction Watch), *http://www.vendio.com*

WebPublicitee, *http://www.webpublicitee.com*

Having stirred the pot regarding Froogle and eBay, I must say that this is not the end of the line. As I write these last pages of this book, Yahoo is about to launch a new Web search initiative to challenge Froogle and eBay. It's called Yahoo Product Search. It isn't a warmed-over version of Yahoo Stores, which has never become popular in a big way. It's similar to Froogle. And, guess what? It takes a free data feed. For more information go to *http://products.yahoo.com.* If you do a search, you will see a link near the top of the page *Merchants: Submit Products Here*, which will lead you to more information. For specific information on the data feed go to: *http://products.yahoo.com/merchants/data-feedspec.html.*

The question is, Does Yahoo constitute a third major marketplace? Google has over 50 percent of the search engine market. Yahoo has only 20 percent? Will Google gain more market share at Yahoo's expense? Or, visa versa? Another question is, Does Amazon.com constitute a third major marketplace? It seems more like an online department store than a diversified marketplace. Will Amazon be able to maintain or increase its market share? Stay tuned folks. This contest is getting interesting.

Right now, I'm calling it a *Two-System Marketplace* (eBay + Froogle). Or, perhaps a more accurate description will be eBay + search engine catalogs (i.e., Froogle and Yahoo). We'll soon see how this works out.

In the meanwhile, if you're an eBay seller, take a serious look at Froogle and Yahoo Product Search to see what they can do for you.

Index

515